As I open this book,
I open myself
to God's presence
in my life.

God's Invitation

God calls me
to be aware of him
in all the people I know,
the places I go,
and the things I do each day.

My Response

When I quiet myself to allow
God's grace to help me,
I see with truth,
hear with forgiveness,
and act with kindness
as God's love works through me.

Thank you God,

for your presence

in my life.

FindingGod

Our response to God's gifts

5

Parish Edition

Barbara F. Campbell, M.Div., D.Min.

James P. Campbell, M.A., D.Min.

LOYOLAPRESS.

CHICAGO

Nihil Obstat
Reverend Patrick J. Boyle, S.J.
Censor Deputatus
August 20, 2003

Imprimatur
Most Reverend Edwin M. Conway, D.D.
Vicar General
Archdiocese of Chicago
August 22, 2003

The *Nihil Obstat* and *Imprimatur* are official declarations that a book is free of doctrinal and moral error. No implication is contained therein that those who have granted the *Nihil Obstat* and *Imprimatur* agree with the content, opinions, or statements expressed. Nor do they assume any legal responsibility associated with publication.

The Ad Hoc Committee to Oversee the Use of the Catechism, United States Conference of Catholic Bishops, has found this catechetical text, copyright 2005, to be in conformity with the *Catechism of the Catholic Church.*

Finding God: Our Response to God's Gifts **is an expression of the work of Loyola Press, an apostolate of the Chicago Province of the Society of Jesus.**

Senior Consultants
Jane Regan, Ph.D.
Richard Hauser, S.J., Ph.D., S.T.L.
Robert Fabing, S.J., D.Min.

Advisors
Most Reverend Gordon D. Bennett, S.J., D.D.
George A. Aschenbrenner, S.J., S.T.L.
Paul H. Colloton, O.P., D.Min.
Eugene LaVerdiere, S.S.S., Ph.D., S.T.L.

Peg Bowman, M.A.
Gerald Darring, M.A.
Brian DuSell, D.M.A.
Teresa DuSell, M.M.
Bryan T. Froehle, Ph.D.

Thomas J. McGrath
Joanne Paprocki, M.A.
Daniel L. Snyder, M.Div., Ph.D.
Christopher R. Weickert
Elaine M. Weickert

Catechetical Staff
Jeanette L. Graham, M.A.
Marlene Halpin, O.P., Ph.D.
Thomas McLaughlin, M.A.
Joseph Paprocki, M.A.

Grateful acknowledgment is given to authors, publishers, photographers, museums, and agents for permission to reprint the following copyrighted material; music credits where appropriate can be found at the bottom of each individual song. Every effort has been made to determine copyright owners. In the case of any omissions, the publisher will be pleased to make suitable acknowledgments in future editions. Continued on page 327.

Cover Design: Think Design Group
Cover Illustrator: Christina Balit
Interior Design: Three Communication Design

ISBN-13: 978-0-8294-1825-5
ISBN-10: 0-8294-1825-3
Copyright © 2005 Loyola Press, Chicago, Illinois.

Manufactured in the United States of America.

LOYOLAPRESS.

3441 N. ASHLAND AVENUE
CHICAGO, ILLINOIS 60657
(800) 621-1008
www.LoyolaPress.org
www.FindingGod.org

08 09 10 11 12 13 Banta 10 9 8 7 6 5 4 3

Table of Contents

Creator and Father

Saint Augustine

Saint Augustine is the patron saint of theologians—people who study about God. Augustine wrote a book about his personal relationship with God. This book is titled *The Confessions*.

Saint Augustine

Although Saint Augustine is a well-known Christian saint, he was not always Christian. He spent his youth getting into trouble with his friends. Eventually he became a teacher, but he was not happy with the life he was living. Then he met Ambrose, the bishop of Milan, who led him to study the Bible. While reading the Bible, Augustine realized that he wanted to be close to Jesus Christ.

At the age of 32, Augustine was baptized a Christian. He thought that he would live as a monk. However, the people of the town of Hippo, North Africa (the region where Augustine had been born), wanted him as their leader. So he became bishop of Hippo. As bishop he preached and helped his people. He also wrote about God and religion. He helped Catholics of his time and of every century since then to understand how much God loves them, as Father, Son, and Holy Spirit.

Until his death in 430, Augustine encouraged his people, telling them to have courage and hope in God. His feast day is August 28.

God Creates Us

Think of all the beautiful things that you enjoy through God's gift of life. What things are special to you? Make a list. Share your list with others in your group. Use this as a way to introduce yourself to them.

 PRAYER

God, source of all that is, let everything around me speak of you. Help me grow in loving you and trusting in your care.

God Created the World

The Bible tells the story of how God created the earth from what was disorder and chaos. This story of creation is found in the first book of the Bible, which is called *Genesis*.

> In the beginning, when God created the heavens and the earth, the earth was a formless wasteland, and darkness covered the abyss, while a mighty wind swept over the waters.
>
> *Genesis 1:1-2*

The beginning of Genesis tells how God created the universe and all the things in it. The story repeatedly uses the phrase "God saw how good it was."

We, too, experience the wonder and beauty of God's creation when we take the time to truly look at the world. When we think about the world and its beauty and order, we can come to realize that we are part of an order beyond ourselves.

So we can come to know God in two ways, from outside and from inside. We can see God's work in the visible world around us. We can look inside ourselves and realize that we are incomplete and are part of a larger plan.

The phrase "God saw how good it was" also shows the value and dignity of work in God's eyes. Our work and efforts, too, are valuable and important.

 ## Reading God's Word

By faith we understand that the universe was ordered by the word of God.

Hebrews 11:3

God Continues to Care for the World

Julian of Norwich was a holy woman who lived in the 1300s. In a vision God asked her to hold a tiny hazelnut in her hand. She held it tenderly. God asked her to imagine that the hazelnut was the size of the whole universe. He told her that just as tenderly as she was holding the hazelnut, he holds the universe in his hands. This is how much he loves all things and continues to love them.

Just as God cares for us, we have the responsibility to care for the world that God has so lovingly created.

Icon of Lady Julian of Norwich, Anna Dimascio

Complete a Circle of Loving and Caring

God is the origin of the circle of loving and caring. Write a few ways in which others show love and care for you. Write a few ways in which you show love and care for others.

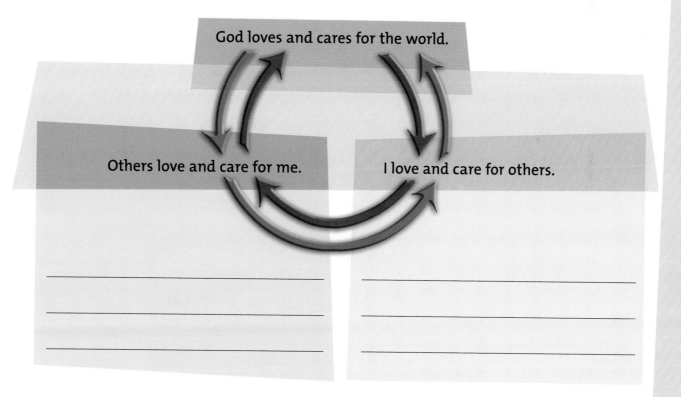

God loves and cares for the world.

Others love and care for me.

I love and care for others.

_____

_____

_____

_____

_____

_____

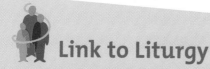 Link to Liturgy

The preface, which recalls God's work in creation, begins the eucharistic prayer.

Reflecting on Creation

A. Use the sentence starters to help you think about God and about the beauty and wonders of God's creation. What things are special to you? Complete the sentences. Have some colored pencils or markers on hand in case you want to use color to express yourself.

I can see _____

_____

I can hear _____

_____

I can touch _____

_____

I can smell _____

_____

I can taste _____

_____

B. What do the beauty and order of creation tell you about God?

_____

_____

C. Write a short prayer to God in thanks and praise of creation.

_____

_____

Creation Is the Work of the Trinity

All that exists is the work of the Trinity: God as Father, Son, and Holy Spirit.

There is only one God, yet there are three distinct persons in God. This is known as the mystery of the Trinity.

Each person of the Trinity has a special mission.

- The Father created the world. He made us and everything in the universe.

- As the Father, God sent his Son, Jesus, who became man, to save us.

- The Holy Spirit gives us grace to believe. The Spirit helps us understand that God is our loving Father and Creator, and that Jesus is the Son of God and our brother.

Holy Trinity, Anonymous, oil on tin, Mexico

Prayers Honoring the Trinity

One way we show our belief in the Trinity is by praying the Sign of the Cross.

Another way is to pray the Glory Be to the Father. This prayer gives praise to the three persons of the Trinity.

Did You Know?

The Glory Be to the Father is also known as the Doxology. A doxology is a prayer of praise.

PRAYER

Prayer is time we spend with God in our minds and hearts. Often we begin this holy time with the Sign of the Cross.

In the name of the Father, and of the Son, and of the Holy Spirit. Amen.

Imagine yourself in your favorite place. See yourself there. Enjoy being there. What does it look like? What do you hear?

You see Jesus coming to meet you. Greet Jesus. Show him around. Tell him why this place is so special to you.

Walk or sit together. Tell Jesus what's on your mind. He listens, then says something to you. You listen. How do you respond? Enjoy each other's company for a while.

Thank Jesus for spending time with you. Thank God for his work of creation. Tell God how glad you are to be able to experience it.

It's time to say goodbye for now. When you are ready, end this prayer time with the Sign of the Cross.

Faith Summary

God created the world and continues to love and care for it and for us. There are three persons in God, but there is only one God. This is the mystery of the Trinity. Each person in the Trinity has a mission. The Father is the creator. The Son continues the Father's work in the world. The Holy Spirit helps us know the Father and the Son.

Ways of Being Like Jesus

Jesus continues the work of God the Father. When you show respect for the things in creation and show love and care for others, you are acting like Jesus.

With My Family

Do something with your family to show your concern and respect for the environment that God created. Plant some flowers in a pot, clean the yard, or pick up garbage. Use your work to praise God.

PRAYER

Thank you, God, for creating me and caring for me. Thank you for giving me all the people who care for me. Let me show my gratitude by caring for all people and things that you have created.

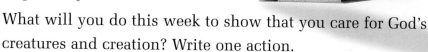

My Response

What will you do this week to show that you care for God's creatures and creation? Write one action.

_____

_____

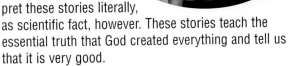

Julian of Norwich holding a tiny nut in her hand

Focus on Faith

God Holds Us Tenderly

Julian of Norwich, who died about 1423, was an English woman who lived alone so that she could pray for the world. In her book *Showings* Julian tells of the vision she received of how much God loves the world. Julian held a tiny hazelnut in her hand, and God asked her to imagine that the tiny hazelnut was the size of the universe. As she held that tiny nut tenderly in her hands, God asked her to imagine how tenderly he holds the whole universe in his. This is the tenderness we experienced holding our children as infants. It is the same tenderness we feel when we see our children's enthusiasm and joy at discovering something new. Each day we have new opportunities to share in the infinite tenderness of God. What opportunity do we have today?

Dinnertime Conversation Starter

Share the experience you had the first time you held a small animal. What were the experiences of the other family members?

Our Catholic Heritage

The book of Genesis in the Bible contains two stories of God's creation of the universe and all the creatures in it. The Church does not interpret these stories literally, as scientific fact, however. These stories teach the essential truth that God created everything and tell us that it is very good.

Hints for at Home

Look through family pictures. Find pictures that illustrate one of these themes: The Beauty of God's Creation or How We Love and Care for One Another. Work with your child to put several of the pictures on a piece of colored paper with the theme labeled on top. Display the resulting art in your home.

Focus on Prayer

Your child is learning about how God cares for the universe and how, as part of God's creation, we love and care for one another. Take time, perhaps at a meal, to say a special prayer of thanks for the people who care for us. Mark the beginning and ending of the prayer with the Sign of the Cross.

God Saves Us

Session 2

Think of some problems that exist in the world. Think of some problems that exist in your neighborhood. What problems do you think are important to solve?

PRAYER

Jesus, my Savior, help me find the way to you through the problems I meet. Sometimes it's really tough. Please show me how to do what is right.

Saint Peter Claver, the "Saint of the Slaves"

Throughout history people have been treated unfairly, sometimes simply because they come from a different place or race or because they are poor or weak. One terrible social crime is slavery. People have long been bought and sold as goods. The Catholic Church teaches that slavery is offensive to God.

Saint Peter Claver was someone who devoted his life to helping slaves. He was born in Spain in 1581. He spent most of his life in South America, where he served as a missionary to slaves.

Peter Claver gave the slaves physical and spiritual care from the moment they arrived from Africa. He met them at the harbor with food and medicine. He tried to persuade their masters to treat them humanely. He also comforted the slaves and taught them about Jesus, encouraging them to live as Christians. By 1615 Peter Claver is said to have baptized more than 300,000 slaves. He died in 1654. His feast day is September 9.

Saint Peter Claver, Robert Lentz, 1989

The Human Condition

All around us there are reports of war, crime in the streets, violence in families, and unfair treatment of certain groups of people. There are also stories of heroism and of people being kind to one another. This is the contradictory nature of the human condition.

The Bible helps explain the human condition to us. It tells us that we are basically good because we are created that way by God. However, we are part of a human family and have a tendency to sin and to do wrong.

The Nature of Sin

To explain human weakness, the Book of Genesis in the Bible tells the story of Adam and Eve. They were the parents of the human race. They gave in to temptation and disobeyed God's command. To reject God was their personal decision. Their sin, which resulted in original sin, damaged the human family.

As a result of original sin, we are inclined to do wrong. However, we still have freedom of choice to say yes or no to God. Saying no to God results in personal sin that can lead us to reject God.

Fall of Man and Expulsion from Paradise (detail), Giusto de Menabuoi, 1370

Study the Story

In *The Confessions* Augustine tells us that, as a young boy, he and some of his wild friends stole some pears from a tree. They did not even intend to eat this fruit. In fact they threw it to the pigs. They stole simply for the fun of doing something that was not allowed.

How does this story relate to what you have just read?

_____

_____

_____

_____

 Link to Liturgy

The litany Lamb of God accompanies the breaking of the bread, just before Holy Communion. Through it we thank God for sending a savior, and we praise God's power to forgive our sins and give us peace.

Sin and the Promise of Salvation

In one of his letters to the early Christian churches, Saint Paul describes how sin came into the world.

> Therefore, just as through one person sin entered the world, and through sin, death, and thus death came to all.

Romans 5:12

Paul is referring to Adam's sin and its devastating effects on all. However, from the beginning, God promised a savior. The savior would restore us to friendship with God. This savior is Jesus, the Son of God who became man.

Paul describes the promise of salvation in another of his letters. He makes a contrast: Just as sin and death came into the world through Adam's choice, victory over sin and death comes from Jesus. Jesus reconciles us to God.

 ### Meet a Saint

Saint Josephine Bakhita was born in Sudan, in northeastern Africa, in about 1870. At the age of seven, she was stolen by slave traders and sold into slavery. She became the property of an Italian diplomat. In Italy she was sent to a convent school and in 1890 was baptized. Eventually, she became a nun. At the convent she did ordinary tasks with a constant smile. She died in 1947 and was declared a saint on October 1, 2000. Her feast day is February 8.

Social Justice Roundtable

You will be assigned to one of four groups.

- Read the problem for your group. Brainstorm as many answers to the question as you can. Think about what a follower of Jesus would do. Write the group's answers.

- Next decide on the two best actions proposed for your problem.

- Be prepared to present your final solutions to the other groups.

Problem 1 Someone of your age makes a racist remark. What do you say or do?

Problem 2 Someone in your class is always bullying other students and telling them how bad they look and how stupid they are. He or she forces the other students to do things for him or her. What do you say or do?

Problem 3 There are several new students from another country in your class at school. They don't speak English well, and they are not chosen to be part of games. What do you say or do?

Problem 4 You read in the newspaper that the manufacturer of a popular brand of sports clothing has a factory in another country, where it pays people a very low wage. What do you say or do?

 ## Reading God's Word

For since death came through a human being, the resurrection of the dead came also through a human being.

1 Corinthians 15:21

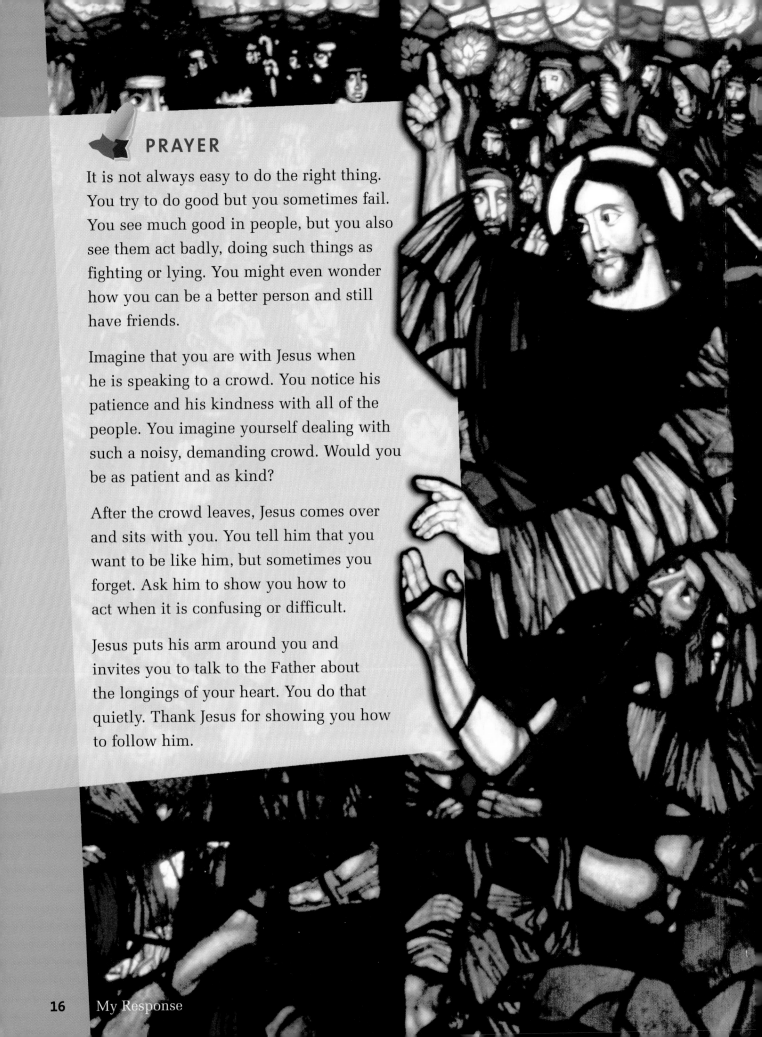

PRAYER

It is not always easy to do the right thing. You try to do good but you sometimes fail. You see much good in people, but you also see them act badly, doing such things as fighting or lying. You might even wonder how you can be a better person and still have friends.

Imagine that you are with Jesus when he is speaking to a crowd. You notice his patience and his kindness with all of the people. You imagine yourself dealing with such a noisy, demanding crowd. Would you be as patient and as kind?

After the crowd leaves, Jesus comes over and sits with you. You tell him that you want to be like him, but sometimes you forget. Ask him to show you how to act when it is confusing or difficult.

Jesus puts his arm around you and invites you to talk to the Father about the longings of your heart. You do that quietly. Thank Jesus for showing you how to follow him.

Faith Summary

The human family is in a weakened condition and is inclined to do wrong because of original sin. However, God gave us a savior, Jesus, who helps us heal our relationship with God.

Ways of Being Like Jesus

Jesus showed he loved and cared for people who were poor, sick, or shunned by society. You can be like Jesus by comforting those who are excluded from a group or who are being treated unfairly.

With My Family

With your family think of someone you know who could use some sort of help. Arrange to do something positive for that person, such as paying a visit or providing for his or her needs.

Living My Faith

PRAYER

Jesus, thank you for being my Savior and bringing me to the Father. Please give me the wisdom and courage to know how to help others, particularly those who are being treated unfairly.

My Response

What is one action that you will take to help others, particularly people who are poor, weak, or being treated unfairly, or those who have a problem at this time? Write your answer.

_____

_____

_____

Focus on Faith

God Is With Us Always

The man who became the Buddha, founder of the Buddhist religious tradition, was sheltered as a youth. His father kept him secluded in a walled house so that he would not see the evils in the world. One day the Buddha went out and saw a man who was starving. He began to ask questions about suffering, and his life was changed. It is probably the hope of all parents to protect our children from all that is wrong in the world, but we have no secluded gardens in which to shield them. The effects of original sin are universal, and we witness their consequences every day. As these effects hit home, it is our task to face the issues in faith. God has not left us alone. Jesus has come to save us, and the Holy Spirit is his abiding presence with us.

Dinnertime Conversation Starter

On days when news of the world has an impact on the whole family, have an open discussion in which everyone's opinion is heard and valued. Discuss ways you can pray as a family for the needs of the world.

Spirituality in Action

With your child decide on a community action to perform. It can be as simple as baking cookies for a new or elderly neighbor, taking food to the local food pantry, or collecting clothing for a local charity. Try to arrange to talk with someone at the organization about the concrete ways in which the charity helps people in the community.

Our Catholic Heritage

The Catholic Church has developed an important body of social teaching. The basic teachings can be found in papal encyclicals (letters) and statements from meetings of bishops. Pope Leo XIII's encyclical "Rerum Novarum" of 1891 affirmed the role of the Church to teach social principles. Here are two principles of Catholic social teaching:

• All people have a fundamental right to life, food, shelter, health care, education, and employment.

• The moral test of a society is how it treats its most vulnerable members, especially poor people.

Focus on Prayer

In silent prayer your child has reflected on sin and how Jesus calls us to do good. At a specific time, perhaps when saying grace before a meal or when saying bedtime prayers, help your child to reflect by suggesting that he or she complete the following sentences privately: I say no to God when I . . . , I say yes to God when I . . . .

God's Revelation

Ancient fortress in Syria

The Old Testament of the Bible tells the story of God's people.

Contemporary Bedouin children in Jordan

What people in the Old Testament can you think of? What stories about them do you know? Share them with the group.

 PRAYER

Gracious God, you are faithful to your people through the ages and now.
Help me to know that I can always count on you.

The Story of Abraham

Abraham was a just man. He and his wife, Sarah, were elderly, and they didn't have any children. One day God spoke to Abraham and told him to leave his home and to travel to a new land.

Abraham heard and obeyed God's call. He and Sarah trusted in God. At each place the pair stopped in their travels, they set up a shrine to worship God. At one of these stops, God told Abraham about the covenant, or agreement, he wanted to make with him. God said that Abraham would become father of many nations and that Abraham and his wife would have a child.

Abraham accepted the covenant. He promised to worship God as the one true God and to obey him.

adapted from Genesis 12:1-17:16

Abraham, Sarah, and the Angel,
Jan Provost, c. 1500

Abraham and Sarah had a son, who was named Isaac. He in turn had a son called Jacob. They were the ancestors of the **Hebrews.** Jesus, the Savior that God promised after the fall of Adam and Eve, was a descendant of Abraham's family.

The story of salvation on earth begins with Abraham. He is considered a holy person by three of the world's religions: **Judaism,** Christianity, and **Islam.** Judaism, the religion of the Hebrews, or **Jews,** reveres Abraham as its father. Christianity, too, honors him. Islam also recognizes Abraham as an important person.

 Reading God's Word

"I am the God of your father," he continued, "the God of Abraham, the God of Isaac, the God of Jacob."

Exodus 3:6

The Old Testament and the Story of Salvation

Many of the stories in the Old Testament tell about Abraham and his descendants, the Hebrews. The Old Testament recounts the story of salvation. It reveals God's plan for the human family and the covenant he made with the Hebrew people. The books in the Old Testament are important to Jews, Christians, and **Muslims** (followers of Islam).

The fundamental belief that Christianity received from the Old Testament is that God is One. The principal prayer of Judaism is "Hear, O Israel, the Lord our God is one Lord." Christians believe that the promise of God's covenant was fulfilled in Jesus Christ. They believe the Old Testament is God's **Revelation,** which the New Testament continues.

A Jewish girl reads the Torah using a Yad at her Bat Mitzvah.

The Old Testament tells the story of God's people before the time of Jesus. It has 46 books. The New Testament tells the story of Jesus and the early Church. It covers a shorter period of time and has 27 books.

Dead Sea Scroll, fragment. (This 2,000 year old Jewish scroll is the earliest manuscript of the Book of Isaiah. The Dead Sea Scrolls were housed in jars like the model shown here.)

Link to Liturgy

The First Reading during Sunday Mass is usually from the Old Testament. The Second Reading is from the New Testament.

The Story of Salvation Continues With Moses

God renewed his covenant with Abraham's descendants many years after Abraham's death. The leader of the Hebrews at the time was Moses. Moses led the Hebrews from slavery in Egypt.

Through Moses, God gave the people rules to follow. Those rules are the Ten Commandments. The rules were not just for Moses' time; they continue to be part of our relationship with God today. Through them, God tells us to love him above all (Commandments 1 through 3) and to be compassionate to our neighbors (Commandments 4 through 10).

Finding Bible Passages

Bible passages are identified by book, chapter, and verse.

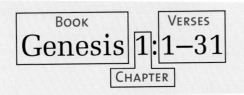

The story of creation begins in Genesis 1:1. Genesis is the first book of the Bible. The number before the colon identifies the chapter, and the number or series of numbers after the colon identifies the verse or verses.

Saint Catherine's Monastery, located at what is thought to be the biblical Mt. Sinai where the Ten Commandments were delivered

Find the following Scripture passages and answer the questions.

1. **Exodus 3:1–4**   How did God appear to Moses?

   _____

2. **Exodus 3:7–8**   What did God promise the Hebrews?

   _____

   _____

3. **Exodus 3:10**   What did God ask Moses to do?

   _____

   _____

The Ten Commandments

Review the list of Commandments at the back of this book. Then find the Commandments in the Bible, Exodus 20:1–20, in which God gives the law to Moses on Mount Sinai.

Moses Presents the Ten Commandments to the Israelites, Raphael

What the Commandments tell you to do:

1. Put God first in your life.

2. Do not swear or say God's name in anger.

3. Worship God publicly.

4. Respect your parents and those in authority.

5. Do not hate others or cause them harm.

6. Love and be faithful to your marriage partner.

7. Do not take something that belongs to someone else.

8. Tell the truth.

9. Do not be jealous and want your neighbor's spouse.

10. Do not be jealous when other people have things you want.

Living by the Commandments

Think about what the Commandments mean to you.

List positive things you can do to keep the Ten Commandments.

_____

_____

_____

List things that would break the Ten Commandments.

_____

_____

_____

PRAYER

Following what God asks of us in the Ten Commandments can be difficult. The Lord's Prayer is a prayer that Jesus taught the disciples. Pray this prayer as the disciples did.

Lord's Prayer

Our Father, who art in heaven,
hallowed be thy name;
thy kingdom come;
thy will be done on earth as it is in heaven.
Give us this day our daily bread;
and forgive us our trespasses
as we forgive those who trespass against us;
and lead us not into temptation,
but deliver us from evil.
Amen.

Jesus invites you to talk to the Father. Talk to God about his holiness and his will for you. Tell God about your daily needs (your "daily bread"). Thank him for his forgiveness. Talk to him about the temptations you need to avoid. Thank the Father for hearing your prayer.

Faith Summary

God promised to send a savior. He made a special covenant with Abraham and his descendants, who became God's people. God gave us the Ten Commandments. The Old Testament tells the beginning of the story of salvation, which is fulfilled in Jesus Christ.

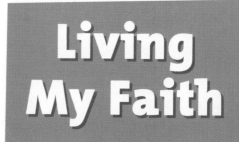

Words I Learned

Hebrews   **Islam**   **Jews**   **Judaism**   **Muslims**   **Revelation**

Ways of Being Like Jesus

You are like Jesus when you obey God's will as expressed in the Ten Commandments. Try to honor God above all things. Try to be kind and compassionate to others.

With My Family

We are each part of a family, and we often know stories from the histories of our families—our parents, our grandparents, even our great-grandparents. With your parents' help, write a family history.

PRAYER

Loving God, thank you for keeping your promise of sending a savior and revealing yourself to us in the Bible. Thank you for showing us how to be good by giving us the Ten Commandments.

My Response

What is one way that you will live the Ten Commandments in a positive way? Choose one commandment. Write how you will live it positively.

a parent page

Abraham, Sarah, and the Angel, Jan Provost

Hints for at Home

Read one of the following stories from the Old Testament with your child: Genesis 12:1–7, the call of Abraham, or Exodus 3:1–17, the call of Moses. Share ideas about it by asking questions such as these: What happens in the story? What does the story teach us about God's plan?

Spirituality at Home

Jesus teaches us that God is our loving Father. In calling God our Father, Jesus is emphasizing the close love and care that God has for us and how he wants to nurture us. This also emphasizes that we as parents are the first example of God's love and concern that our children experience. When they hear of God's loving concern as Father, they filter it through the lens of their experience of us as their parents. In what kind of atmosphere are we raising our children? How will they experience God's fatherly concern for them based on what they experience from us as the primary examples of that concern?

Focus on Prayer

Pray the Lord's Prayer with your child. Then spend a few minutes thinking or talking—whichever is more comfortable for your child—about what it means. The exact words for the Lord's Prayer can be found at www.FindingGod.org.

Focus on Faith

Journeys of Faith

Were we to explore the histories of our families, we would find at least one story of a long and difficult journey. At some point our ancestors crossed a body of water. They crossed either the Bering Strait north of Alaska or the Atlantic or Pacific Oceans. On this journey they were sustained by their faith. The faith of our ancestors is now part of our Catholic heritage. As parents, we ask ourselves how our children will grow in the faith. Telling stories of the journey in faith that is your family heritage is the best way to begin to help your child.

In this session the children have learned about Abraham and Sarah's journey in faith. You can show your child that, in your own life and in the lives of your family members, this journey continues.

Dinnertime Conversation Starter

Share a favorite story about a grandparent, an aunt, or an uncle. Invite your child to do the same.

Saint Jerome, Giotto di Bondone

Our Catholic Heritage

Around A.D. 400, Saint Jerome translated the Bible into Latin. An English-language translation of that version, with comparisons to the original Hebrew and Greek, was made in the late 1500s and early 1600s. Called the Douay-Rheims Version, it was the Bible that was most widely used by English-speaking Catholics for centuries. *The New American Bible,* commissioned by the U.S. bishops, was translated from the original languages in the 20th century. It is a contemporary American translation.

God Directs Our Lives

We all depend on one another in many ways.
Think of ways that you depend on people like your
parents, caregivers, teachers, and classmates. Make a list.
On whom do you depend? Think about how those same people
and others depend on you. Make a list of ways.

 PRAYER

*Creator God, I depend on you for everything, starting with my life.
Lead me to gladly search out and follow your will for me, and help me
serve your kingdom.*

Saint Philip Neri, the Saint of Joy and Humility

Philip Neri, born in 1515 in Florence, Italy, was a down-to-earth man who taught us that being holy does not mean being serious all the time. He loved a good joke. In fact his favorite books were the New Testament and a joke book. When he taught young people about their faith, he told them, "Be good—if you can."

Philip himself achieved a great deal of good. He moved to Rome and cared for sick and poor people.

Then Philip became a priest. He encouraged people to be humble and to receive the sacraments often to be close to Jesus. He also encouraged people to be happy, often saying, "Worrywarts and long faces, stay away from here." His feast day is May 26.

Saint Philip Neri, shown with the little dog he used to help teach humility and a sense of proportion to the young aristocrats who took it for walks, Robert Lentz

Following the Example

How did Philip Neri serve God's kingdom? List two ways.

_____

_____

Did You Know?

In his life and community Saint Philip Neri lived out one form of Christian spirituality. Saints like Ignatius of Loyola, Francis of Assisi, and Dominic formed their own communities to live out Christian spirituality in distinct and diverse ways.

Jesus, the Child, and the Kingdom

Jesus' disciples asked him, "Who is the greatest in the kingdom of heaven?" So he used an example to explain the nature of his kingdom to them—and to us.

Jesus called a child over and told the disciples,

> Amen, I say to you, unless you turn and become like children, you will not enter the kingdom of heaven. Whoever humbles himself like this child is the greatest in the kingdom of heaven.
>
> *Matthew 18:1-5*

What do Jesus' words mean? Why did Jesus use the example of a child?

At the time Jesus lived, children counted for almost nothing. They were completely dependent on their families. So in giving a model of a child as having the highest place in his kingdom, Jesus is speaking of someone who is totally dependent and trusting.

Jesus asks the disciples to be humble. This means to recognize our dependence on God and trust in him. It means letting go of our selfish ambitions and trusting that God cares for us.

Jesus and the Children,
Enrique de la Vega

 Reading God's Word

Amen, I say to you, whoever does not accept the kingdom of God like a child will not enter it.

Mark 10:15

The Members of God's Kingdom

Jesus' words tell us what belonging to God's kingdom means. Members of God's kingdom accept God's direction for their lives.

God revealed that direction first in the Old Testament—especially in the Ten Commandments. The Old Testament law is completed in the New Testament. To live the New Law means to practice Christian virtue and live in the grace of the Holy Spirit.

The Son of God became man to proclaim the Kingdom of God. Jesus gave God's direction for us under the New Law in the Beatitudes. They tell us how to share in God's life and be happy. They teach Christian virtue.

How can we grow in virtue? We can study the meaning of the Beatitudes, live out their values, and keep on trying when they are difficult to follow. Through the Holy Spirit, we receive the grace we need to practice Christian virtue, which the Beatitudes express.

When we live the Beatitudes, we are living as members of God's kingdom. We are acting as a sign of God's goodness in the world. We are bringing happiness to others—and to ourselves.

Find the Beatitudes

The Beatitudes are part of Jesus' teaching in the Sermon on the Mount. Read them in Matthew 5:3–12.

The Sermon on the Mount, Claude Lorrain, ©The Frick Collection, New York

The Meaning of the Beatitudes

Read the Beatitudes in the back of the book. Match each action or attitude below with one of the Beatitudes. Write the beatitude.

1. We feel sad when we see people in bad situations.

   _____

   _____

2. We work to end bad feelings and arguments.

   _____

   _____

3. Our possessions are not the most important things in our lives.

   _____

   _____

4. We do not get angry easily. We are kind and gentle with others.

   _____

   _____

5. We do our best to see that everyone is treated fairly.

   _____

   _____

6. We forgive those who hurt us. _____

   _____

7. We do something good even when others laugh at us.

   _____

   _____

8. We are loyal to God's commands and act with good intentions.

   _____

   _____

PRAYER

We can ask God for the grace we need to practice Christian virtue, which the Beatitudes express. When we wake up each day, we can pray the Morning Offering to greet God and to dedicate our day to him.

Morning Offering

My God, I offer you my prayers, works, joys,
*   and sufferings of this day*
in union with the holy sacrifice of the Mass
*   throughout the world.*
I offer them for all the intentions of your
*   Son's Sacred Heart,*
for the salvation of souls,
reparation for sin,
and the reunion of Christians.
Amen.

After you pray the Morning Offering, spend some time with God. Tell God what you will be doing for the rest of the day. Ask for his help and blessing on yourself and on all whom you meet.

Faith Summary

Jesus taught us how to serve God's kingdom. We are called to be dependent on God and trust in him. Jesus gave us the Beatitudes to show how to share God's life fully and be happy.

Ways of Being Like Jesus

You are like Jesus when you are humble and recognize that you depend on God for all things. You are like Jesus when you live the Beatitudes. You show concern for others by loving and caring for them.

With My Family

Talk with your family about how you can live the Beatitudes. For example, how can you be a peacemaker? How can you be poor in spirit?

 PRAYER

Thank you, Jesus, for giving me the Beatitudes to show me how to live. Please help me live them in my life every day.

My Response

Reread the Beatitudes. Which one has a special meaning to you? Write one way you can live that beatitude.

_____

_____

_____

Living My Faith

RAISING FAITH-FILLED KIDS
a parent page

Focus on Faith

Following Jesus' Way

Jesus told his disciples that unless they became like children they would not enter the Kingdom of God. Jesus was not promoting some starry notion of childlike innocence. Jesus was speaking here of children as those who need direction in life. Our journey to God is not one that we can travel by choosing our own ways. We have to take direction from God in order to follow him. God has given us the Ten Commandments, and Jesus has given us the Beatitudes as fundamental signposts. They tell us how to worship God truly and to care for others. We want our children to follow God's way. We are the most important examples they have of what this means.

Dinnertime Conversation Starter

Discuss with your child how important signs are in life. Point out how the signs we obey each day (for example, traffic lights, stop signs, right-of-way signs, walk and don't-walk signs) help to keep us safe. Relate these signs to the Ten Commandments and Beautitudes, which God gives us to help us follow Jesus.

Spirituality in Action

Encourage your family members to think of ways to help someone you know who might be dependent on others for basic needs or who might appreciate some help. For example, you could visit an elderly or homebound relative or visit a neighbor to give the person company or to run errands for him or her.

Focus on Prayer

Your child is learning the Morning Offering, which is a prayer to remind us to stay close to God during daily activities. You might pray the prayer together when it is possible—perhaps at the breakfast table or while in your car commuting. You will find the exact words to the prayer at www.FindingGod.org.

Hints for at Home

With your child, discuss a beatitude that has a special meaning to him or her. Help your child do an art project related to that beatitude. For example, your child might write it out in special script or type it using a special font on the computer. Display the resulting work in your home.

Review

The Father, the Son, and the Holy Spirit created us and continue to care for us. God's Son, Jesus, came to save us from original sin. Jesus calls us to serve God's kingdom of grace and love as a sign to the world of God's goodness.

 PRAYER

Help me know you more and more, my great and loving God. Thank you for the help the Ten Commandments and the Beatitudes give me.

Faith Summary

God created the world and continues to love and care for it. Each person in the Blessed Trinity has a mission in the world. The Father created everything. The Son became man for the sake of our salvation. The Holy Spirit helps us know the Father and the Son.

People are inclined to sin because of original sin. But God promised a savior, Jesus, who would heal our relationship with God. Through Adam, sin and death came into the world. In contrast, through Jesus' life, death, and resurrection, we are saved.

Because God promised to send a savior, he made a covenant with Abraham and his descendants. They became God's people. The Old Testament tells the story of these people. God gave rules, the Ten Commandments, for the people to follow. The story of salvation, begun with Abraham, is fulfilled in Jesus.

When he was on earth, Jesus gave us the Beatitudes to show how to live fully and be happy. With the help of the Holy Spirit, we can live the Beatitudes.

Dear Diary . . .

You have met some important Bible characters in this unit—Adam and Eve, Abraham and Sarah, and Moses. Now it's time to find out more about them.

Using your imagination, you and a partner will write diary entries as these characters. One of you will write entries for Adam and Sarah, the other will write for Eve and Abraham. You will both write entries for Moses. Reread their stories to refresh your memory: Adam and Eve (Genesis 2:5–9,15–25; 3); Abraham and Sarah (Genesis 12:1–9; 17:1–8,15–17,19); and Moses (Exodus 3:1–10).

As you describe the events in the life of each person, be sure to include details about where you live, with whom, what your relationships with other people are like, and how you interact with God. You might even include some questions about things that you don't understand.

When you have written the diary entries, share them with your partner.

Adam and Eve, created by a child in Russia for Children of the World Illustrate the Bible

In Other Words

Below are descriptions of persons or things you have learned about in this unit. Read them, and on the line write who or what is being described.

1. Son of Abraham _____

2. The religion of the Hebrews, or Jews _____

3. Another name for the Glory Be to the Father _____

4. Through this man God gave the Hebrews the Ten Commandments. _____

5. There is only one God, yet there are three distinct persons in God. What is this mystery called? _____

6. A saint who spent his youth partying, but who converted to Christianity at age 32 _____

7. The first book of the Bible, which contains the two creation stories _____

8. A prayer in which we ask God to give us our daily bread _____

9. We are practicing Christian virtue when we follow these. _____

10. A prayer you can say to offer your day to God _____

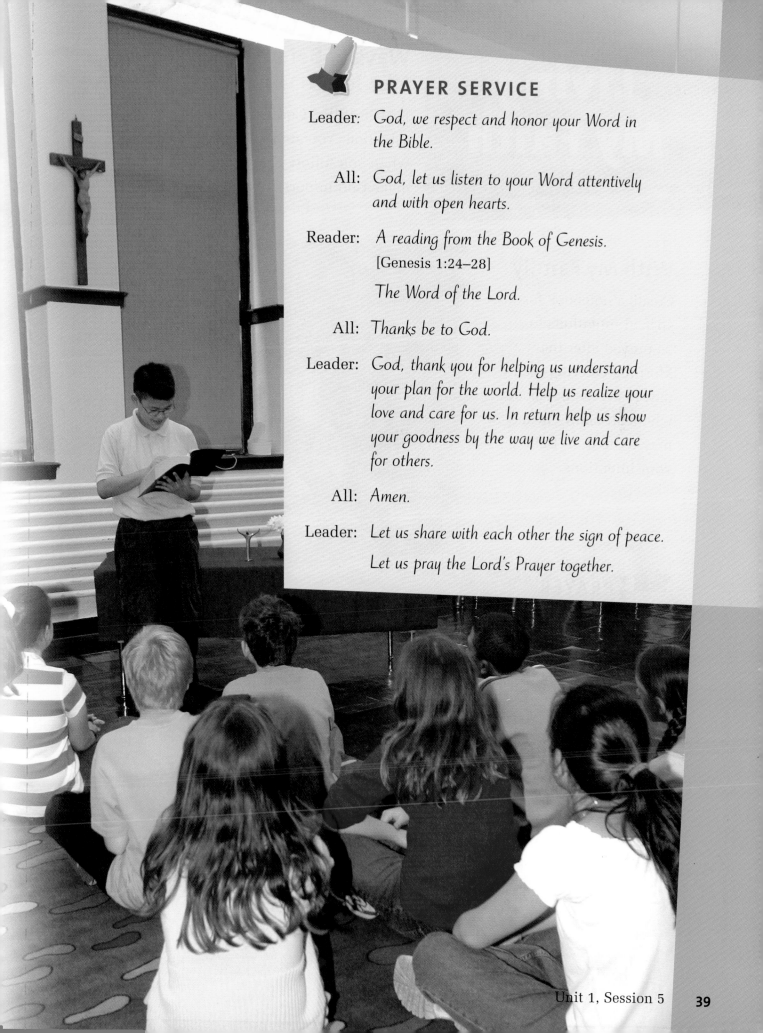

PRAYER SERVICE

Leader: God, we respect and honor your Word in the Bible.

All: God, let us listen to your Word attentively and with open hearts.

Reader: A reading from the Book of Genesis.
[Genesis 1:24–28]

The Word of the Lord.

All: Thanks be to God.

Leader: God, thank you for helping us understand your plan for the world. Help us realize your love and care for us. In return help us show your goodness by the way we live and care for others.

All: Amen.

Leader: Let us share with each other the sign of peace.

Let us pray the Lord's Prayer together.

Living My Faith

Ways of Being Like Jesus

Jesus fulfilled God's plan of salvation. You are like Jesus when you follow God's plan and make God important in your life.

With My Family

Create a notebook for special intentions to be prayed after the Morning Offering each day. Place the notebook where all family members may write in it. Date your intentions.

 PRAYER

Loving God, thank you for your actions in the world and your plan of salvation. Most of all, God, thank you for letting me know you, the almighty, maker of heaven and earth, of all things seen and unseen.

My Response

How will you try to be closer to God because of what you learned in this unit? How have you tried already?

_____

_____

_____

Son of God, Son of Mary

Saint Alphonsus Liguori

Saint Alphonsus Liguori was a Doctor of the Church, influential for his writings. He wrote about making good moral choices and about ways to pray.

Lawyer and Preacher

Alphonsus Liguori was born into a noble Italian family in 1696. A brilliant student, he received a degree in law at the age of only 16. He became a famous lawyer. Then he lost a case because of a major oversight. Alphonsus came to see this loss as God's call for him to be humble and to seek a path besides law. Alphonsus prayed to know God's will, and finally at Scala, in Italy, he had a vision of his vocation and decided to become a priest.

Saint Alphonsus with Saint Gerard Majella, J. W. Printon C.S.S.R.

Despite many difficulties, he founded an order of priests and brothers called the Redemptorists. He became a bishop known for preaching and bringing people back to God. At the end of his life, Alphonsus had many physical sufferings and went through a period of spiritual discouragement, but he did not turn from God. He died in 1787 and was canonized in 1839. His feast day is August 1.

Alphonsus taught people to pray by imagining themselves with Jesus in the Gospels and just talking with him. He taught them to open their hearts to Jesus. He also encouraged people to pray often before the Blessed Sacrament.

Alphonsus's personal outpouring of love for Jesus was expressed in hymns. One of these is still a popular Italian Christmas song: "You came down from the stars, O King of Heaven, to a bitterly cold cave."

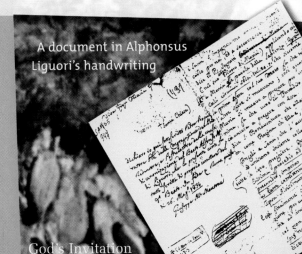

A document in Alphonsus Liguori's handwriting

SCALA

New Life in Jesus

These images of Jesus are from churches. What do they tell you about Jesus?

What other images of Jesus have you seen? What do they tell you about Jesus?

le Beau Dieu
(The Beautiful Lord),
a sculpture,
Chartres Cathedral,
Chartres, France

Jesus as the Good Shepherd,
painting on canvas,
Church of the Messiah,
Copenhagen, Denmark

The Risen Jesus,
stained glass,
Trinity Lutheran Church,
Cloquet, Minn.

PRAYER

Dear Jesus, you lived your life the way God our Father wanted. Help me to do the same thing with my life.

Jesus' Mission on Earth

The Son of God became man to fulfill a mission. With the sin of Adam, there was a break in the relationship between God and humanity. The Son of God came to heal that relationship. The **mystery** of God becoming man while remaining divine is called the **Incarnation.** (A mystery is something we believe although we do not completely understand it.)

Through his life, death, and resurrection, Jesus reconciles humanity to God. This is the reason Jesus lived on earth. In fact, the name *Jesus* means "God saves."

Jesus is both divine and human, true God and true man. As divine, Jesus is our Lord and Savior and speaks for God. As human, Jesus speaks for us. He knows our needs as well as our ability to love.

Jesus' Church Continues His Mission

Jesus' mission on earth continues for all time. Through the Holy Spirit, Jesus established a Church to carry on his mission.

The Church passes on the principles of faith taught by the apostles, Jesus' followers. It has carried on this role for centuries. In addition the Church speaks to the present needs in the world. As the sign and symbol of God's presence in the world, the Church is called to address all that concerns God: this includes speaking for justice and working for peace.

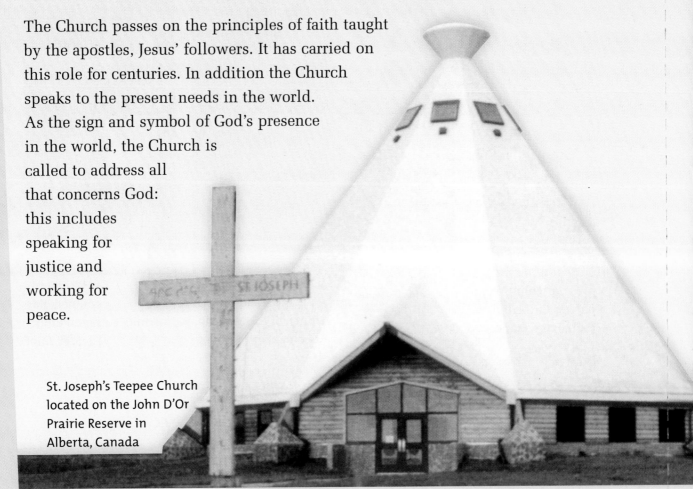

St. Joseph's Teepee Church located on the John D'Or Prairie Reserve in Alberta, Canada

Jesus'—and Our—Role in the Church

The New Testament uses a special image to show the Church's nature.

> So then you are no longer strangers and sojourners, but you are . . . members of the household of God, built upon the foundation of the apostles and the prophets, with Christ Jesus himself as the capstone. Through him the whole structure is held together and grows into a temple sacred in the Lord; in him you . . . are being built together into a dwelling place of God in the Spirit.
>
> *Ephesians 2:19-22*

This passage compares the Church to a temple of living stones. In this temple Jesus is like a keystone. Without that stone the building could not stand. This shows the unity between Jesus and the Church. Other images are also used to show this unity. These images are the Church as Body of Christ and the Church as Bride of Christ. The Church lives from, in, and for Jesus; Jesus lives with the Church and in the Church.

As the people of God, we are like stones in the temple that is the Church. We are the living sign of God's presence in the world. As believers, we have an important role in the Church.

A keystone with a carved face supports this arch.

 Reading God's Word

Therefore, thus says the Lord GOD:
See, I am laying a stone in Zion,
a stone that has been tested,
A precious cornerstone as a sure foundation;
he who puts his faith in it shall not be shaken.

Isaiah 28:16

The Role of the Holy Spirit in Jesus' Mission

The Holy Spirit continues Jesus' mission on earth. With the help of the Spirit, the Church carries on the teaching of Jesus.

The Spirit also works through individuals. In Baptism and Confirmation the Spirit gives us the help we need to fulfill our mission to be living signs of Jesus on earth. This help is called **sanctifying grace.** This special grace is a free gift from God that we cannot earn through our own efforts.

 Meet a Holy Person

Angelo Roncalli was elected pope in 1958. His papacy was a turning point in modern Church history. As Pope John XXIII, Roncalli wrote important encyclicals—pastoral letters that are written by the pope—that emphasized the need to work for economic justice and peace. His greatest achievement was calling the Second Vatican Council, whose purpose was to renew the Church. John XXIII died in 1963 and was beatified in 2000.

The Apostles' Creed

From its very beginning—from the time of the apostles—the Church has taught people about God's plan. The basic teachings of the Church are found in the Apostles' Creed. The Apostles' Creed summarizes our beliefs as Christians.

Christ Preaching, Rembrandt, c. 1650

What Does the Apostles' Creed Say?

Review the Apostles' Creed, which is found in the back of the book. Write **T** for true or **F** for false for each statement below about the Creed.

_____ 1. It recognizes that there are three persons in one God.

_____ 2. It describes the Father as Creator.

_____ 3. It talks about Adam and Eve.

_____ 4. It refers to the mystery of the Incarnation.

_____ 5. It mentions that the Bible is the Word of God.

_____ 6. Jesus' work of salvation is summarized.

_____ 7. The Last Supper is described.

_____ 8. It says Jesus returned to the Father after his life on earth.

_____ 9. The role of the pope is explained.

_____ 10. It mentions that after death there is resurrection.

 Link to Liturgy

The word *creed* comes from the Latin word *credo*, which means "I believe." The creed we pray at Mass is called the Nicene Creed. It gets its name from Nicaea, an ancient city in what is now Turkey, where the first Church council was held in the year 325.

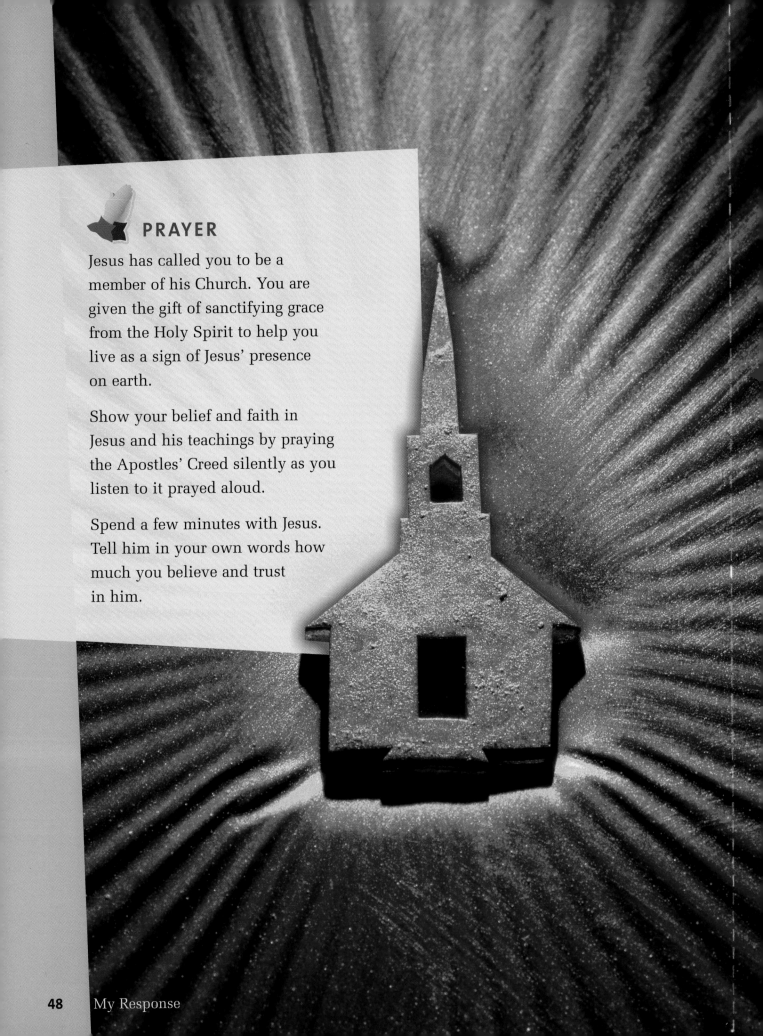

PRAYER

Jesus has called you to be a member of his Church. You are given the gift of sanctifying grace from the Holy Spirit to help you live as a sign of Jesus' presence on earth.

Show your belief and faith in Jesus and his teachings by praying the Apostles' Creed silently as you listen to it prayed aloud.

Spend a few minutes with Jesus. Tell him in your own words how much you believe and trust in him.

Faith Summary

The mystery of God becoming man in Jesus is called the Incarnation. Jesus' mission on earth continues through his Church. As members of the Church, we are signs of Jesus' presence on earth. God, through the Holy Spirit, gives us sanctifying grace, which helps us live like Jesus.

Words I Learned

Incarnation   mystery   sanctifying grace

Ways of Being Like Jesus

Jesus followed the practices of Judaism during his life, actively participating in Holy Days and following traditions. You can be like Jesus by being an active participant in your parish.

With My Family

Take a ride to two or three churches near you. Pick up church bulletins, and compare how these churches are trying to live out Jesus' mission.

PRAYER

Jesus, thank you for loving and caring for us so much that you became one of us to save us. Thank you for making me a living sign of God's presence in the world.

My Response

Think of ways that you can be closer to Jesus. These ways might be inward, such as prayer; or outward, such as helping at home. Write an action that you will do in the next week.

Focus on Faith

What Is God Like?

Children can ask what may seem like impossible questions. One of these is "What is God like?" All sorts of abstract answers come to mind. Words such as *all-powerful* and *almighty* swirl in our heads. The Christian answer is to look to Jesus Christ. He is the one who came to tell us and show us what God is like. God is our loving Father. Jesus shows us how to love. Our children are receiving their fundamental understanding of what God is like from the way we relate to them. From us they are learning how a loving parent acts. From us they are learning the dignity of being a brother or sister in Jesus.

Our Catholic Heritage

The Second Vatican Council was a major event in the recent history of the Catholic Church. This meeting of bishops from around the world was called by Pope John XXIII in 1959. The council opened on October 11, 1962. It instituted numerous changes in liturgical practices, the most striking of which was the use of native languages—instead of Latin—in celebration of the Eucharist and other sacraments. Greater understanding and communication among Christian churches was another major outcome of the Council.

Dinnertime Conversation Starter

Encourage your child to ask questions about God and about your family's religious practices. Together look for answers to puzzling questions.

Focus on Prayer

Renew your belief in Jesus' saving mission by saying the Apostles' Creed together with your child. You can find the exact words to the Apostles' Creed at www.FindingGod.org.

Spirituality in Action

Visit the cathedral in your diocese or a shrine or any other special place of worship. Help your child see that he or she is united in Christ with many people in many other places who share the same faith and liturgy.

Meeting Jesus

We sometimes use special gestures to make contact with other people. The gestures show that we are connected. What do the pictures show about people making connections? What similar gestures do you use?

PRAYER

Jesus, help me recognize the many ways you are present in the world and how you touch my life every day. Let me pass your love and goodness on to the people I meet.

Jesus Heals Jairus's Daughter

One day Jesus arrived in a town where a crowd gathered around him. Jairus pushed through the crowd and fell down at Jesus' feet. "My daughter is at the point of death. Please, come and lay your hands on her that she may get well and live."

Jesus went with Jairus. The crowd followed. On the way, people from Jairus's house met them and said, "Your daughter has died. Why trouble the teacher any longer?" Jairus was downcast, but Jesus looked at him and said, "Be not afraid. Just have faith." Jairus trusted in Jesus.

Near Jairus's house they heard loud weeping. Jesus said to the people there, "Why are you crying? The child is not dead but asleep." The people made fun of him for this.

Jesus entered the child's room. He took her by the hand, saying, "Little girl, I say to you, arise." The girl got up immediately and walked around. Jesus told the astonished parents to give their daughter something to eat. Then Jesus left the house.

adapted from Mark 5:21-24,35-43

📖 Reading God's Word

Jesus did this . . . and so revealed his glory, and his disciples began to believe in him.

John 2:11

Jesus' Presence in the Sacraments

The raising of Jairus's daughter shows God's healing power through Jesus' touch and words. Jesus touches our lives today through the sacraments. In the sacraments we celebrate the presence of Jesus. The words proclaim the meaning of the celebration. The physical objects—water, bread and wine, oil, and hands of blessing—are the signs of Jesus touching our lives. The sacraments call us to give witness to Jesus' presence in the world.

In the sacraments we recognize that God the Father is the source of all blessings (favors or good things). The sacraments are blessings we receive from God in his generosity and unshakable love. Jesus is the Father's greatest blessing to us. Through the Holy Spirit, we are made adopted children of God.

Finding Your Blessings

We are constantly receiving numerous blessings from God. The help and blessings we give each other reflect this. Write about one special blessing you have received from someone else. Tell why it is important to you.

_____

_____

_____

_____

The Seven Sacraments

Our lives are touched by Jesus Christ when we receive the sacraments. Each sacrament is associated with signs: objects, words, and actions. Each sign brings God's grace and blessings in a special way.

Baptism

In Baptism we receive new life in Christ. Baptism takes away original sin and gives us a new birth in the Holy Spirit. Its signs are water, oil, a candle, and a white garment.

Confirmation

In Confirmation the Holy Spirit strengthens our life of faith. Its signs are laying hands on a person's head (most often by a bishop) and anointing with chrism, oil mixed with perfume. Like Baptism, Confirmation is celebrated only once.

Eucharist

The Eucharist nourishes our life of faith. Its signs are the bread and wine we receive— the Body and Blood of Christ.

 Did You Know?

New adult members of the Church are traditionally welcomed during the Easter Vigil service. Unbaptized adults receive Baptism, Confirmation, and Eucharist at that time. The entire process of becoming a new Church member is found in the Rite of Christian Initiation of Adults (RCIA).

Penance

In the Sacrament of Penance, we celebrate God's forgiveness. Forgiveness requires being sorry for our sins. In this sacrament Jesus' healing grace is received through absolution by a priest.

Anointing of the Sick

This sacrament unites a sick person's sufferings with those of Jesus and brings healing and forgiveness of sins. A person is anointed with the oil of the sick and receives the laying on of hands from a priest.

Holy Orders

In Holy Orders men are ordained as priests to be leaders of the community, as bishops to shepherd the Church, or as permanent deacons to serve the community. The sacrament involves the laying on of hands for all three and the anointing with oil for bishops and priests.

Matrimony

In Matrimony a baptized man and woman are united with each other as a sign of the unity between Jesus and his Church. Matrimony requires the consent of the couple, as expressed in the marriage promises.

PRAYER

Recall the story of Jesus' raising of Jairus's daughter.

Imagine you are one of the people present in the crowd when Jairus arrives to talk to Jesus. Jairus really believes that Jesus can help. And he's right.

Jesus touches the girl. She awakens and gets up. Jesus tells the parents to get her something to eat. Jesus really cares for her.

He cares for you too. In what ways do you need Jesus' care? In your heart ask Jesus for what you need.

Listen for his answer. Thank him for his love.

Jesus Raising Up the Daughter of Jairus,
Gustave Doré

Faith Summary

Jesus' touch healed people and brought them life and peace. The sacraments celebrate Jesus' presence among us today. A sacrament is a sign by which Jesus shares God's life and blessings—grace—with us.

Ways of Being Like Jesus

You can be like Jesus when you bring healing and peace to others. You can give words of comfort to those who are sick and help with some of their needs.

With My Family

Have a family prayer time. Gather in a circle and hold hands. Say a memorized prayer or make up your own prayer. You can pray for people or intentions that are of particular importance to your family.

PRAYER

Jesus, thank you for the sacraments so that I can experience your presence in my life and receive your blessings.

My Response

The sacraments are opportunities to share in Jesus' life. What is one thing you can do this week to share Jesus' life with another person?

_____

_____

Living My Faith

RAISING FAITH-FILLED KIDS

a parent page

Focus on Faith

Becoming a Source of Blessing

At meals we begin with a prayer of blessing. We ask God to bless us and the gifts we receive. In saying this prayer, we recognize God as the source of all blessings. He is the source of all that we have and all that we share. God blesses us because he cares for us. What God asks of us is to share the blessings that we have received. We can do this with our children by blessing them with the Sign of the Cross every day. When this becomes an important practice in our homes, we show our children that the love we share is not limited to what we give them materially. God's love flows into us and overflows to others.

Dinnertime Conversation Starter

With your family do a quick recall of how God blesses you personally or as a family. Starting at one end of the dinner table, ask each person to mention a blessing, either spiritual or material. Continue around the table until you run out of things to mention. Then thank God for his generosity.

Hints for at Home

Sacramentals are sacred signs of the Church. With your child, obtain a religious image or object—a picture, a statue, a crucifix—that has a special meaning for you and your family. Choose it together, doing research and talking about it. Place the chosen image or object in a prominent place in your home.

Our Catholic Heritage

The term *sacrament* comes from the Latin word *sacramentum*. A *sacramentum* was a solemn oath or pledge of obedience such as that given by a Roman soldier to his commander. This was the visible sign of his allegiance. The term was adopted by the early Church to signify that the sacraments are visible signs of Christ's presence in the Church.

Focus on Prayer

Your child reflected on the story of Jesus' raising of Jairus's daughter (Mark 5:21–24, 35–43). Together read the story and then spend a few minutes silently reflecting on Jesus' healing presence and care for others, as well as on Jesus' presence in your lives.

Doré

Baptized Into Christ

How do you become part of a group? What ceremonies do you go through when you join? What are the duties and responsibilities of members of a group?

What do you know about how someone becomes a member of the Church?

 PRAYER

Jesus, through Baptism, you made me part of your community, the Church. Through my actions help me show that I am learning to accept my responsibilities as a member of your Church.

Peter Calls for Repentance and Baptism

Not long after Jesus ascended into heaven, the Holy Spirit came upon the disciples, who were in Jerusalem. There was a loud noise like a strong, driving wind as the Spirit came upon them. Wondering what the commotion was, many people came to see what was happening. They heard the disciples speaking. The people asked, "What is going on?"

Peter told the gathering crowd the story of Jesus—his work among people, his teachings, and his miracles. Peter told the people that Jesus, who had been crucified in Jerusalem, was the chosen one of God, the Savior that God had promised. Peter testified that Jesus had risen from the dead and had returned to the Father. From heaven Jesus Christ sent the Holy Spirit.

Moved deeply by the story of Jesus' suffering, death, and resurrection, the crowd asked Peter, "What are we to do?"

Peter said to them, "Repent and be baptized, every one of you, in the name of Jesus Christ for the forgiveness of your sins; and you will receive the gift of the holy Spirit."

adapted from the Acts of the Apostles 2:1-13,22-38

 ## Meet a Saint

Saint Francis Xavier was one of the first Jesuits. He worked in India and Japan, preaching the word of Jesus. Like the poor people, he slept on the ground in a hut and lived on rice and water. He visited prisons and hospitals, and he taught children about God's love.

Francis told many people about Jesus' call to a new life, and many answered the call. As a missionary, he baptized more than 40,000 people.

Francis became ill on the way to China and died on December 3, 1552. His feast day is December 3.

Saint Francis Xavier Resurrecting an Inhabitant of Cangoxima in Japan, Nicolas Poussin

Jesus, Salvation, and the Sacraments of Initiation

When he spoke to the crowd, Peter stated basic Christian beliefs: Jesus died on the cross for our salvation. He rose from the dead and lives in a new way beyond time and space. Peter's sermon ends in hope: Jesus Christ sends the Spirit and calls all to a new relationship with God. Jesus Christ shares his divine life with us.

We share in Jesus' divine life through the Sacraments of Initiation: Baptism, Confirmation, and Eucharist. These sacraments bring us into the fullness of the Spirit as we become members of the Church.

Linaiuoli Tabernacle: Peter Preaching with Mark, Fra Angelico, 1433

 ## Reading God's Word

Then afterward I will pour out my spirit upon all mankind.

Joel 3:1

The Sacrament of Baptism

Baptism is a call to a new birth and life—life in the Holy Spirit. Baptism unites us with the death and resurrection of Jesus, is necessary for salvation, and welcomes us into the Church.

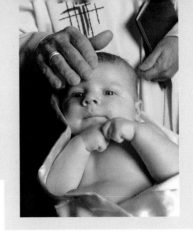

The Rite of Baptism

Water is the main sign of Baptism. Water is necessary for human life, but it can also destroy, as with floods. In nature then, water can be a sign of both life and death. So water is an appropriate sign to show our dying and rising with Jesus.

In the celebration of Baptism, a person is immersed in water. He or she goes all the way into the water and then comes out. This action is a symbol of dying to sin and rising to a new life in Christ. Sometimes water is poured over a person's head. The celebrant calls on the Trinity: "I baptize you in the name of the Father, and of the Son, and of the Holy Spirit."

The person being baptized puts on a white garment. It symbolizes that the person is a new creation, now clothed in Christ.

A child being baptized is anointed with two oils: the **oil of catechumens** is put on the chest, and **chrism** is put on the top of the head. Oil is a symbol of strength and healing.

A candle is lit during the celebration. This shows that the person baptized is asked to keep the flame of faith alive in his or her heart.

The Effects of Baptism

Through Baptism a person receives forgiveness of original sin as well as personal sins. The baptized person receives sanctifying grace. Baptism seals the person with a permanent spiritual mark. That is why the sacrament can be celebrated only once.

What Baptism Calls Us to Do

Baptism makes us members of the Church, whose mission we share.

One of our duties as members is **stewardship.** Stewardship calls Catholics to share their time, money and goods, and talents to contribute to God's kingdom on earth.

How Are You a Steward?

1. You can practice stewardship by giving service to the Church. List some ways that people of your age give service to the Church.

   _____

   _____

2. List two special talents that you have.

   _____

   _____

3. List two ways that you think you can use your talents to serve the Church.

   _____

   _____

 Did You Know?

Catechumens are people learning about the Christian life and preparing to live as Christians. Signed with the cross, they have a special relationship with the Church.

PRAYER

One of the signs of Baptism is a lit candle. It shows our responsibility to keep the flame of faith burning and to be the living sign of Jesus on earth.

Pause and think about the symbol of the lit candle. See it in your mind.

Your parents were given a lit candle at your Baptism. These are some of the words that were said when they were given the candle: "You have been enlightened by Christ. Walk always as children of light and keep the flame of faith alive in your heart."

Think about these words. Which of them have special meaning for you today?

Ask Jesus to help you walk as a child of light.

Faith Summary

Baptism is a call to a new life in Jesus Christ through the Holy Spirit. Baptism unites us with the death and resurrection of Jesus and welcomes us into the Church. Baptism makes us children of the Father, members of the Church, and temples of the Holy Spirit.

Words I Learned

chrism   oil of catechumens   stewardship

Ways of Being Like Jesus

Jesus accomplished his mission on earth. He devoted himself entirely to teaching about God and his kingdom. You can share in Jesus' mission as a baptized person by offering your talents and giving service to the Church and the community.

With My Family

Talk with your family about your Baptism. Try to find some pictures of the celebration. If you still have your baptismal candle, you might light it while you do this.

 PRAYER

Loving God, thank you for welcoming me into your community, the Church, through Baptism.

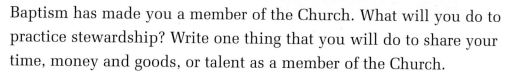

My Response

Baptism has made you a member of the Church. What will you do to practice stewardship? Write one thing that you will do to share your time, money and goods, or talent as a member of the Church.

Focus on Faith

Brothers and Sisters in Christ

It was not very long ago that your child was welcomed into your family. There are the memories of birth, the first days at home, and the gentle expectation surrounding the new life. These memories can be stirred when you run across photos or videotapes of the event or a baptismal certificate.

The child in your arms was initiated into new life in Christ. Your child became permanently bonded in Christ through Baptism. In the process your relationship with your child became deeper than that of parent to child. You and your child became brothers and sisters in Jesus Christ. How does your awareness of this deeper bond influence your relationship with your child?

Spirituality in Action

Your child is learning about stewardship—giving time, treasure, and talents in the service of the Church and the community. Encourage and help your child in any appropriate service he or she undertakes. Try to set an example for your child by using your own talents in some way for the Church. For example, you might help at Mass or cook for community dinners.

Dinnertime Conversation Starter

Place a photo, a candle, or other baptismal memorabilia for each child in the center of the dinner table. Share with each child a memory of his or her Baptism. Tell each child why his or her Baptism was an important choice for you.

Focus on Prayer

Your child has reflected on how to be a living sign of Jesus on earth, how to show his or her faith to the world. Spend time in prayer with your child as each of you completes the following sentences privately. "I show my faith in Jesus and the Church when I . . . " "I give service to the Church and to the community when I . . . "

Hints for at Home

With your child, review stories of your Baptism. Talk about the choice of your name, your godparents, and your baptismal gown. View photos or a video of the Baptism and end with a prayer of thanks for the gift of faith.

Growing in the Spirit

As you grow up, you have more and more responsibilities as a member of your family and your community. What responsibilities and duties do you have now that you didn't have one year ago? Two years ago?

In what ways are you "growing up" in your faith?

 PRAYER

Jesus, teach me what it means to be holy. May your Holy Spirit, whom I received at my Baptism, help me be strong in my faith.

The Story of Pentecost

After Jesus' ascension into heaven, the apostles' mission was to spread the news of salvation to the world and act as witnesses to Jesus. The Holy Spirit came to aid them in their mission. This happened when the apostles, Mary, and the other disciples were gathered during the Jewish feast of Pentecost, which marked the time when God gave Moses the Commandments.

> And suddenly there came from the sky a noise like a strong driving wind, and it filled the entire house in which they were. Then there appeared to them tongues as of fire, which parted and came to rest on each one of them. And they were all filled with the holy Spirit and began to speak in different tongues, as the Spirit enabled them to proclaim.

Acts of the Apostles 2:2-4

The Holy Spirit moved the apostles to proclaim the good news about Jesus and the new covenant that fulfills the promise God made to Abraham.

The Holy Spirit came as a driving wind, which is a symbol of a new kind of action of God in the story of salvation. The Spirit also came as tongues of fire. The symbolism of fire goes back to the Old Testament. When God gave Moses the Ten Commandments on Mount Sinai, smoke rose from the mountain as though it were on fire. At Pentecost, the fire again shows God acting in the world.

Pentecost, Giotto di Bondone, 1267

Our Mission as Christians

Just as the apostles were given a mission, all Christians have a special mission, a call to **holiness.** This means living a life dedicated to God and to the mission of the Church, which is to proclaim the good news of salvation offered through Jesus Christ.

Just as the Holy Spirit helped the apostles fulfill their mission, the Spirit acts in our lives and calls us to continue the mission of Jesus.

Our Mission and Confirmation

We can lead holy lives only with the help of God's grace, which we receive in the sacraments. We first received sanctifying grace in Baptism. Through that sacrament our sins were forgiven, and we received the help we need to live for God and others. Confirmation continues and completes Baptism. In Confirmation, as in Baptism, we receive sanctifying grace.

Through Confirmation our relationship with God is strengthened. We ask God to send us the Holy Spirit, the **Advocate** or Helper, to give us the **Gifts of the Holy Spirit: wisdom, understanding, counsel, fortitude, knowledge, piety,** and **fear of the Lord.** In Confirmation our bond with Jesus is made stronger, so that we can better witness to Christ. We are witnesses to Christ when our actions reflect Jesus' presence in the world and show our faith in God.

Did You Know?

Different countries have observed various customs at Pentecost. In Italy rose petals, symbolic of the fiery tongues, were scattered from the ceilings of churches. In France trumpets were blown during Mass to recall the sound of the strong, driving wind that accompanied the arrival of the Holy Spirit.

Pentecost window, T. C. Esser
St. Thomas More Church, La Crosse, Wis.

The Sacrament of Confirmation

Confirmation is a Sacrament of Initiation in which baptized Christians receive help from the Holy Spirit to fulfill their mission.

Who Can Be Confirmed?

The person being confirmed

1. has reached the age of reason, which is defined as about the age of seven.

2. professes the faith and wants to receive the sacrament.

3. is in the state of grace, a state of friendship with God.

4. is ready to live as a witness to Christ.

As in Baptism, a person can celebrate Confirmation only once.

The Rite and Signs of Confirmation

A bishop is the usual celebrant of the Sacrament of Confirmation. The bishop first extends his hands over those to be confirmed and calls on God: "Send your Holy Spirit upon them to be their helper and guide."

Each person being confirmed is then anointed with chrism. The bishop makes the Sign of the Cross on the forehead of the person as he says: "Be sealed with the Gift of the Holy Spirit."

The Effects of Confirmation

Confirmation gives sanctifying grace. We deepen the life of the Holy Spirit and form a closer bond with Jesus. The Holy Spirit helps us believe, pray, love, and perform good acts.

What Confirmation Calls Us to Do

Just as at home and in your community you take on greater
responsibility as you grow older, you take on more responsibilities
with Confirmation. You are called to show Jesus' presence by
participating more fully in the mission of the Church and by working
for justice and peace.

Understanding the Sacraments

Complete the chart about Baptism and Confirmation.
Look back at Session 8 if necessary.

	Baptism	Confirmation
Grace received		
Signs during the rite		
Number of times received		
What it calls us to do		

 Reading God's Word

The wind blows where it wills, and you can hear the sound it makes,
but you do not know where it comes from or where it goes; so it is
with everyone who is born of the Spirit.

John 3:8

PRAYER

The Holy Spirit guides you in your life.
The Spirit helps you in your call as a
Christian to live a holy life and be a sign
of the living presence of Jesus on earth.

Pray the Prayer to the Holy Spirit:

Come, Holy Spirit, fill the hearts of your faithful.
And kindle in them the fire of your love.
Send forth your Spirit and they shall be created.
And you will renew the face of the earth.

Lord,
by the light of the Holy Spirit
you have taught the hearts of your faithful.
In the same Spirit
help us relish what is right
and always rejoice in your consolation.
We ask this through Christ our Lord.
Amen.

Faith Summary

In Confirmation we are sealed with the Holy
Spirit, and we receive the strength we need to
give witness to the faith. Confirmation completes
Baptism. Through the Spirit we receive the grace
to fulfill our call as Christians, to live holy lives
and to participate in the Church's mission.

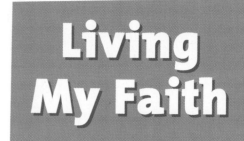

Living My Faith

Words I Learned

Advocate   holiness

Gifts of the Holy Spirit

counsel   fear of the Lord   fortitude   knowledge

piety   understanding   wisdom

Ways of Being Like Jesus

During his life, Jesus prayed to the Father,
comforted and healed others, and forgave
those who hurt him. You are like Jesus when
you forgive those who hurt you.

With My Family

Ask your parents and other family members
to share their memories of Confirmation. Ask
them if they chose new names for Confirmation
and why they chose these names.

PRAYER

*Dear Holy Spirit, thank you for being the Lord and Giver of Life. Thank you
for giving me the strength to be a living sign of Jesus' presence in the world.*

My Response

How will you try to live a holy life? Write one action you plan to take.

Focus on Faith

The Wind Blows Where It Wills

We see change going on every day. The child who came home from school is different from the child you sent to school. Each day life becomes more complex. We can easily become nostalgic for the time when things were simpler, when problems could be settled with a hug and a few comforting words. The promise of the Holy Spirit in our lives, however, is not that things will remain static. It is that as change happens, we have God's promise that his Spirit will be with us. Jesus compares the presence of the Holy Spirit in our lives with the wind that blows where it wills. We don't know where it comes from or where it is going. The image is one of mystery, movement, and change.

Dinnertime Conversation Starter

Sometimes we can make change happen. Ask your child and other family members what changes for the better they would like to make in your family life.

Hints for at Home

One of the symbols of the Holy Spirit is wind because you can feel it but you don't know where it comes from or where it goes, and it is known by its effects. Have a fun day with your child and fly kites, noting that the wind directs the kites as the Holy Spirit guides our lives.

Focus on Prayer

Your child is learning the Prayer to the Holy Spirit. Pray the prayer aloud together as a family. You can find the exact words for the Prayer to the Holy Spirit at www.FindingGod.org.

Our Catholic Heritage

Doré

In the Jewish tradition Pentecost was the celebration of the receiving of the Law from God. It was at the time of this festival that the Holy Spirit came upon the disciples. We celebrate the feast of Pentecost on the Sunday closest to 50 days after Easter to mark the Spirit's coming.

Review

The Son of God, while remaining divine, became man. He healed our relationship with God by his suffering, death, and resurrection. The Church continues his mission. Jesus continues to be present in the sacraments, which call us to a new life.

 PRAYER

Jesus, help me share your love and goodness so that I will show your presence through my example.

Faith Summary

God so loved the world that he sent his Son Jesus to save the human family. The mystery of the Son of God becoming man in Jesus is called the Incarnation. Jesus' mission on earth continues through the Church, of which he is the head. As members of the Church, we are living signs of Jesus on earth. God, through the Holy Spirit, gives us a special gift called sanctifying grace, which helps us live like Jesus.

Jesus' touch healed people and brought them life and peace. Jesus touches our lives today through the celebration of the sacraments. A sacrament is a sign by which Jesus shares God's life and blessings—grace—with us. The sacraments celebrate Jesus' presence among us. Two Sacraments of Initiation that relate to our "birth" in the community of Christians are Baptism and Confirmation.

Baptism is a call to a new life in Jesus Christ through the Holy Spirit. It unites us with the death and resurrection of Jesus, and it welcomes us into the Church. As members of the Church, we are asked to share our time and talents for the good of the Church community. We are also asked to work for peace and the equal sharing of the earth's goods by all.

In Confirmation we receive the Holy Spirit, our bond with Christ is made stronger, and we are better able to give witness to the faith. Confirmation completes Baptism. Through the Spirit, we receive the grace to live our call as Christians: to live holy lives dedicated to God and to participate in the Church's mission of proclaiming the good news about Jesus.

Know Your Faith Crossword

Solve the crossword puzzle.

Across

5. The Apostles' ____ summarizes our beliefs as Christians.

6. The main sign of Baptism is ____.

7. The Sacraments of ____ are Baptism, Confirmation, and Eucharist.

9. In Baptism we first receive ____ grace.

10. The oil used in both Baptism and Confirmation is called ____.

Down

1. Baptism unites us with the death and ____ of Jesus.

2. The act of sharing our time, money, and talents to contribute to God's kingdom on earth is called ____.

3. The mystery of the Son of God becoming man is called the ____.

4. In Baptism a person receives ____ of original sin.

8. Fortitude is a ____ of the Holy Spirit received in Confirmation.

Jesus' Work on Earth

You have learned about Jesus' work as a healer and as a teacher. You have also learned that Jesus performed miracles. Find the following passages in the New Testament. Write them on the lines. Then write whether the passage shows Jesus as a healer, as a teacher, or as a worker of a miracle in nature.

Jesus and the Fishermen by an 11-year-old in Honduras

Luke 8:23–24

_____

_____

_____

_____

Shows Jesus as: _____

Mark 8:23–24

_____

_____

_____

Shows Jesus as: _____

Matthew 5:43–44

_____

_____

_____

_____

Shows Jesus as: _____

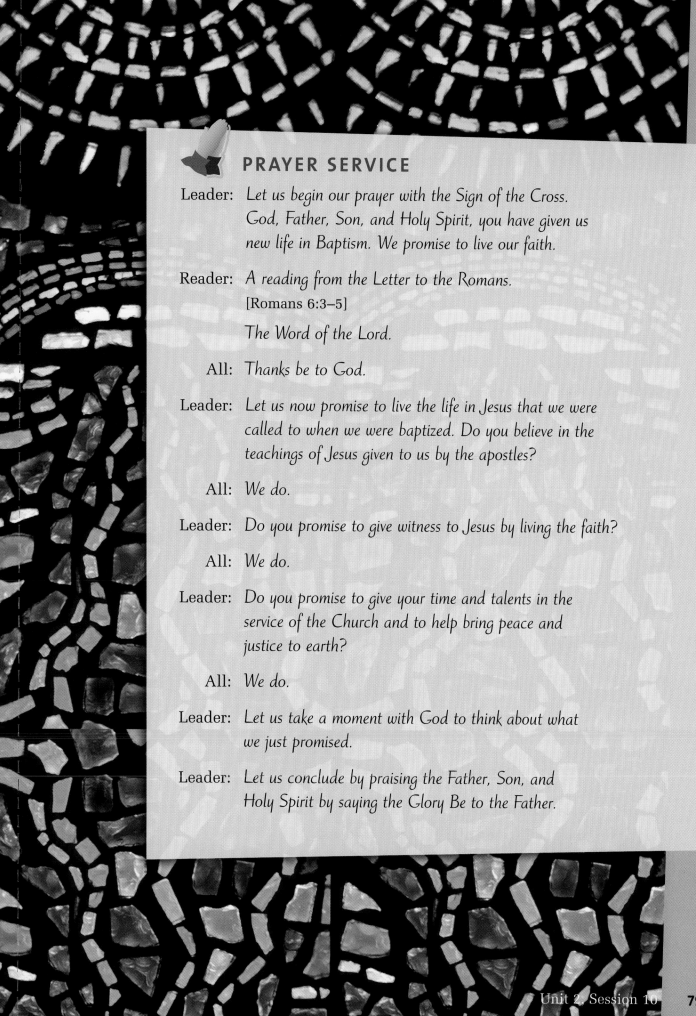

PRAYER SERVICE

Leader: Let us begin our prayer with the Sign of the Cross. God, Father, Son, and Holy Spirit, you have given us new life in Baptism. We promise to live our faith.

Reader: A reading from the Letter to the Romans.
[Romans 6:3–5]

The Word of the Lord.

All: Thanks be to God.

Leader: Let us now promise to live the life in Jesus that we were called to when we were baptized. Do you believe in the teachings of Jesus given to us by the apostles?

All: We do.

Leader: Do you promise to give witness to Jesus by living the faith?

All: We do.

Leader: Do you promise to give your time and talents in the service of the Church and to help bring peace and justice to earth?

All: We do.

Leader: Let us take a moment with God to think about what we just promised.

Leader: Let us conclude by praising the Father, Son, and Holy Spirit by saying the Glory Be to the Father.

Living My Faith

Ways of Being Like Jesus

The Son of God became man and wants us to be with him and share in his new life. We are like Jesus when we share our time, talents, and possessions with others.

With My Family

Tell your family about the ways to be like Jesus that you have learned. Share with your family the ways you have tried or might try. Ask your family about the ways they try to be like Jesus.

 PRAYER

Jesus, thank you for calling me to a new life, and for continuing your presence in my life through the sacraments.

My Response

You have learned and thought about many ways to be like Jesus. Which way seems important for you? How will you try to put that way into practice in your life? Write your ideas.

_____

_____

_____

Community of Jesus

Saint Ignatius of Loyola

Saint Ignatius of Loyola was the founder of an order of priests and brothers called the Jesuits, whose mission is to serve the Church.

Saint Ignatius of Loyola

Ignatius of Loyola, born in 1491 in Spain, started his career as a soldier in service to his king. A wound to his leg meant he had to spend months in bed. He had only two books to read. One was about Jesus and the other was about the saints. Studying them changed his life. He decided to devote himself to God's service; his goal was to imitate Jesus.

Ignatius developed a plan of meditation in a work called the *Spiritual Exercises*. This work aims at helping people find out God's will for them and at giving them the courage to follow God's call. People are first guided through meditations on sinfulness and living the Ten Commandments, and then they are asked to put themselves in the Gospel and follow along with Christ's life, death, and resurrection. The goal is to help lead people to a life of generous service, prompted by love of Christ and desire to follow him.

Ignatius's vision and ideas attracted a band of followers, and he eventually founded a community of priests and brothers called the Society of Jesus. Its members are called the Jesuits. Since Ignatius's time, Jesuits have been dedicated to service to the Church community—establishing schools and sending members to bring the Good News about Jesus throughout the world. Saint Ignatius's feast day is July 31.

The Church Is One

Mexican Day of the Dead altar

Sunday Mass, Nairobi, Kenya

What do you know about different ways to celebrate Church holidays and various customs in different places around the world? Share your information with the group.

Philippine passion play during the Lenten season

PRAYER

Jesus, help me see that I am a brother or sister of all people you have called. Help me accept and appreciate all the members of your Church.

Unity and Diversity in the Church

The Church is called the Body of Christ to show the unity between Jesus and his Church. As Church members, we share in this unity. We are all brothers and sisters in Christ and part of his Body. In the Church there is both unity and diversity. Saint Paul explains this.

> Just as a body has many parts but is still one body, so it is with Jesus Christ. No matter what your nationality, we are all one, because we are all baptized by the Holy Spirit into the same body.

adapted from 1 Corinthians 12:12-13

Paul emphasizes that the source of unity in the Church is the Holy Spirit. We are alike by sharing in divine life. This unity with God is made possible by grace, which is a gift from God and not something that we can achieve through our own efforts.

Paul also recognizes the diversity in the Church. Church members come from many different cultures and speak many different languages. They possess a variety of gifts from the Holy Spirit. In the Church, members have different roles.

 Did You Know?

The liturgy is celebrated in many languages, including the Native American languages of Navajo and Choctaw.

The Different Roles for Church Members

There are many ways to answer God's call to holiness. All baptized people are called to be holy and are part of the priesthood of believers.

- The pope, bishops, priests, and deacons receive the Sacrament of Holy Orders and form the **clergy.** Bishops and priests form the **priesthood.**

- Some people lead a **religious life,** living in a community and following its practices. They make promises called **vows.** Through the vows of poverty, chastity, and obedience, they promise to live simply, to bind themselves under the pain of sin to live in a chaste manner, and to obey those in authority.

- Members of the Church who are not priests or in religious life form the **laity.** The laity are called to be witnesses to Christ in the world and to foster gospel values in society.

Bishop MacFarland poses with a newly confirmed boy and his mother.

United in Beliefs

The Church keeps its unity by being faithful to the teachings of the apostles. In the back of your book, read the part of the Apostles' Creed that begins with the words "I believe in the Holy Spirit." It focuses on God's continuing action in the world. Match each phrase with its meaning.

_____ 1. The holy Catholic Church   a. God gives us pardon.

_____ 2. Communion of Saints   b. We will share new life in Jesus after death.

_____ 3. Forgiveness of sins   c. The Church is for all.

_____ 4. Resurrection of the body   d. All the holy—living and dead—are united.

 ## Reading God's Word

There is neither Jew nor Greek, there is neither slave nor free person, there is not male and female; for you are all one in Christ Jesus.

Galatians 3:28

The Pope's Role in the Church's Unity

A visible sign of the unity in the Church is the pope, together with the bishops who administer local dioceses. The pope and bishops receive their authority as successors of the apostles. They ensure fidelity to the apostles' teachings. The pope is the successor of Saint Peter, whom Jesus chose as the leader of the Church. As such, the pope has full authority over the Church.

The Servant of the Servants of God

Gregory the Great (540–604) was a pope who devoted himself to pastoral work. He lived at a time of political disorder, and he took on the task of providing for people's needs, including distributing food.

Gregory encouraged people to pray. He promoted an early form of devotion to the **Stations of the Cross,** in which the steps of Jesus on the way to his crucifixion are retraced. Gregory reformed the liturgy and added the Lord's Prayer to the Mass. His name was given to the religious music known as Gregorian chant.

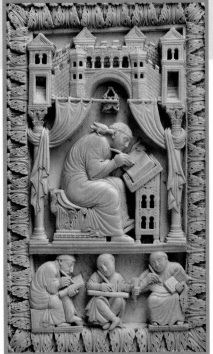

Saint Gregory the Great and three scribes, German ivory carving

Gregory was also interested in **evangelization,** spreading the news about Jesus. According to one famous story, he sent missionaries to Britain after seeing people from that island in the slave market in Rome. Gregory himself is noted as a writer who gave practical advice to help bishops and leaders serve their communities.

Gregory called himself the "servant of the servants of God," a title still used by popes. He set an example for later popes to follow.

Music of a Gregorian chant

Attending Liturgy in the Eastern Tradition

Different traditions were a part of the Church from its beginning, as the result of the division of the Roman Empire into west (Rome) and east (Constantinople, present-day Istanbul, Turkey). Read this report from a fifth-grader who sometimes attends Mass in a church that follows the Eastern tradition.

Sometimes I go to Mass on Sunday with my grandmother to a church in her neighborhood. There's one big difference from Mass in my parish—the liturgy is in Ukrainian. If you walked into the church, you would notice other differences: There is a screen across the front of the altar. Gates in the screen are opened at the start of the liturgy, but the priest stays behind the gate most of time, with his back to the congregation. A choir and the congregation sing responses throughout the liturgy, but there are no musical instruments—just voices. We stand, sit, and

Sts. Volodymyr and Olha Ukrainian Catholic Church, Chicago, Illinois

kneel during the liturgy—for example, we stand when we pray the Nicene Creed and kneel for the eucharistic prayers. When I receive the Eucharist, I first kiss an icon (a holy picture) and a crucifix, which are placed on a special table in front of the screen. The priest gives me the Eucharist on a spoon—there is a cube of bread and some wine on it. After Mass, my grandmother talks with her friends, and I see my cousins. I am happy that I can understand Ukrainian and be part of this community.

Examining the Eastern Tradition

On a separate sheet of paper, list the similarities and differences between the liturgy of this Eastern church and that of the church you usually attend. Then write what have you learned about unity and diversity in the Church from the story.

An icon picturing Christ

PRAYER

The Apostles' Creed is the prayer of faith.

When you pray the Creed, think about each sentence as you pray it. Pause after each sentence to think about what the words mean to you.

Think particularly about the meaning of these lines: "I believe in the holy catholic Church, the communion of saints."

Think about all the people you know in your parish. You see them at Mass. What are their names? Where are they from? What do they do?

Think about how we are all brothers and sisters in Christ despite our differences in ages, places of birth, talents, and interests.

Now spend a few minutes with Jesus. What do you want to say to him? Tell him whatever is on your mind. Be sure to thank him for always being with you.

Faith Summary

The Church has members in many different places with different roles and gifts. Church members are united in beliefs, as expressed in the Apostles' Creed and Church teachings, and by sharing in divine life through grace. A visible sign of Church unity is the pope with the bishops, who are successors of the apostles.

Words I Learned

clergy   evangelization   laity   priesthood
religious life   Stations of the Cross   vows

Ways of Being Like Jesus

In his public life Jesus called all people—rich and poor, young and old, leaders and outcasts. We are like Jesus when we respect and accept all people.

With My Family

With your family choose a culture about which you would like to know more, and research some of its religious customs. Talk about how these customs are similar to or different from the religious customs of your family's culture.

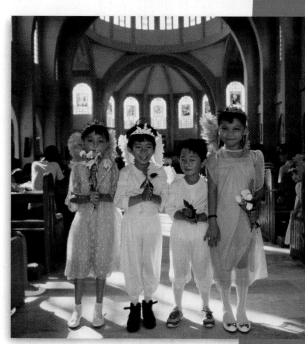

Young Philippine children in angel costumes stand in the aisle of their Catholic church.

PRAYER

Jesus, thank you for calling me to be a member of your Church and part of a community that unites people from many places and times.

My Response

As Christians we are brothers and sisters in Christ. Write one action you will take to show that you are willing to be a brother or sister to all.

Painting of the Virgin Mary holding baby Jesus, St. Mark's Coptic Orthodox Church of Chicago

Our Catholic Heritage

The motto of Saint Ignatius of Loyola and the Jesuits is *Ad Majorem Dei Gloriam.* Abbreviated AMDG, it means "For the greater glory of God." This motto refers to the Jesuit way of deciding which action, from an array of many good actions, to take. The action to take is the one that will most reveal God's glory.

Hints for at Home

Your child is learning about the diversity of peoples who make up the living Church. With

your child attend a service that reflects a tradition different from your own. It might be a liturgy in an Eastern Catholic church, such as a Ukrainian or an Armenian church, or a liturgy in a different language. Talk about how the service shows the diversity and unity in the Church.

Focus on Faith

Unity in Diversity

America has often been called a melting pot for people of many ethnic origins. Perhaps the image of a salad bowl might be more fitting, as each distinct flavor adds to the flavor of the whole. The Catholic Church is also a community of diverse cultures. Along with the experience of the Roman Catholic Church, there are some 20 Eastern Catholic churches celebrating the liturgy in languages such as Armenian, Coptic, Arabic, and Malayan. In the Roman Catholic Church, diverse spiritualities are clustered around the mission of religious orders such as the Passionists, the Dominicans, and the Jesuits. This diversity is possible because the central core of Catholic teaching within the apostolic tradition finds its unity in the pope and the bishops as successors to the apostles.

Dinnertime Conversation Starter

Share with your children the different experiences of Catholic spiritual~~ity~~ that you have had—for example, a retreat experience with a particular religious community, participation in a Catholic youth rally, or a role in a Christmas pageant or the living Stations of the Cross.

Focus on Prayer

In this session your child prayed the Apostles' Creed, which is a prayer that unites us in faith. Say the prayer aloud with all the members of your family, holding hands as a sign of being united in belief. You can find the exact words for the Apostles' Creed at www.FindingGod.org.

Called to Holy Orders

People such as police officers, teachers, and doctors give particular kinds of services to the community. How do the people in the pictures give service? How do priests give service to the community of believers?

PRAYER

Dear God, please bless all those who serve the community. Especially bless the priests who help bring us closer to you.

The Apostles Choose a New Member

Jesus chose 12 men to be apostles. One of them, Judas, betrayed Jesus and then hanged himself. After Jesus' ascension, the apostles had the important mission of spreading the news about Jesus. But they were lacking one member. Here is how the apostles chose a replacement:

Extraordinary Synod: Pope John Paul II Meets with Bishops,
Franklin McMahon, 1985

Peter informed a large group of Jesus' followers that a replacement for Judas was needed. He explained that this person needed to have been a witness to Jesus' life, death, and resurrection. Two people were proposed, Justus and Matthias. Peter and the apostles prayed for the Lord to show them whom to choose. Matthias was chosen; he became the new apostle.

adapted from Acts of the Apostles 1:15-26

The disciples chose a new Church leader to be a witness to Jesus Christ and continue his work. Today the pope and the bishops have been chosen to continue Jesus' work; they are successors of the apostles.

 Reading God's Word

And so I say to you, you are Peter, and upon this rock I will build my church, and the gates of the netherworld shall not prevail against it.

Matthew 16:18

Sacraments at the Service of Communion

People can devote themselves to service to others through two sacraments, Holy Orders and Matrimony. These two sacraments are called **Sacraments at the Service of Communion.** The mission of these sacraments is to serve the Kingdom of God. Holy Orders and Matrimony contribute to the personal salvation of those who receive them, through service to others.

Men who receive Holy Orders have an important role in serving the community; they help continue Jesus' presence on earth in the tradition of the apostles. Although priests are leaders, all members of the Church participate in the priesthood of believers through Baptism.

The love between married couples is a reflection of the love of Christ for his Church.

Cardinal Francis George ordains a new priest.

Meet a Saint

Turibius of Mogrovejo (1538–1606) was the bishop of Lima, Peru. Originally from Spain, he went to the Americas to help people in the new Spanish colonies there. As bishop, Turibius helped poor people and defended the rights of natives. He traveled constantly through his diocese to care for his people. He built churches and hospitals and set up the first seminary to train priests in the Americas. He is said to have baptized 500,000 people. Turibius was declared a saint in 1726. His feast day is March 23.

The Sacrament of Holy Orders

Holy Orders is the sacrament by which men are called by the Holy Spirit to serve the Church. Through the Rite of **Ordination,** they receive a permanent spiritual mark, called a **character,** marking them as representing Jesus' presence in the Church.

There are three kinds of participation in the Sacrament of Holy Orders: as bishop, as priest (from *presbyter,* which is Greek for "elder"), and as **deacon.**

Priests blessing deacons at an ordination ceremony

- A bishop receives the fullness of the Sacrament of Holy Orders. He is head of a local church. The local area entrusted to him is called a diocese. He is also part of the episcopal college: This is the group of bishops who, with the pope, guide the Church.

- Priests serve the community in various ways, such as presiding at liturgies, preaching, administering sacraments, counseling, serving as pastors, and teaching.

- Deacons help and serve bishops by serving the needs of the community, proclaiming the gospel, teaching and preaching, baptizing, witnessing marriages, and assisting the priest celebrant at liturgies.

Deacons are ordained for service in the Church. There are two types of deacons. Transitional deacons are studying to become priests. Permanent deacons are called to remain deacons for life and to serve the Church in this capacity.

The Rite of the Sacrament of Holy Orders

Priests receive the Sacrament of Holy Orders in the Rite of Ordination. The bishop lays his hands on the head of the candidate and says a prayer asking for an outpouring of the Holy Spirit. In one part of the rite, the candidate lies in front of the altar while the Litany of the Saints is sung or recited. In another part of the rite, a new priest's hands are anointed with chrism. In the rite for a bishop, the new bishop's head is anointed.

Window depicting Holy Orders, St. Patrick's Cathedral, Ontario, Canada

Knowing Your Church Leaders

Complete the following chart of your personal Church leaders. Fill in the names.

Pope: _____

Name of your diocese: _____

Your bishop: _____

Name of your parish: _____

Your pastor and parish priest(s): _____

Deacon(s) in your parish: _____

 Sacred Site

Mary is honored in Costa Rica as Our Lady of the Angels. On August 2, 1635, the feast of the Holy Angels, a poor woman found a three-inch-high stone carving of Mary beside a footpath. This statue was removed five times, and five times it mysteriously reappeared where it had been found. Taking this to mean that Our Lady wanted a shrine built there, the locals built a shrine, which soon became a site of pilgrimage. The shrine, which is now a basilica, is located near the town of Cartago.

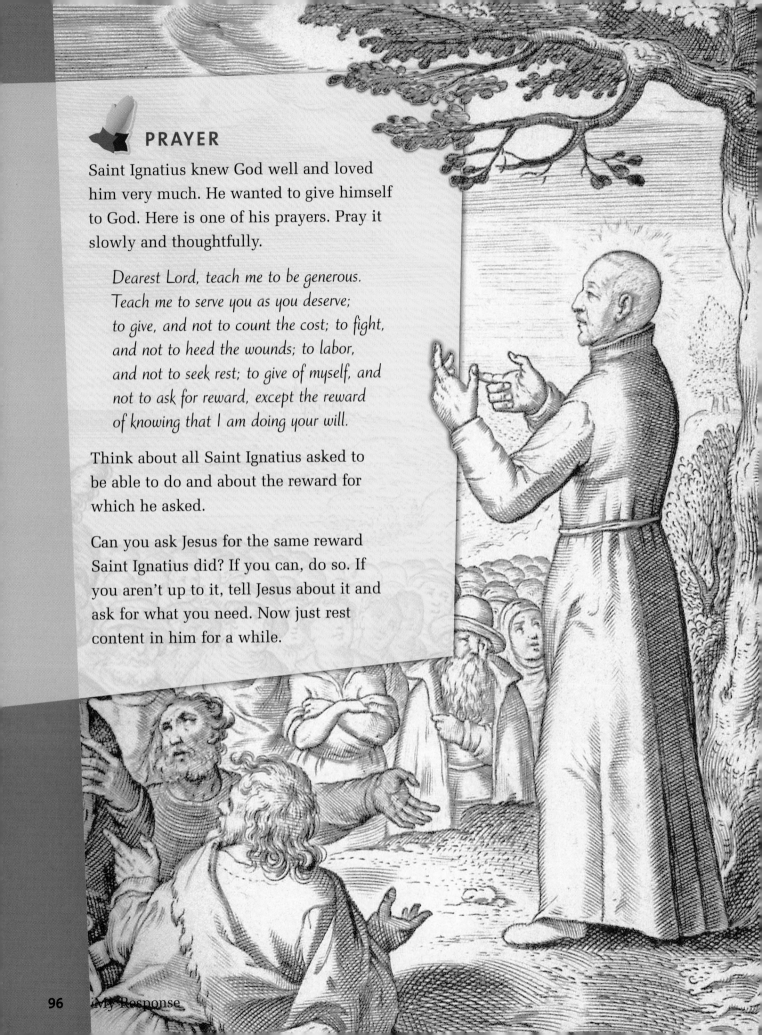

🕊 PRAYER

Saint Ignatius knew God well and loved him very much. He wanted to give himself to God. Here is one of his prayers. Pray it slowly and thoughtfully.

Dearest Lord, teach me to be generous. Teach me to serve you as you deserve; to give, and not to count the cost; to fight, and not to heed the wounds; to labor, and not to seek rest; to give of myself, and not to ask for reward, except the reward of knowing that I am doing your will.

Think about all Saint Ignatius asked to be able to do and about the reward for which he asked.

Can you ask Jesus for the same reward Saint Ignatius did? If you can, do so. If you aren't up to it, tell Jesus about it and ask for what you need. Now just rest content in him for a while.

Faith Summary

The Sacraments at the Service of Communion are Holy Orders and Matrimony. Through these sacraments people help serve God's kingdom by service to others. Holy Orders is the sacrament in which men are called to serve the Church as bishops, priests, and deacons.

Words I Learned

character   deacon   ordination
Sacraments at the Service of Communion

Ways of Being Like Jesus

We are like Jesus when we promote the mission of the Church. This can be as simple as providing a good example by participating reverently in liturgy or helping others learn more about Jesus.

With My Family

Priests and deacons preach a homily at liturgies on Sunday, helping us understand God's plan for us and Jesus' call to us. Listen to the homily on Sunday and share with your family how the homily is meaningful to you.

Living My Faith

 PRAYER

Dearest God, thank you for all those who serve the church. Help me to serve you and to know that I am doing your will.

My Response

You have learned about specific ways in which priests help the community. Write about one action you can take to serve the Church community.

Focus on Faith

God Calls Us All

A young man was sharing with his parents his plans for school and for a profession. As he finished, his father said, "There are many ways to respond to God's call, but have you ever considered serving Christ as a priest or brother?" The young man broke down and cried tears of joy. That had been his dream all along. A week later he joined a religious community. God calls each of us to a vocation in life. He calls many young men to serve as priests or religious brothers. He also calls young women to religious life. As parents, we can create an atmosphere of acceptance and love so that our children can hear God's call and answer it with a loving heart.

Dinnertime Conversation Starter

A sk your child what he or she would like to do as an adult. Listen with an open heart and explore with your child directions to take to realize that dream.

Our Catholic Heritage

Solanus Casey (1870–1957) was an American priest who has been named venerable—the first step toward sainthood. He had trouble with academic work and had a difficult time preparing to be a priest, but his superiors reluctantly allowed him to be ordained in 1904. However, he was not allowed to preach or hear confessions. He was given the job of porter, or doorkeeper, for his Capuchin community. In this job he welcomed the sick, the poor, and the homeless people who came for help. He was understanding and cheerful, and people came to him with their problems. Over time he gained a reputation as a healer of bodies and souls.

Hints for at Home

The letter to Titus (Titus 1:7–9) contains a list of qualities for good Church leaders. With your child, read this list. Talk about what each quality means. Talk about ways you and your child can demonstrate these qualities yourselves.

Focus on Prayer

Your child prayed a prayer to promote service to the community. Together pray silently in thanks for those who serve the Church community as priests and deacons. Ask that everyone answer God's call to serve.

The Domestic Church

How is your family like a small community? What activities do you do together? What are your duties? How do you learn from one another? How do you help one another? How do you show your love?

 PRAYER

Jesus, my helper, show me how to love, forgive, and share within my family, so that I can help my family be a place where your love can be found.

Jesus in the Temple as a Child

Jesus grew up in a family, with his parents Mary and Joseph. His family was faithful to the traditions of Judaism, observing the feasts and praying together. The Gospel of Luke tells how the 12-year-old Jesus remained in Jerusalem after the festival of Passover.

When the festival days had ended, Mary and Joseph began their return journey to Nazareth, unaware Jesus was not with them. When they discovered he was not among those in the caravan, they returned to Jerusalem. After searching for Jesus for three days, they found him in the Temple speaking with and listening to the teachers, who were impressed with Jesus' wisdom and understanding.

When Joseph and Mary saw Jesus, Mary asked him why he had done this and worried them so. Jesus replied, "Why were you looking for me? Did you not know that I must be in my Father's house?" His parents were astonished.

Jesus returned to Nazareth with his parents and was obedient to them. In Nazareth he grew up, gradually gaining understanding and wisdom.

adapted from Luke 2:42-52

Jesus Among Doctors, Jean Auguste Dominique Ingres

The story tells of the time when Jesus as a child began his mission in the world as given to him by his Father. The rest of the time he lived with his parents as a loving, obedient child.

 Sacred Site

The original Temple in Jerusalem housed the Ark of the Covenant, which contained the Ten Commandments. Before Jesus' time the Temple had been destroyed and rebuilt. It was destroyed for the last time by the Romans in A.D. 70.

The Family as the Domestic Church

Maria

There is a long tradition in Christianity that calls the family the **domestic church.** This is where children first learn to worship God, to love and forgive, and to work together.

In a family, children receive their introductions to the faith. Cooperating with the Holy Spirit, the family forms a community of grace and prayer. It is a school in which children learn about how to live a holy life and how to be loving.

Luigi

Luigi Beltrame Quattrocchi (1880–1951) and Maria Corsini Beltrame Quattrocchi (1884–1965) show us how a family forms a domestic church. Married in Rome in 1905, they had four children, three of whom entered religious communities.

Luigi, a lawyer, was an example of dedication to family and work. He was active in serving the community and promoting Christian values. Maria was also very active in the community, ministering to people's needs, as well as writing on education and teaching about God.

Beltrame Quattrocchi family photo, Rome, Italy, 1922

This married couple is an example of how to create an atmosphere of faith in the home and how to serve the community. Although their life was ordinary, they lived it in an extraordinary way. They were the first married couple to be named "blessed" together. (Being named "blessed" is a step toward sainthood.)

The Sacrament of Matrimony

In the Sacrament of Matrimony, a man and a woman celebrate their commitment of lifelong love for each other. The Sacrament of Matrimony is a sign of a special vocation: God has called the couple to a life of love in a community. Matrimony builds the people of God. As a result, like Holy Orders, Matrimony is called a Sacrament at the Service of Communion.

Matrimony is based on the personal decision of a man and woman, who promise to dedicate themselves to each other for their lives. As a sacrament, the couple's union is a reflection of the love of Christ for his Church.

Because marriage is important in building the people of God, the celebration of a couple's love takes place before a priest or another witness approved by the Church. In the ceremony itself the couple exchanges promises. They are the ministers of the sacrament.

Celebrating Matrimony

Matrimony often takes place during the celebration of a eucharistic liturgy. The couple exchanges promises. Here is one example:

"I, [name], take you, [name],
to be my wife/husband.
I promise to be true to you
in good times and in bad,
in sickness and in health.
I will love you and honor
you all the days of my life."

 Reading God's Word

" . . . wherever you go I will go"

Ruth 1:16

In the Sacrament of Matrimony, the couple receives the grace they need to love each other with a love similar to that with which Christ loves the Church. The grace of the sacrament perfects the human love of the couple. The Holy Spirit is the source of love and gives the couple the strength of enduring love.

Building the Domestic Church

The Holy Spirit also helps us to build the domestic church. Make a promise about how to live your role in the domestic church, which is your family.

I promise to help make my family a place of prayer by

_____ .

I promise to help make my family a place of sharing by

_____ .

I promise to help make my family a loving community by

_____ .

I promise to help make my family a forgiving community by

_____ .

I promise to help make my family a serving community by

_____ .

 ## Link to Liturgy

We form a community of prayer when we gather together to celebrate liturgy. A family forms a community of prayer when, for example, it prays grace before and after meals.

PRAYER

A family forms a special community called the domestic church. Part of being a domestic church is praying together as a family.

You can pray as a family before and after meals with the following prayers.

Prayer Before Meals

Bless us, O Lord, and these your gifts
which we are about to receive from your goodness.
Through Christ Our Lord.
Amen.

We get nourishment, energy, and enjoyment from the foods we eat and from each other's company. All these gifts are from God. Take some time now to thank God for his generosity.

Conclude with the following prayer of thanksgiving:

Prayer After Meals

We give you thanks for all your gifts, almighty God,
living and reigning now and for ever.
Amen.

Faith Summary

The Sacrament of Matrimony is based on the promise of a man and a woman to a lifelong love and gives a couple the grace from the Holy Spirit to fulfill their promise. The couple's union reflects the enduring love between Jesus and the Church. The couple, together with their children, make up what is called the domestic church.

Word I Learned

domestic church

Ways of Being Like Jesus

We can be like Jesus when we respect our family and promote love and closeness within it.

With My Family

Talk with your family about various ways you can make your family a place of prayer, love, sharing, and forgiving. Share some of your thoughts from the activities you did in this session with them.

 PRAYER

Jesus, thank you for letting me be part of a special community of love and prayer with my family. Thank you for putting others in my life so that together we may grow closer to you.

My Response

A family can be a place of prayer, love, and service. Write one way in which you will help or do something special for a member of your family during the next week.

RAISING FAITH-FILLED KIDS

a parent page

Focus on Faith

What Our Children Are Learning

Luke tells the story of the young boy Jesus in the Temple, listening to the teachers and impressing them with his wisdom and understanding. When Mary and Joseph come looking for Jesus, he tells them that he is doing his Father's business. Nevertheless, Jesus goes home and is obedient to them. Consider the source of Jesus' wisdom and understanding. Jesus learned all of these things within the context of his loving home. Mary and Joseph shared with him their understanding of God. They taught him the traditions of his people. Jesus' insights were based on his daily experience in the home. When our children leave home for school or play, they take with them the wisdom and understanding that we have taught them. What are we teaching them that they will share?

Dinnertime Conversation Starter

Share with your child traditions that you bring from your childhood home and that you hope will become his or her traditions as well. Explain why these traditions are important to you.

Spirituality in Action

Share with your child pictures and memories of your marriage ceremony. What were your hopes and dreams as your family grew?

Focus on Prayer

Your child is learning the prayers to pray before and after meals. Pray them together as a family at mealtimes. You can find the exact words for these prayers at www.FindingGod.org.

Hints for at Home

Your child has thought of some ways to make your home a place of prayer, love, and sharing. Talk with your child about those ways. Also think of ways that you yourself can work toward this goal. They could be as simple as spending more time doing things together or setting aside a certain time for prayer. You might want to prepare a weekly or monthly sheet, with headings such as those shown below, on which family members can write personal promises.

This week/month I will share my time with my family by . . .
This week/month I will give to my family by . . .
This week/month I promise to keep my home a place of peace by . . .

God Calls Us

The title of this sculpture is *Universal Call to Holiness.* It is a 37-ton, 780-square-foot relief carved in marble. It is at the National Shrine of the Immaculate Conception in Washington, D.C.

What does it tell about the role of the Holy Spirit? What does it tell you about the role of Mary among those who received God's call?

PRAYER

Jesus, help me understand your call to service for me personally, so that I may respond to it, as Mary your Mother did.

The Universal Call to Holiness

In 1988 Pope John Paul II wrote about the vocation to holiness as something every person is called to. Because the Spirit is in us, we are all called to live holy lives within such areas as politics, mass media, economics, science, and the arts. In their vocation as laypeople, single or married, the laity seek the Kingdom of God by engaging in everyday affairs following gospel values.

Assembling a Sculpture

On November 4, 1999, Cardinal James Hickey, the archbishop of Washington, D.C., led the dedication for the sculpture *Universal Call to Holiness.* (See previous page.) This work was created by the American sculptor George Carr. First, Carr designed a small model for approval. Then Carr made a full-scale clay model.

This large model was sent to Tuscany, Italy, where 22 skilled sculptors used it to carve the design out of huge slabs of marble. The slabs were then transported to the United States, where architect Anthony Segreti and construction consultants put the huge pieces into place. Workers moved the pieces with hand-operated pulleys since the abrupt on-and-off thrusts caused by electric pulleys could have damaged the pieces. The work was possible because of the cooperation of people with diverse backgrounds and skills.

Cooperating on a Project

Have you ever worked as part of a team or on a group project? What talents did you share? How did the project come out? Choose one experience, and write a few sentences about it.

The huge marble slabs are chosen, sculpted, and then carefully lowered into place.

Using One's Talents for Service

In the early Church some people who received special gifts from the Spirit did not use their gifts well, and there was disorder in some communities. Saint Paul wrote to address the problem:

> Now you are Christ's body, and individually parts of it. Some people God has designated in the church to be, first, apostles; second, prophets; third, teachers; then, mighty deeds; then, gifts of healing, assistance, administration, and varieties of tongues. Are all apostles? Are all prophets? Are all teachers? Do all work mighty deeds?
>
> *1 Corinthians 12:27-29*

Saint Paul recognizes that Church members have different gifts and roles. He is telling everyone to use their talents in the interest of the community and not to make proud shows of themselves. He is emphasizing that each person has something to offer the community. Paul goes on to mention that the greatest gift of all is love—a gift that all can put into action.

All Christians are called to a life of mission and service. There are various callings, or vocations, such as being a priest or member of a religious community, a married or a single person. Each vocation serves the people of God and God's kingdom.

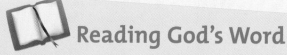 Reading God's Word

The LORD came and revealed his presence, calling out as before, "Samuel, Samuel!" Samuel answered, "Speak, for your servant is listening."

1 Samuel 3:10

Sharing Talents

Write a few special talents and interests you have.

My talents: _____

_____

My interests: _____

_____

Write how you can live Jesus' call now and use your talents for service in these places:

At home: _____

_____

At school: _____

_____

In my parish: _____

_____

In my community: _____

_____

 ## Sacred Site

Mary is the patroness of Cuba, where she is honored as Our Lady of Charity of Cobre. According to legend, in 1600 a statue of Mary appeared at sea to three men in a canoe. She was holding the child Jesus on her right arm and a gold cross in her left hand. The statue itself was fastened to a board that read, "I am the Virgin of Charity." As a symbol of Cuban nationality, today images of her bear the colors of the Cuban flag: white, blue, and red. Her sanctuary, which is now a basilica, is located in the town of Cobre.

The Blessed Virgin Mary

Mary was called to a special vocation: She was called at the time of the Annunciation to be the mother of Jesus. By saying yes, Mary cooperated with God in the history of salvation. In saying yes to God, Mary was filled with the Holy Spirit and received the grace to fulfill her vocation as the virgin Mother of God.

Mary is special among human beings. From the very first moment of her conception and her life in her mother's body, she was preserved from original sin. This is called Mary's Immaculate Conception. She remained totally dedicated to God and free from personal sin throughout her life.

When Mary's life on earth was completed after Jesus' Ascension and the coming of the Holy Spirit, she was taken into heaven, body and soul. This is called Mary's **Assumption.** Mary now reigns as Queen of Heaven.

Mary intercedes and prays for us as we work to fulfill the vocations given to us by God. We can ask for her help in prayers such as the Hail Mary and the Rosary.

Mary, Queen of Heaven,
Master of the Saint Lucy Legend

 Did You Know?

The patroness of the United States is Mary, under the title of the Immaculate Conception.

PRAYER

God called Mary to be the Mother of Jesus. She accepted his call. God has a personal call for you too.

Imagine that you are talking with Mary. Ask her how it felt to be called by God. What does she say to you?

Ask her how it felt to say yes to God's call. What does she tell you?

Talk with her about your call to serve. What does she say to you? What things does she want you to do to serve the community now? What do you tell her?

Sit quietly with Mary, aware of her love and guidance.

Assumption Mosaic, National Shrine

Faith Summary

As baptized members of the Church, we are all called by the Holy Spirit to serve the community. Each vocation—priest, religious community member, married, or single—helps develop the people of God as a whole. Mary accepted the vocation of being the Mother of Jesus. Mary was preserved from original sin and was free from sin throughout her life.

Word I Learned

Assumption

Ways of Being Like Jesus

We are like Jesus when we answer his call to contribute to God's kingdom and when we listen to and act on God's call to us through the Spirit.

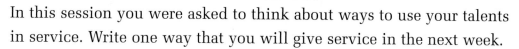

Living My Faith

With My Family

With your family make a list of ways that they think you can use your talents to contribute and serve at home, at school, at church, and in the community.

 PRAYER

Jesus, thank you for giving us Mary as an example for following God's will. Help me follow her example and show God's love to others.

My Response

In this session you were asked to think about ways to use your talents in service. Write one way that you will give service in the next week.

Focus on Faith

Jesus Calls Us to Serve

As a family sat down to dinner, the parents looked at each of their children. One was not very good in math but had a big heart and took great responsibility for his younger brothers and sisters. Another could be a bit severe but was determined to learn and even taught herself to read at a young age. One of the boys had wonderful religious insights, but sometimes his parents wondered whether his head would ever leave the clouds. The parents inwardly sighed with joy but with some concern. Just as God called Mary to her vocation as the Mother of Jesus, God would call each of these children to serve in some unique way. How can you best nurture each of your children so that the talents God has given each one will flourish?

Dinnertime Conversation Starter

Give your children opportunities to dream out loud about their goals. Listen to their dreams in a nonjudgmental way to discover their talents and brainstorm about ways to nurture them.

Our Catholic Heritage

Upon the end of her life on earth, Mary was assumed into heaven. The Church celebrates the feast of Mary's Assumption on August 15. It is a Holy Day of Obligation. The Assumption was proclaimed a doctrine of the Church in 1950 by Pope Pius XII.

Spirituality in Action

As your child thinks of ways to use his or her talents for service, think of one way that you can give service and put it into action as an example to your child. An example of something you might do is help a community organization put out its monthly newsletter.

Focus on Prayer

In this session your child learned about how Mary accepted God's call and how she will pray for us and help us listen and act on God's call. As a family, pray the Rosary or pray one decade of the Rosary a day for five days to ask for help in understanding and following God's call. The Mysteries of the Rosary can be found at www.FindingGod.org.

Review

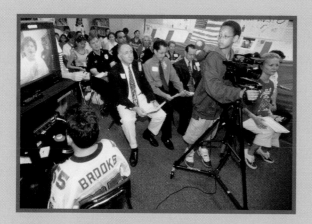

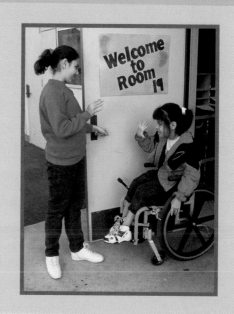

Everyone is called to be part of God's people and to serve his kingdom. People are called to give service in many different ways. What are some ways you have learned?

 PRAYER

Jesus, you have called me to be part of your Kingdom. Help me appreciate all who contribute to your community, and help me find the vocation that is your choice for me.

Faith Summary

The Church is diverse and united. Its members are in many different places with different roles and gifts. Yet the Church remains united by the guidance of the Holy Spirit. Church members are united in beliefs, as expressed in the Apostles' Creed and Church teachings. A visible sign of Church unity is the pope with the bishops.

The Sacraments at the Service of Communion are Holy Orders and Matrimony. Through these sacraments people help serve God's kingdom by service to the community.

Holy Orders is the sacrament in which men are called to serve the Church as bishops, priests, and deacons. They are the means by which Jesus' presence in the Church continues through the sacraments.

The Sacrament of Matrimony is based on the promise of a man and a woman to a lifelong love and gives a couple the grace to fulfill their promise. The couple, together with their children, make up the family, or domestic church.

As baptized members of the Church, we are called by the Holy Spirit to serve the community in a special way. Each vocation—priest, religious community member, married, or single—serves the people of God as a whole.

Mary was called to the vocation of being the virgin Mother of Jesus. She humbly cooperated with God's plan. Mary was preserved from original sin and was free from sin throughout her life.

Service · Mission

Unity

Community Acrostic

Read the clues. Write the correct words in the blanks to complete the puzzle.

1. The geographic area for which a bishop has responsibility

2. A man ordained to assist bishops and priests

3. The special community formed by a married couple and their children is called the _____ church.

4. A word used to describe how Mary was taken into heaven, body and soul

5. One Sacrament at the Service of _____ is Matrimony.

6. When a priest is anointed by a bishop

7. Someone who has received the fullness of the Sacrament of Holy Orders

8. The ancient Jews' sacred place to worship God

9. Church members who are neither ordained nor members of religious communities

1. __ __ __ **C** __ __ __

2. __ __ __ __ **O** __

3. __ __ **M** __ __ __ __ __ __

4. __ __ __ __ **M** __ __ __ __ __

5. __ __ __ __ __ **U** __ __ __

6. __ __ __ __ **N** __ __ __ __ __

7. __ **I** __ __ __ __ __

8. **T** __ __ __ __ __

9. __ __ __ __ __ **Y**

Bless This Home

Your family forms a community of grace and prayer, a domestic church. The place where your family lives is special. It is where your parents or caregivers share their faith with you, where you learn about God and his goodness, and where you can grow in the light of God's love.

Many things make your home a good place. Ask God to bless your home and those who live in it.

Write a blessing of your own for your home. Create a border in colors and shapes of your liking. Write your blessing inside this border. Sample home blessings are provided below.

Take your blessing home and show it to your family. Together choose a prominent place near the front door where it can be displayed.

Sample home blessings:

Bless this home with love.
Fill its rooms with bright sunshine,
its table with good food,
its beds with happy dreams.
Let those who live here
find in it rest and laughter.
May they live long and happily
within its walls.

May this home be a place
of laughter and good health,
of support in difficult times.
May those who live here
be slow to anger,
generous with their forgiveness,
and unconditional in their love.

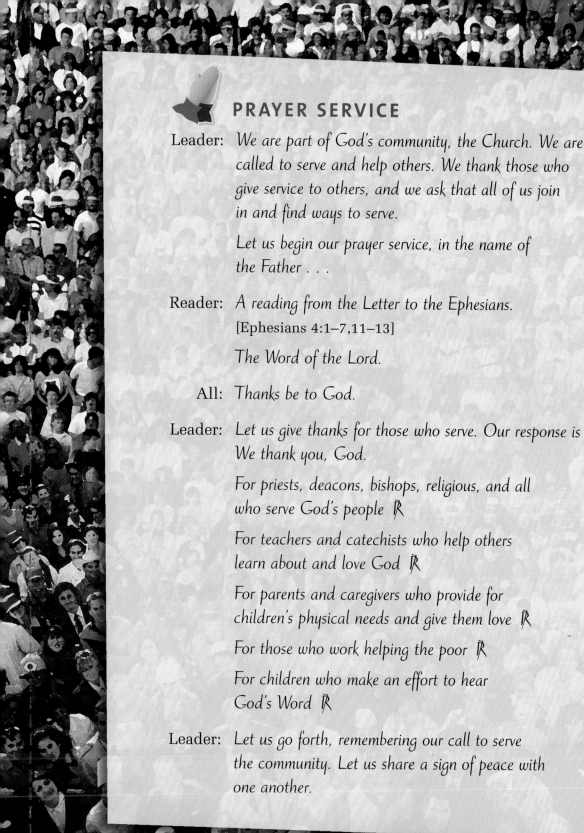

PRAYER SERVICE

Leader: We are part of God's community, the Church. We are called to serve and help others. We thank those who give service to others, and we ask that all of us join in and find ways to serve.

Let us begin our prayer service, in the name of the Father . . .

Reader: A reading from the Letter to the Ephesians. [Ephesians 4:1–7,11–13]

The Word of the Lord.

All: Thanks be to God.

Leader: Let us give thanks for those who serve. Our response is We thank you, God.

For priests, deacons, bishops, religious, and all who serve God's people ℟

For teachers and catechists who help others learn about and love God ℟

For parents and caregivers who provide for children's physical needs and give them love ℟

For those who work helping the poor ℟

For children who make an effort to hear God's Word ℟

Leader: Let us go forth, remembering our call to serve the community. Let us share a sign of peace with one another.

Living My Faith

Ways of Being Like Jesus

You are like Jesus when you actively contribute to the communities of which you are a part.

With My Family

Talk with your family about how your family can work together to help the Church community and the wider community. You might consider things like ushering at Mass, presenting the gifts, and helping to hand out the church bulletin at the end of Mass. You might also consider participating in a fundraiser for a charitable cause or helping clean up a park in your neighborhood. Set a date to do some of these things together.

 PRAYER

Dear Jesus, thank you for letting me be one of your people, a member of your family, the Church.

My Response

You have learned and thought about many ways to serve the community. Right now, in what way is it very important for you to serve? How will you try to put that way into practice in your life?

Meeting Jesus

Saint Bernadette

Bernadette Soubirous was a poor girl to whom Mary appeared in 1858 at Lourdes in southern France. The shrine at Lourdes has been a place for healings and prayer ever since.

Saint Bernadette

Bernadette Soubirous came from a poor peasant family in southern France. On February 11, 1858, while she was gathering wood, she had a vision of Mary. This was the first of 18 visions that the 14-year-old girl experienced that year. Mary, who called herself the Immaculate Conception, asked that people do penance for the conversion of sinners and requested that they visit Lourdes, the site of the visions, on pilgrimage. Mary instructed Bernadette to dig for a hidden spring. She did so, and a spring was discovered whose waters healed the sick.

Bernadette herself suffered a great deal as a result of the visions. Many people doubted that Mary had ever appeared to Bernadette and sought to test her; others were jealous of her and treated her unkindly. Through it all, Bernadette steadfastly affirmed the existence of the "lady in white" and was humble and patient. Recognizing that she had received a call to be a nun, she entered a convent, where she lived a life of holiness and simplicity. When a new basilica was opened at Lourdes in 1876, she chose not to attend the celebration because she did not want to attract any attention.

Bernadette died at the age of 35 and was canonized in 1933. She was the first saint to be photographed, and in 1942 a Hollywood film was made about her life. Her feast day is April 16.

The New Passover

What do these pictures have in common? What do the pictures tell us about the kinds of food we eat? What do they tell us about sharing food with others?

When do you eat together with others, sharing food? At what kinds of special events do you share food?

PRAYER

Jesus, help me see how you give us spiritual food. May I come close to you in celebrating the Eucharist with others and in receiving you in Holy Communion.

Jesus Feeds the Crowd

One day Jesus went up on a mountain with his disciples. Jesus saw that a large crowd was gathering, and he knew that the time for a meal was near.

He asked his disciple Philip, "Where can we buy enough food for the people to eat?" Philip answered, "Two hundred days' wages worth of food would not be enough for each person to have just a little." Another disciple Andrew said, "There is a boy here who has five barley loaves and two fish, but what good are these for so many?" Jesus said, "Have the people sit down." So about five thousand people sat down on the grass.

Then Jesus took the loaves, gave thanks, and gave them to the crowd; he did the same with the fish. Those present ate as much as they wanted. Then Jesus said to his disciples, "Gather the leftovers, so that nothing will be wasted." So the disciples collected the remaining food, which filled 12 wicker baskets.

When the people saw what Jesus had done, they said, "This is truly the Prophet, the one who is to come into the world." They wanted to make him king. They said to him, "Sir, give us this bread always." Jesus said to them, "I am the bread of life; whoever comes to me will never hunger, and whoever believes in me will never thirst."

adapted from John 6:1-15, 34-35

Jesus Feeds the Crowd, Monica Liu

Jesus, the Bread of Life

During Jesus' time, bread was a sign of abundance and hospitality. The abundance of bread in the story is a sign that God's kingdom had come in Jesus. When Jesus identifies himself as the bread of life, he means that he himself is the abundance that God offers the world.

In the story the people who eat do not understand Jesus' mission. They ask Jesus if he is like Moses, who gave the Hebrews bread when they were wandering in the desert after being freed from slavery in Egypt. That bread was called *manna*, and daily it fell from heaven for the Hebrews to gather.

Jesus answers that although the Hebrews at the time of Moses ate bread, they still died. Jesus says that he is the living bread who came down from heaven, and that whoever eats this bread will live forever. Jesus is referring to the Eucharist, which he was to institute at the Last Supper, the night before he suffered and died.

In Jesus' time, sharing bread with others was a sign of being reconciled with one another. In sharing the bread of Jesus in the Eucharist, Christians are reconciled with God and with one another.

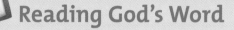

Reading God's Word

Jesus said to him, "Have you come to believe because you have seen me? Blessed are those who have not seen and have believed."

John 20:29

Passover, the Last Supper, and the Eucharist

Jesus instituted the Eucharist at the Last Supper during the season of **Passover,** the central celebration of the Jewish people. It recalls God's liberation of the Hebrews from slavery in Egypt at the time of Moses.

God called Moses to lead his people out of Egypt, but the ruler of Egypt refused to hear Moses' request to free the Hebrews. So God sent the Egyptians a series of plagues, including frogs, flies, and locusts. Finally the angel of God's judgment brought death to the firstborn males of the Egyptians, while "passing over" the houses of the Hebrew families. The Hebrew families had been asked to sacrifice a lamb and place its blood over their doors so the angel would know which houses to pass over. The Egyptian ruler finally relented and let the Hebrews go.

This event is celebrated in the Passover meal. At the meal, Jewish people view God's liberating acts as taking place not just in the past but also in their own lives.

Christians see the story of Passover as anticipating the events of the Last Supper and of Jesus' Passion. The Hebrews were saved at the time of the first Passover meal by the sacrifice of the lamb. All people are saved by Jesus' sacrifice.

Last Supper, J. Lambert-Rucki, 1947

More About Passover

1. Read Exodus 12:5–8. What was eaten at the Passover Meal?

_____

2. Read Exodus 12:5–8,12–13. What were Jews asked to put over their

   doors to show they followed God? _____

The Eucharist as Celebration and Sacrament

The story of Jesus feeding the crowd shows Jesus providing for people's physical needs. At the Last Supper, Jesus provides for our spiritual needs by instituting the Eucharist. He tells us, "This is my body. This is my blood." The Eucharist is the focal point of Christian life.

The word *Eucharist*, which comes from a Greek word that means "thanksgiving," can refer both to the entire liturgy of the Mass and to the sacrament celebrated at the Mass. The bread, made of wheat, and the wine, made of grapes, are consecrated during the liturgy, and these become the Body and Blood of Jesus Christ, or Holy Communion.

Priest consecrating the Eucharist

Jesus is present in the eucharistic celebration in the person of the ordained priest; in the **assembly,** which consists of the people present; in the word proclaimed; and in the consecrated bread and wine.

The Eucharist is the central celebration in the life of Catholic Christians. Because of the central importance of the Eucharist in their lives, Catholics are obliged to attend Mass on Sundays and on Holy Days of Obligation. The Eucharist is offered for the living, as well as for the dead.

The Liturgical Year

Just as the celebration of the Eucharist commemorates the Last Supper, the entire **liturgical year** commemorates the life of Jesus from his coming and birth (Advent and Christmas), to his death and resurrection (Lent, Holy Week, and Easter), through his Ascension and his sending of the Spirit at Pentecost. Our call to follow Jesus day by day as his disciples is celebrated in Ordinary Time.

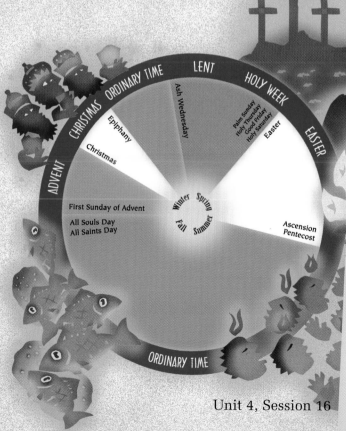

PRAYER

Recall the story of Jesus feeding the crowd with loaves and fishes.

Imagine you are in the crowd when the disciples distribute the food. You are sitting on the grass. You eat and are filled.

You notice that there are many baskets of food left over, even though there had been only a few loaves of bread and some fish to begin with.

What goes through your mind?

Then you hear Jesus say, "I am the bread of life; whoever comes to me will never hunger, and whoever believes in me will never thirst."

What is Jesus saying? Think about his words and about who he is.

Someone has come to sit next to you. It is Jesus. He smiles, says your name, and asks, "What do you want to talk about?"

Tell Jesus whatever is in your heart. He is listening. What does he tell you? Thank Jesus for his help.

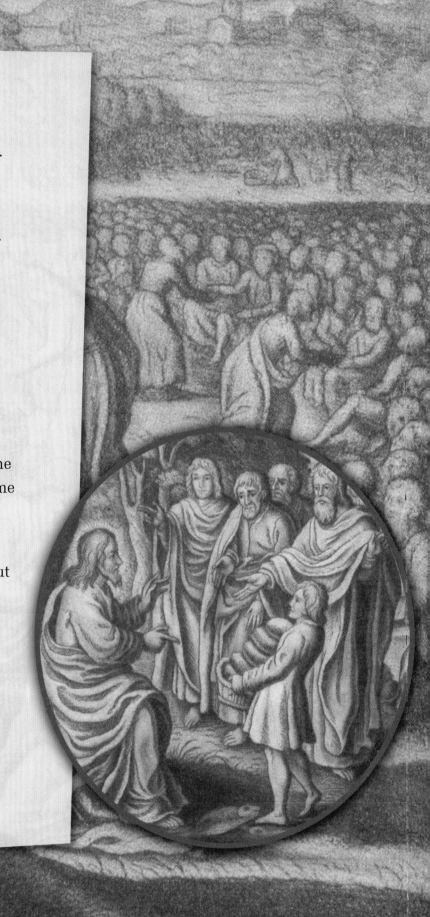

Faith Summary

Jesus is the bread of life. Just as he miraculously fed the crowds with bread and fish, he provides us with spiritual food in the Eucharist, which he instituted at the Last Supper. Celebrating the Eucharist is the source and summit of Christian life. It is both the liturgy that is celebrated and the sacrament whose signs are bread and wine. In the eucharistic celebration, Jesus is present in the priest, the assembly, the Word of God, and in a special way in the consecrated bread and wine.

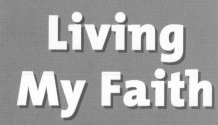

Living My Faith

Words I Learned

assembly   liturgical year   Passover

Ways of Being Like Jesus

You are like Jesus when you are alert to the needs of others and act to do what you can to fill those needs. Sometimes you can help others just by listening to them, or sometimes you can give time and help even though you haven't been asked.

With My Family

You and your family can show your concern for the poor by making an effort to live more simply. You can start with the food you eat. Prepare only as much as will be eaten, so there is no waste. If there are leftovers, save them and eat them the next day.

 PRAYER

Jesus, thank you for your gift of the Eucharist that helps me stay close to you.

My Response

Write one thing that you will do to show that you appreciate the gift that Jesus gives us in the Eucharist.

Focus on Faith

"I Am the Bread of Life"

A priest, giving instruction to a young woman about the faith, explained that Catholics believe that the Eucharist is the Body and Blood of Jesus Christ. The woman said, "You believe that? Why, that's ridiculous!" Then she left the session. The priest commented that although she did not believe the teaching, she understood what Jesus meant when he said, "I am the bread of life." In the Eucharist, Jesus Christ offers himself as our food to bring us to eternal life.

Dinnertime Conversation Starter

S hare with your child your memories of your First Communion.

Our Catholic Heritage

The Church's liturgical calendar lists the feast days of saints. A feast day is the day set aside in the liturgy to honor the life of a saint. This day is almost always the day on which the saint died, since this is considered the saint's "birthday" into heaven. For example, April 16 is the feast of Saint Bernadette of Lourdes, who died on that day.

Sainte Bernadette

Hints for at Home

Do activities at home to celebrate the liturgical year and keep awareness of Jesus' presence in your lives and home. For example, in your home hang a calendar that highlights religious feasts. Other ideas are to have an Advent calendar or a wreath for Advent, a crucifix displayed for Lent, a container into which you put savings for the people during Lent, and a picture of the risen Jesus for Easter.

Focus on Prayer

Your child has reflected on the story of Jesus' feeding the crowd with loaves and fishes (John 6:1–15, 34–35). Read the story together, and then spend a few minutes thinking about Jesus' continuing presence in the Eucharist and its central importance in our lives as Christians.

Celebrating the Eucharist

Ceremonies and rituals are a part of our everyday lives. What are some ceremonies in which you have taken part? What was the purpose of these ceremonies?

PRAYER

Jesus, help me realize how important it is for me to receive you in the Eucharist. May I always grow closer to you.

The Eucharist Calls Us to Share

The principal celebrant of the Eucharist is an ordained priest. Jesus Christ himself, acting through the ministry of the ordained priest, offers the eucharistic sacrifice. All Catholics participate as part of the priesthood of believers. The eucharistic liturgy commemorates, or recalls, the sacrifice of Jesus and makes it present to us. The Eucharist, a **memorial** of this sacrifice, is offered in reparation for the sins of all people—living and dead—and offers spiritual and temporal benefits from God

According to Saint Paul, Christians cannot truly celebrate the Eucharist unless they are ready to love and share with one another. He was especially critical of the rich, who would gather with the community to eat but not to share what they had.

> Therefore whoever eats the bread or drinks the cup of the Lord unworthily will have to answer for the body and blood of the Lord. A person should examine himself, and so eat the bread and drink the cup. For anyone who eats and drinks without discerning the body, eats and drinks judgment on himself.

1 Corinthians 11:27-29

By "discerning the body," Paul means that those celebrating the Eucharist must understand that Jesus died for all people. To receive the Body and Blood of Christ worthily, we should not have had anything to eat for one hour, we should have confessed any mortal sin we have committed, and we should be ready to live like Jesus.

 Reading God's Word

Therefore, if you bring your gift to the altar, and there recall that your brother has anything against you, leave your gift there at the altar, go first and be reconciled with your brother, and then come and offer your gift.

Matthew 5:23-24

Thomas Aquinas Teaching,
Zanobi di Benedetto
Strozzi

A Saint Devoted to the Eucharist

Saint Thomas Aquinas (1225–1274) was a distinguished thinker and writer about God. He is most famous for a great book, *Summa Theologica,* which summarizes the teachings of the faith at his time.

Thomas had a great love for the Eucharist. He helped to explain the nature of Jesus' presence in the Eucharist. He also wrote a beautiful hymn in praise of the Eucharist called the *Pange Lingua* ("Sing, My Tongue"). His feast day is January 28.

Saint Thomas
Aquinas,
Botticelli

Jesus' Presence in the Eucharist

During the Mass, the priest proclaims the words of Christ: "This is my body. This is the cup of my blood." Through these words and through the power of the Holy Spirit, bread and wine become Christ's Body and Blood. Through the eucharistic prayer Jesus is really present in what was bread and wine. This is called the **Real Presence** of Jesus in the Eucharist. The term used to express this belief is **transubstantiation.** Thomas Aquinas used this term to teach that, while the bread appears to be bread and the wine appears to be wine, they both become the Body and Blood of the risen Jesus at the time of consecration.

Did You Know?

You may hear some parts of the Mass referred to by their Latin names: the *Gloria* is the hymn of praise in the introductory rite; the *Sanctus* is the Holy, Holy, Holy after the preface; and the *Agnus Dei* is the Lamb of God. *Kyrie eleison* are Greek words for "Lord have mercy." *Hosanna* is a Hebrew acclamation for "save, we ask."

The Order of the Mass

The Mass is the high point of the Catholic Christian life, and it follows a set order.

Introductory Rite

The Mass begins with a procession, the Sign of the Cross and greeting, and may include a prayer of sorrow for sins (Pentitential Rite), an acclamation of praise for God's mercy (Kyrie), and a hymn of praise (Gloria). It concludes with an opening prayer.

Liturgy of the Word

We hear the story of God's plan for salvation, in the readings from the Old and New Testaments, from a book called the Lectionary. A story from Jesus' life is read from one of the Gospels. The homily helps us understand God's Word and connects it with our lives. We make a profession of faith (the Creed) and offer general intercessions to pray for our needs and the needs of the world.

Liturgy of the Eucharist

Preparation of the Altar and Gifts

A chalice (for the wine) and a paten (for the bread) are placed on the altar. Members of the assembly carry bread and wine to the priest or deacon who places them on the altar. The priest concludes with a prayer over the gifts.

Eucharistic Prayer

This is the heart of the liturgy. During this prayer the words of Christ from the Last Supper and the invocation of the Holy Spirit change the bread and wine into the Body and Blood of Christ. It begins with the preface (a prayer of praise to God) and its acclamation Holy, Holy, Holy—the hymn of the angels. At the center of the eucharistic prayer is the consecration. The assembly responds, "Christ has died, Christ is risen, Christ will come again" (memorial acclamation). The eucharistic prayer concludes with a song of praise to the Trinity and the assembly's Great Amen.

Communion Rite

At this time we express our unity with God and one another. The Communion Rite consists of the Lord's Prayer, the sign of peace, the breaking of the bread, the asking for mercy (Lamb of God), the sharing of the Body and Blood of Jesus Christ as a community, and the prayer after communion.

Concluding Rite

The Concluding Rite consists of a blessing from the priest and a dismissal (often "Go in peace to love and serve the Lord"). It sends us forth on our mission as Christians.

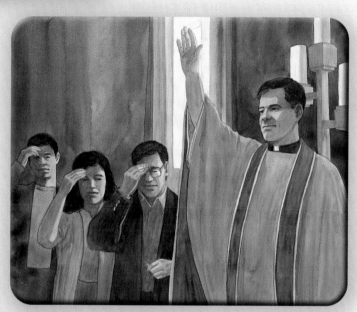

Identifying the Parts of the Mass

Write the part of the Mass in which each occurs:
the Introductory Rite (**I**), the Liturgy of the Word (**W**),
the Liturgy of the Eucharist (**E**), or the Concluding Rite (**C**).

_____ 1. memorial acclamation

_____ 2. the words *This is my body*

_____ 3. opening prayer

_____ 4. dismissal

_____ 5. sign of peace

_____ 6. Gospel

_____ 7. Gloria

_____ 8. Creed

_____ 9. Holy, Holy, Holy

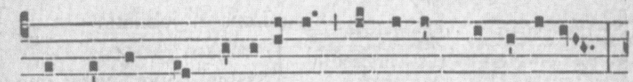

Pange lingua

Pange língua glo-ri-ó-si   Córpo-ris mysté-ri-um,
Sing (my) tongue (the) glorious   Body's   mystery,

PRAYER

We adore Jesus in the Eucharist, where our faith tells us Jesus is really present. The following prayer expresses adoration of Jesus in the Eucharist. This prayer is called *Tantum Ergo*. It is the last part of the *Pange Lingua*, written by Saint Thomas Aquinas.

Tantum Ergo

With heads bowed let us now worship a sacrament so great;
And let the old teaching give way to the new;
Let faith reinforce our belief where the senses cannot.

To the Father and the Son let there be praise and jubilation,
Salvation, honor, virtue, and also blessing;
To the Holy Spirit let there be equal praise.

Many say that seeing is believing. But we can believe without seeing. Think about things you believe in even though you can't touch, see, or hear them.

Talk to Jesus. He is with you right now waiting for your questions. Talk to him about your faith or about something else that is in your heart. Ask him any questions you may have. Listen for his answers.

Thank Jesus for spending time with you.

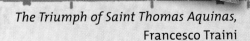

The Triumph of Saint Thomas Aquinas,
Francesco Traini

Faith Summary

When we celebrate Mass, we celebrate the Real Presence of Jesus under the appearance of bread and wine. The liturgy commemorates, or recalls, the sacrifice of Jesus. At the consecration the bread and wine become the Body and Blood of Jesus. To receive the Body and Blood of Christ worthily, we should not have had anything to eat for one hour, we should have confessed any mortal sin we are aware that we have committed, and we should be ready to live like Jesus.

Words I Learned

memorial   Real Presence   transubstantiation

Ways of Being Like Jesus

We are like Jesus when we are aware of the presence of God in our lives and pray to stay close to him. One way for us to do this is by receiving the Eucharist frequently.

With My Family

On a Sunday before you participate in Mass with your family, make a list of the special intentions for which you will pray. Bring your list to Mass. Silently include your special intentions with the general intercessions.

 PRAYER

Jesus, thank you for your presence in the Eucharist and in my life.

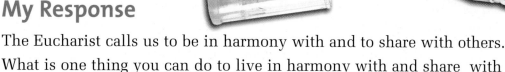

My Response

The Eucharist calls us to be in harmony with and to share with others. What is one thing you can do to live in harmony with and share with another person?

Focus on Faith

Saint Thomas Aquinas and the Eucharist

Saint Thomas Aquinas was born to a noble family in Italy. His parents wanted Thomas to become the abbot for a great Benedictine monastery. Instead, Thomas ran away to become a Dominican. A brilliant teacher and scholar, he helped define the meaning of the Real Presence of Jesus Christ in the Eucharist. Late in his life, while celebrating Mass, Thomas had a vision of Jesus. He realized then that any words he could use were like straw compared with the great mystery of God's love for us.

St. Thomas Aquinas, Carlo Crivelli

Dinnertime Conversation Starter

Ask your child what he or she hopes to be and do as an adult. Discuss how a person's dreams can help shape his or her life.

Our Catholic Heritage

Hymns and songs are important parts of our Catholic tradition. One of the most ancient and beautiful hymns of praise is the *Te Deum.* Some people say that it was written by Saint Ambrose (339–397), who baptized Saint Augustine. It begins with the words *Te Deum laudamus* ("You are God: we praise you").

Spirituality in Action

To show the importance of Jesus in the Eucharist in your lives, plan to visit the Blessed Sacrament together as a family at some time other than a Sunday and spend at least 15 minutes in prayer and meditation.

Focus on Prayer

Your child has reflected on the eucharistic hymn *Tantum Ergo*, written by Saint Thomas Aquinas. It speaks of how faith enables us to see what our senses cannot: the bread and wine as the Body and Blood of Christ. Talk with your child about what he or

she remembers about this hymn and about how faith often brings us beyond what we can see and understand.

Celebrating Reconciliation

What are some times when you are called on to forgive? Is it easy to forgive? Why or why not?

 PRAYER

Jesus, help me remember that you are always ready to forgive me when I do something wrong.

Jesus Brings Us Peace and Forgiveness

The apostles were gathered together after Jesus died, afraid of what the authorities might do to them as Jesus' followers.

> On the evening of the first day of the week, when the doors were locked, where the disciples were, . . . Jesus came and stood in their midst and said to them, "Peace be with you." When he had said this, he showed them his hands and his side. The disciples rejoiced when they saw the Lord. [Jesus] said to them again, "Peace be with you. As the Father has sent me, so I send you." And when he had said this, he breathed on them and said to them, "Receive the holy Spirit. Whose sins you forgive are forgiven them, and whose sins you retain are retained."
>
> *John 20:19-23*

Risen Christ with disciples, All Saints Episcopal Cathedral, Albany, New York

The risen Jesus brings peace: This gift of the Holy Spirit helps people live in harmony with others and with themselves. This is reconciliation, the returning of harmony to our broken relationships with God, with others, and even with ourselves. In the Gospel story Jesus gives the apostles the authority to forgive sins and reconcile people with God and with one another. The Church celebrates that gift of reconciliation in the Sacrament of Penance.

 ## Link to Liturgy

In the sign of peace that we share with one another during the Communion Rite of the Mass, we are sharing the peace that Jesus shared with the disciples.

Jesus Brings a Healing Presence Into Our Lives

During his life Jesus was a healer. He worked many **miracles,** such as healing sick people. Miracles show God acting in the world.

This healing is continued in the Church through the power of the Holy Spirit. It is continued particularly in the **Sacraments of Healing,** which include the Sacraments of Penance and Anointing of the Sick.

The Meaning of Sin in Our Lives

We are in need of healing because of the existence of sin in our lives. Every day we make decisions about whether to live in harmony with God and others. We can destroy this harmony and break our relationships by acts of disobedience and self-centeredness. Sin is an offense against God.

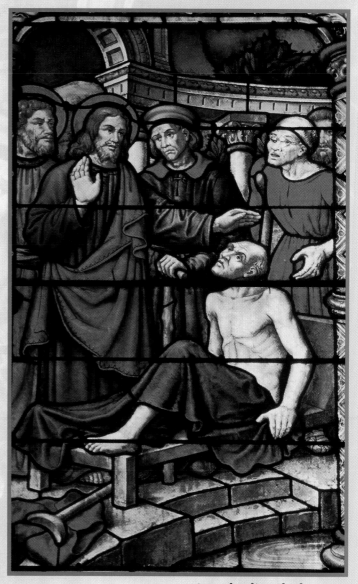

Jesus healing the lame, Saint Etienne Cathedral, France

Totally rejecting God and others in our lives is a grave, or mortal, sin. When the rejection is not so total or serious, we commit venial sin. Continually committing venial sin gets us in the habit of saying no to God and can lead to mortal sin.

God calls us to repentance in the Sacrament of Penance. When we repent because we love God above all, it is called perfect contrition. When we repent for other reasons—for example, the fear of Hell—it is called imperfect contrition. When we accept the grace to repent and celebrate the Sacrament of Penance, we can live in peace with God and others and contribute to peace in the world.

The Sacrament of Penance

The essential parts of the Sacrament of Penance are contrition, confession, satisfaction made by the penitent (the person confessing sins), and the absolution by the priest, who is sworn to keep in confidence what he has been told. *Contrition* means being sorry for sins; *confession* means telling one's sins; *satisfaction* means doing what is possible to repair the harm a sin has caused to another person and to yourself.

The Rite of Penance

Before confessing their sins, penitents make an examination of conscience. They think of how they have done wrong or failed to do good. They can ask the Holy Spirit to help them make a good confession. When a person confesses sins to a priest, here is the typical process:

1. The penitent prays the Sign of the Cross.

2. The priest invites the penitent to trust in God. He may also read from Scripture.

3. The penitent confesses his or her sins. Grave or mortal sins must be confessed. The priest may help and counsel the penitent. The priest gives the penitent a penance to perform, which is often in the form of an action to complete or prayers to pray.

4. The penitent expresses sorrow for sins, usually by reciting the Act of Contrition.

Outdoor confessions at World Youth Day

5. The priest gives absolution using special words that include "Through the ministry of the Church may God give you pardon and peace and I absolve you from your sins in the name of the Father, and of the Son, and of the Holy Spirit." The penitent responds, "Amen."

6. At the end, the priest and penitent praise God for his mercy. Then the priest dismisses the penitent with words such as these, "The Lord has freed you from your sins. Go in peace."

Forgiveness in the Gospels

Read the Parable of the Forgiving Father from the Gospel of Luke (15:11–24). Complete the activity.

What is the passage about?

_____

_____

_____

_____

_____

_____

_____

_____

_____

_____

_____

_____

Forgiving Father,
Frank Wesley,
India

What does the passage teach you about forgiveness?

_____

_____

_____

Reading God's Word

If you forgive others their transgressions, your heavenly Father will forgive you.

Matthew 6:14

PRAYER

You pray the Act of Contrition when you celebrate
the Sacrament of Penance. In this prayer you tell God
you are sorry for having done wrong. Pray this prayer
now slowly, thinking about the words as you say them.

Act of Contrition

My God,
I am sorry for my sins with all my heart.
In choosing to do wrong
and failing to do good,
I have sinned against you
whom I should love above all things.
I firmly intend, with your help,
to do penance,
to sin no more,
and to avoid whatever leads me to sin.
Our Savior Jesus Christ
suffered and died for us.
In his name, my God, have mercy.

God is happy to forgive your sins. He wants you to be close to
him. He can help you avoid those things that lead you to sin.
Ask God how you can avoid them. What does he tell you?

Perhaps you have your own words to tell God you are sorry
for your sins. If you do, try using them now to make your
own prayer for forgiveness. Sit quietly and be aware
of God's love.

Faith Summary

In the Sacrament of Penance, we can heal our relationships with God and others by being sorry for our sins, confessing them to a priest, receiving absolution, and trying to do better. We help bring peace and forgiveness to the world by being sorry for our sins and living in harmony with others.

Words I Learned

miracle   Sacraments of Healing

Ways of Being Like Jesus

Jesus brought peace and forgiveness into the world. We are like Jesus when we forgive those who hurt us. We can try to keep open lines of communication with those who have done wrong to us.

With My Family

Praying for people helps us forgive them. With your family make a Forgiveness Box. Write prayers for those people who have angered or wronged you. Ask God to bless these people. Place these prayers in the Forgiveness Box. Continue to pray for the strength to forgive these people.

 PRAYER

Jesus, thank you for forgiving me when I do wrong. Thank you for helping me be at peace with myself, others, and you.

My Response

The Sacrament of Penance helps fix broken relationships and brings peace to ourselves and others. Write one thing that you will do to fix a broken relationship in the next week.

Focus on Faith

Reconciling Meals

In the Scriptures an invitation to a meal and eating together is a sign of reconciliation. That is why people were upset when Jesus ate with Zacchaeus (Luke 19:1–10), and why religious leaders criticized Jesus for eating with people whom they considered sinners. John 21:1–19 tells the story of Jesus' preparing a meal for Peter and some disciples after the Resurrection. Peter and the others were fishing when they saw Jesus on the shore. Jesus invited them to a breakfast of bread and fish. This invitation and the meal they ate together was in itself a sign of forgiveness and reconciliation. Taking time to prepare and have a meal together creates opportunity for families to remain reconciled and live in harmony.

Our Catholic Heritage

Father Lawrence Jenco provides an example of what forgiveness means. Jenco was held hostage in Beirut, Lebanon, for 564 days, enduring beatings and threats to his life. He was kept in solitary confinement for six months. Once during his captivity, a guard asked Jenco for forgiveness. Jenco admitted to the guard that there were times when he hated his captors, but while talking, Jenco realized that he was able to forgive and ask for forgiveness in return. Jenco wrote that he knew at that moment that he was freed. After his release he wrote a book about his experiences titled *Bound to Forgive*. Jenco died in 1996 at the age of 61.

Dinnertime Conversation Starter

With your child plan a meal that you can prepare together to celebrate the oneness of your family.

Spirituality in Action

With your family read one of the following passages from Matthew, Chapter 18: the lost sheep (10–14) or the unforgiving servant (21–35). Then say a prayer of forgiveness together. Make a promise as a group that you all will try to bring a spirit of peace into your family.

Focus on Prayer

Your child is reviewing the Act of Contrition. Say the prayer aloud as a family. You will find the words to this prayer at www.FindingGod.org.

Jesus Heals Us

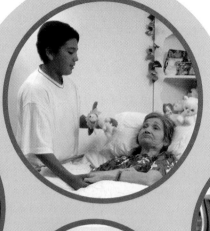

How have others acted as healers for you? How can you bring healing to others?

PRAYER

Jesus, help me see how you have brought healing to the world and continue to heal us through the sacraments.

The Apostles Heal in Jesus' Name

Now Peter and John were going up to the temple area for the three o'clock hour of prayer. And a man crippled from birth was carried and placed at the gate of the temple called "the Beautiful Gate" every day to beg for alms from the people who entered the temple. When he saw Peter and John about to go into the temple, he asked for alms. But Peter looked intently at him, as did John, and said, "Look at us." He paid attention to them, expecting to receive something from them. Peter said, "I have neither silver nor gold, but what I do have I give you: in the name of Jesus Christ the Nazorean, [rise and] walk." Then Peter took him by the right hand and raised him up, and immediately his feet and ankles grew strong. He leaped up, stood, and walked around, and went into the temple with them, walking and jumping and praising God. When all the people saw him walking and praising God, they recognized him as the one who used to sit begging at the Beautiful Gate of the temple, and they were filled with amazement and astonishment at what had happened to him.

Acts of the Apostles 3:1-10

The healed man's response to God's act was overwhelming joy, expressed in an outpouring of praise to God. God continues to heal in the Church through the Holy Spirit. By uniting our prayers with Jesus in the Spirit, God will always hear us and answer in some way.

Reading God's Word

They drove out many demons, and they anointed with oil many who were sick and cured them.

Mark 6:13

Jesus Heals and Saves

The name *Jesus* means "God saves." The name emphasizes that Jesus is the one who has come to save all. *Christ* means "anointed." The name shows that God the Father has given Jesus a mission and endowed him with power to save and power to heal. Jesus' whole life was aimed at saving people. His words and actions are the foundation of the saving grace we now receive in the sacraments.

The sacrament that helps unite those who are suffering with Jesus' saving and healing power is the Anointing of the Sick. Through this sacrament people receive forgiveness for their sins and comfort in their suffering; they are restored in spirit; and sometimes they even experience the return of physical health. The sacrament teaches us that God wants us to give comfort to the suffering and wants us to work to relieve suffering where we can.

 Sacred Site

Lourdes, in southern France, is where Mary appeared to Bernadette Soubirous in 1858 and where many people have experienced healings of various kinds. The Church officially recognizes more than 60 of these healings as miraculous after having subjected them to rigorous medical study. Some people leave their crutches as an evidence of their cure. Some bathe in the waters of the spring in the grotto where Mary appeared, and many drink the water in hopes of a cure. About six million pilgrims visit Lourdes every year.

The Sacrament of Anointing of the Sick

In the Sacrament of Anointing of the Sick, the priest anoints the seriously ill, injured, or the aged with the oil of the sick.

In addition to the anointing, the person is often offered Holy Communion. When the person is dying, the Communion is called viaticum. For a dying person, the sacrament is preparation for passing over to eternal life.

Anointing sometimes occurs in a church and is given to the sick or aged in a community. It often takes place in homes, nursing homes, and hospitals. For example, a person who is going to have surgery may be anointed. The sacrament may be received more than once, such as when a sick person's condition worsens.

The Rite of Anointing of the Sick

In the Rite of Anointing of the Sick, the priest anoints the sick person on the forehead, saying, "Through this holy

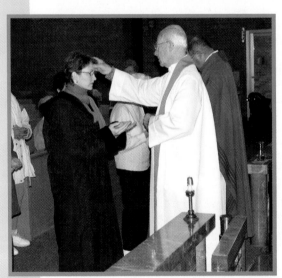

anointing may the Lord in his love and mercy help you with the grace of the Holy Spirit. Amen." He also anoints the sick person on the hands, saying, "May the Lord who frees you from sin save you and raise you up. Amen."

The "raising" refers to spiritual healing, as well as to any physical healing that may take place.

Communal anointing in church is pictured above. At right a pastoral sick call set is shown.

Did You Know?

The oil of the sick is a special oil used for the Sacrament of Anointing of the Sick. It is blessed by the bishop at the Chrism Mass during Holy Week.

Comparing the Two Sacraments of Healing

The following statements are about the Sacraments of Penance and Anointing of the Sick. Identify which statements are true and which are false by placing a **T** or an **F** on the line. Look back at Session 18 if needed.

_____ 1. The priest may never repeat what the penitent has confessed.

_____ 2. The Act of Contrition is used to express joy to praise God.

_____ 3. Anointing of the Sick is only for those who are near death.

_____ 4. The absolution by the priest is one of the essential parts of the Sacrament of Penance.

_____ 5. *Contrition* means being sorry for your sins.

_____ 6. The Holy Communion offered to a dying person is called viaticum.

_____ 7. In the Rite of Anointing of the Sick, the priest anoints the sick person on the forehead and the hands.

_____ 8. Before confessing sins, the penitent makes an examination of conscience.

_____ 9. Anointing of the Sick takes place only in church.

_____ 10. The Sacrament of Anointing of the Sick may be received only once.

 Link to Liturgy

As part of the Mass, we say we need God's help. We do this before we share Holy Communion, when we say the words, "Lord, I am not worthy to receive you, but only say the word and I shall be healed."

PRAYER

Jesus heals us and helps us. He healed many people during his life on earth. He brought Jairus's daughter back to life, and he cured the man who was paralyzed from birth. Jesus continues to heal and help us today.

Imagine that you are walking with Jesus. As you walk, you see people who are sick, suffering, grieving, disappointed, lonely, and excluded. You may know some of the people.

How do you think Jesus looks at these people? What does he feel toward them? What do you think he says to them? How does he bring comfort to them?

Take a while and talk to Jesus. Tell him what you thought about the people you passed. Ask him to help you find ways to help them.

You might need some help or healing yourself. If you do, ask Jesus for it.

Listen for his answer.

Torchlight procession at Lourdes

Faith Summary

In the Sacrament of Anointing of the Sick, the ill, injured, or aged are anointed with oil by a priest. As a result, they receive forgiveness for their sins, comfort in their suffering, and spiritual—and sometimes even physical—healing. Suffering is part of life, but Jesus unites our suffering with his passion and death so that through our suffering we can participate in his saving and healing work.

Ways of Being Like Jesus

During his life Jesus showed special sympathy to those who were sick, and he healed the sufferings of many. We are like Jesus when we show concern for sick people and help them by comforting them or befriending them.

With My Family

With your family make a few fun, colorful cards for some of the sick children at a hospital. Bring them to the hospital to be distributed by a nurse, doctor, or volunteer.

 PRAYER

Jesus, thank you for your healing presence in our lives. Help me to see other people through your loving eyes.

My Response

You have learned how the Sacrament of Anointing of the Sick brings comfort. What is one way that you can help a sick person?

Focus on Faith

Jesus Came to Heal

When serious illness strikes one individual in the family, the whole family is in need of Jesus' healing touch. Through the Sacrament of the Anointing of the Sick, the Church brings Jesus' healing—spiritual, emotional, and sometimes even physical—to those who are seriously ill and to their families. The Sacrament of the Anointing of the Sick assures the family of the continued care, concern, and prayers of the Church.

A priest who came to celebrate the Sacrament of the Anointing of the Sick with a family in his parish described the reaction of one of the children, who said, "Father, my grandmother is sick. First she had a doctor, then she had a nurse, and now she needs a priest." The Sacrament of the Anointing of the Sick, once referred to as Extreme Unction and thought of as a sacrament for the dying, is a prayer of healing and may be celebrated individually and communally.

Spirituality in Action

With your child, visit a person in a nursing home. You might play cards with this person or participate in a craft activity with him or her. Try to do this on a regular basis if it is possible.

Our Catholic Heritage

Two miracles performed through the intercession of a person are required before that person can become a saint. A miracle is defined as an extraordinary happening showing divine intervention in human affairs. A healing cure is one example. This must be a complete cure—occurring without medical intervention. Medical specialists are asked to give testimony about the occurrence of a miracle.

Focus on Prayer

Your child has reflected on how Jesus might view suffering, grieving, disappointed, lonely, and excluded people and on how a person might try to look at them with Jesus' eyes. Mention this and then spend time together thinking about how Jesus saves and heals and welcomes all and about the response that calls from us.

Review

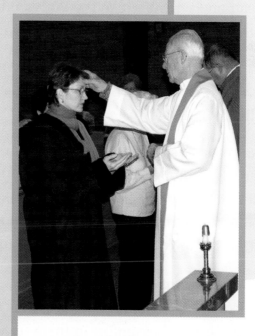

Why are the sacraments important to you? How do you show that they are important to you?

PRAYER

Jesus, help me trust in your healing presence now and always.

Faith Summary

Jesus is the bread of life. Just as he miraculously fed the crowds with bread and fish, he provides us with his Body and Blood in the Eucharist. In the eucharistic celebration, Jesus is present in the priest, the assembly, the Word of God, and in a special way in the consecrated bread and wine.

When we celebrate the Eucharist, we recognize the Real Presence of Jesus under the appearance of bread and wine. The liturgy commemorates, or recalls, the sacrifice of Jesus, who died to make reparation for our sins. The bread and wine become the Body and Blood of Jesus. This is called transubstantiation. To celebrate the Eucharist properly, we must first confess any mortal sin we remember having committed.

Penance and Anointing of the Sick are called Sacraments of Healing.

Jesus helps us to stay friends with God through the Sacrament of Penance. Even though we sin and say no to God, our relationship with God and others is healed by our being sorry for our sins, confessing them to a priest, and trying to do better. We receive absolution for sins from a priest through the Sacrament of Penance.

In the Sacrament of Anointing of the Sick, the ill, injured, and aged are anointed with oil by a priest. As a result, they receive forgiveness from sin, comfort in their suffering, and spiritual—and sometimes even physical—healing. Jesus unites our suffering with his passion and death so that through our suffering, we can participate in his saving and healing work.

The Order of the Mass

The Order of the Mass is partially provided in the chart below. Listed are parts of the Mass that are missing. Fill in the missing parts in the order that they occur in the Mass.

Blessing

Breaking of the bread

Dismissal

General Intercessions

Gloria

Gospel

Holy, Holy, Holy

Lord's Prayer

Memorial Acclamation

Penitential Rite

Preface

Profession of Faith

Sign of Peace

The Order of the Mass

Introductory Rites

Entrance Procession

_____

Kyrie

_____

Liturgy of the Word

Readings

_____

Homily

_____

_____

Liturgy of the Eucharist

Preparation of the Gifts

Eucharistic Prayer

_____

_____

Consecration

_____

Great Amen

Communion Rite

_____

_____

_____

Communion

Concluding Rite

_____

Forgiveness Acrostic

Read the clues. Write the correct letters in the blanks to complete the puzzle.

1. Penance and Anointing of the Sick are called Sacraments ___ ___.

2. The Jewish ___ recalls the Hebrews' Exodus from Egypt under Moses.

3. The total rejection of God is called ___ sin.

4. The ___ year is the yearly cycle of the Church's remembrance of Jesus' life.

5. A divine action in the world, such as the healing of a sick person, is called a ___.

6. A less serious form of sin is called ___ sin.

7. The eucharistic liturgy remembers, or recalls, Jesus' suffering and death on the cross. It is a ___ of Jesus' sacrifice.

8. Before confession, we need to make an examination of ___.

9. The mystery of Jesus coming to us under the appearance of bread and wine is called the ___ ___.

10. The oil used in the Anointing of the Sick is called the oil of the ___.

11. The people gathered to celebrate the Eucharistic liturgy are called the ___.

1. __ **F** __ __ __ __ __ __ __

2. __ __ __ __ **O** __ __ __

3. __ __ **R** __ __ __

4. __ __ __ __ __ **G** __ __ __ __

5. __ **I** __ __ __ __ __

6. **V** __ __ __ __ __

7. __ **E** __ __ __ __ __ __

8. __ __ **N** __ __ __ __ __ __ __

9. __ __ __ __ __ __ **E** __ __ __ __ __

10. **S** __ __ __

11. __ __ **S** __ __ __ __ __

PRAYER SERVICE

Leader: Let us gather to thank God for his willingness to forgive us and to ask for his forgiveness.

Reader: A reading from the Gospel of Luke.

[Luke 15:11–24]

The gospel of the Lord.

All: Praise to you, Lord Jesus Christ.

Leader: Merciful is the Lord, abounding in kindness.

All: Merciful is the Lord, abounding in kindness.

Group One: As the heavens tower over the earth, so God's love towers over the faithful.

All: Merciful is the Lord, abounding in kindness.

Group Two: As far as the east is from the west, so far have our sins been removed from us.

All: Merciful is the Lord, abounding in kindness.

[adapted from Psalm 103]

Leader: Let us ask the Father for forgiveness by praying the Lord's Prayer, the prayer Jesus taught us.

All: Our Father, . . .

Leader: As we go forth to be people of forgiveness, let us offer each other the Lord's peace.

Living My Faith

Ways of Being Like Jesus

Jesus gave himself completely to others and gave us the sacraments to make the mystery of his life, death, and resurrection present in our lives. You are like Jesus when you try to live in helpful, friendly relationships with family, friends, and acquaintances and try to mend broken relationships.

With My Family

With your family make a list of ways that you can bring forgiveness and healing to your neighborhood. You might say hello (with a smile) to a neighbor or bring flowers to someone who is unable to leave his or her home.

PRAYER

Jesus, thank you for continuing your presence in the world through your sacraments. Keep me mindful that you are with me to bring me back when I sin, to pick me up when I fall, and to walk with me always.

My Response

You have thought about forgiveness and healing in this unit and talked about ways to live them in your life. Write one action you will take to make these ideas a real part of your life.

Living Like Jesus

Saint Isaac Jogues

Isaac Jogues, a French Jesuit, was one of a number of Christian missionaries martyred in the Americas. He was convinced that his call to service was to teach Native Americans about Jesus.

Saint Isaac Jogues

Isaac Jogues (1607–1646) was educated in Jesuit schools in France, and he chose to dedicate his life to God by becoming a Jesuit priest. He had a great desire to spread the Gospel to the Americas, and in 1636 he was sent to work in what is now Canada and the northeast United States.

He learned the language of the Hurons, a Native American nation, and he traveled as far west as Lake Superior. The missionary work was difficult because some Native Americans viewed the missionaries with suspicion. They believed that the missionaries, in their black robes, were evil spirits who brought disease. Conflicts among various Native American nations made the work even harder.

On one mission Isaac Jogues was captured by the Mohawks, along with René Goupil, a lay worker trained in medicine, and a number of Hurons. The captured group was subject to unbelievable tortures: Their fingernails were removed and fingers cut off, and they were beaten with clubs. René Goupil was killed. Although in captivity and treated as an enslaved person, Isaac Jogues continued to preach and tend to others' needs. He eventually escaped and went back to France.

Because of the state of his hands, Isaac Jogues could no longer hold the host, and he had to be given special permission to say Mass. He could have stayed in France, but convinced his mission was in the Americas, he chose to go back. Not long after his return, Isaac Jogues was captured by the Mohawks and killed along with his companion, Jean de la Lande.

Isaac Jogues and his lay companions René Goupil and Jean de la Lande were declared saints in 1930. Their feast day is October 19.

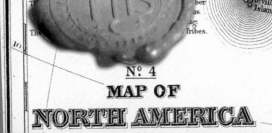

Making Moral Decisions

What choices do you have to make in your everyday life about doing what is right? What choices do you have to make to avoid doing wrong?

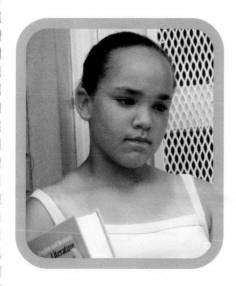

 PRAYER

Jesus, I want to learn how to follow you. Please give me the strength and courage to make choices that bring me closer to you.

Saint Francis of Assisi

As a young man in the Italian town of Assisi, Francis (1181–1226), the son of a silk merchant, liked to have fun with his friends. He eventually decided on what seemed to him to be a glamorous life—that of a soldier. But he was captured and held as a prisoner.

Back in Assisi after his release from prison, Francis no longer felt he fit in. He began to notice the poor and sick people, and he began to help them. One night in a dream he received a call from Jesus to help rebuild his Church. Francis thought Jesus meant the small, rundown chapel at the edge of town. So he sold some goods from his father's shop to pay for the rebuilding. His father, very angry at Francis's action, disowned Francis as his son. Francis gave back his possessions to his father—even his clothing. He wore only a brown cloak belted with a rope.

From then on Francis dedicated his life to God and to the care of poor people. Although some of his old friends made fun of him, seeing him in such humble clothes and in the company of sick and poor people and the lowly, Francis was happy and even danced with joy. Eventually many others followed him, and he became the center of a community dedicated to helping others. Francis's simple brown cloak became the habit, or unifom, of his community.

Francis is one of the best loved of all saints. He appreciated nature— he is said to have preached to the birds— and is the patron saint of ecologists, animals, and zoos. His feast day is October 4.

Legend of St. Francis 5: Renunciation of Worldly Goods,
Giotto di Bondone

Putting Our Lives on a Firm Foundation

In the Gospel of Matthew, Jesus uses a forceful image to tell us of the importance of having him as the foundation of our lives.

> "Everyone who listens to these words of mine and acts on them will be like a wise man who built his house on rock. The rain fell, the floods came, and the winds blew and buffeted the house. But it did not collapse; it had been set solidly on rock. And everyone who listens to these words of mine but does not act on them will be like a fool who built his house on sand. The rain fell, the floods came, and the winds blew and buffeted the house. And it collapsed and was completely ruined."
>
> *Matthew 7:24-27*

This passage makes it clear that we need to make Jesus central in our lives as Saint Francis did by following his teachings and trying to be like him. Jesus compares those who follow his teachings to a house on a firm foundation— the storms may come, but believers can withstand the danger. They know that they are friends with Jesus. Those who ignore Jesus' teachings as handed down by the Church or who do not act on them discover there is little to help them when the storms of life come upon them.

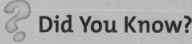

Did You Know?

You each have an inner voice, your conscience, where you can be alone with God. Your conscience is what helps you decide if an action is right or wrong. You develop it throughout your lifetime with the help of the Scriptures, the Gifts of the Holy Spirit, the advice of others, and the teachings of the Church. When you have a decision to make, taking quiet times alone with God can help you hear the voice of your conscience.

Making Choices

As believers in Jesus Christ, we are called to a new life and are asked to make moral choices that keep us close to God. With the help and grace of the Holy Spirit, we can choose the ways to act to keep us friends with God, to help other people, and to be witnesses to Jesus in the world.

Making good choices and acting on them is often not easy. Sometimes the right choices are not clear. Sometimes we are pressured by other people to do something we may not feel is right, or sometimes we may just want to go along with the crowd, whether they are doing right or wrong.

When your conscience tells you what is the right thing to do, you must follow it.

If you want to decide how God wants you to act, there are certain things you can do. You can

1. ask the Holy Spirit for help.

2. think about God's law and the Church's teaching.

3. think about what will happen as a result of your decision. When you think about the consequences, ask yourself, will they make you closer to or further from God? Will they hurt someone else?

4. ask for advice from people who live the faith.

5. remember Jesus Christ is with you.

6. think about how your decision will affect your life with God and others.

Choosing the right friends is a very important decision.

Making Choices: Roundtable Discussion

You will be divided into three groups. Each group will be assigned a problem.

- Read the problem. Discuss the choices.

- Next, decide on one or two good courses of action for the problem.

- Then present your ideas to the larger group. Discuss these solutions.

1. One day some of your friends decide that it would be fun to try to steal from a store. Each of you is supposed to take something. You don't want to lose your friends or be excluded.

   _____

   _____

2. You want to watch a big game on TV tonight, but you haven't done a report that's due tomorrow. There is a report of your brother's on the computer. You know you could use it, and no one would ever know that it was not yours.

   _____

   _____

3. A classmate in school has a cool, new portable CD player—and brings it to school to show off. Your friend takes the player, secretly shows it to you, and brags about taking it.

   _____

   _____

 ## Reading God's Word

When the tempest passes, the wicked man is no more;
   but the just man is established forever.

Proverbs 10:25

PRAYER

We are faced with choices every day. What should I wear? Do I want a soda or a lemonade? Should I see this movie or that one? Many of our choices are fairly easy to make. But some of them are harder; some of them are choices between doing right or wrong.

Invite Jesus to be with you while you reflect.

When was a time when you faced a hard choice about doing right or wrong? What happened?

If you think you made the right decision, thank Jesus for giving you the knowledge and courage to do the right thing.

If you think that you made the wrong choice or did the wrong thing, tell Jesus you are sorry. Think about other choices you could have made or what would have helped you make a better choice. Tell Jesus your thoughts.

You know that you can trust Jesus to help you make good choices. Ask him for his help.

Listen in your heart for his answer.

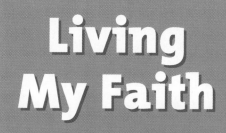
Living My Faith

Faith Summary

As Christians, we are called to make moral choices that influence our relationships with God and others. We believe that we have a new life in Jesus and are called to follow his teachings and to try to be like him. We each have a conscience that helps us make good choices. Our consciences are formed by the Word of God, the Gifts of the Holy Spirit, the advice of others, and the teachings of the Church.

Ways of Being Like Jesus

We are like Jesus when we say no to pride and selfishness and yes to doing God's will.

With My Family

Saint Francis gave up all his material possessions and lived his life in poverty helping poor people. Think of something you and your family can give up to help the poor. For example, you could give up drinking soda and put money in a jar each time you would like to have a soda but do not. After a certain amount of time, your family could donate this money to an organization dedicated to helping poor people.

PRAYER

Jesus, thank you for being with me and helping me make the right choices.

My Response

Think about how you will respond the next time you have a difficult choice to make about doing right or wrong. What steps will you take to help you make the right decision?

Focus on Faith

Francis of Assisi Makes a Choice

Saint Francis of Assisi was born into a wealthy family. He used his father's wealth to support a pleasure-seeking lifestyle. While a soldier, Francis was taken prisoner. In prison he reconsidered his life and determined to base his life on God. Upset because Francis sold some of his goods to rebuild a church, Francis's father complained to the bishop. The bishop told Francis that it was wrong to use his father's goods without permission. In response Francis gave everything back to his father, even his clothes, and left home. He wore only a brown cassock, belted with rope, which became the model for the Franciscan habit worn today. Francis's father did not support his call from God. When your children come to ask you to support their vocations, how will you answer?

Dinnertime Conversation Starter

Explore with your child his or her various vocation options. What are your child's hopes, inclinations, interests? How can the family support and help him or her?

Saint Francis, Master of Saint Francis

Our Catholic Heritage

Saint Maximilian Kolbe (1894–1941), a Polish priest, made a heroic choice: He offered to die in the place of someone else. He was in the Nazi death camp at Auschwitz during World War II. Ten prisoners were chosen to be killed in punishment for an escape attempt. Kolbe took the place of a younger man who had children, and he was murdered. Kolbe, a Franciscan, had been the leader of a movement to bring people back to Jesus through Mary and had worked to spread the gospel in Japan. He was put in the camp for speaking up against the Nazis.

Spirituality in Action

Make your family active in its charity by adopting a needy family in your parish. You could take the family to dinner occasionally and give its members gifts at the holidays.

Focus on Prayer

Pray the Peace Prayer of Saint Francis together as a family. You will find this prayer at www.FindingGod.org. Afterward, focus on the good choices your child has made this week. Let your child know that you noticed and support these choices.

Living a Moral Life

How do others' words affect you? How do you feel when people say good things about you? How do you feel when people criticize and tease you? Have you ever found out that people were saying unkind things about you behind your back? How did you feel?

PRAYER

Jesus, help me use my words to encourage and comfort others, to bring goodness and peace.

Words Out of Control

This version of an old Jewish folktale tells about the effects of spreading rumors.

One day a man went to a rabbi—a religious leader—to ask for help. The man was a shopkeeper, and he had found out that people were saying he used inaccurate weights to overcharge customers. The man said that the story wasn't true.

The rabbi investigated and found out that a woman of the town had started the rumor. He went to her and told her that he believed that she was spreading an untrue story. The woman felt bad, and she said that she would go to everyone she had told and say that her story was wrong.

The rabbi thought for a moment, and then said, "First, get a pillow and go to the top of the hill and let out all the feathers. Then pick up the feathers and bring them back to me. Be sure to get them all."

The woman did as she was told. But the wind got hold of the feathers, and the air was soon full of feathers going in all directions. The woman tried and tried, but she realized that she could never catch them all.

The woman told the rabbi what had happened. He replied that just as it was impossible to retrieve all the feathers, it is impossible to find all who had heard the false story about the shopkeeper. However, he encouraged her to do what she could to remedy the situation. So the woman went to shop at the man's store every day and praised the goods she bought there.

Using Words for Bad or Good

The letter of James deals with the wrong use of words. It uses many images to show the power of the tongue to do harm.

> The small bit in the mouth of a horse guides the direction in which it trots, and the small rudder on a ship guides the direction in which the entire ship sails. In a similar way, the tongue is a small part of our body but it can affect the entire person.
>
> Consider how a small fire can set a huge forest ablaze. The tongue is also like a fire. It can harm our entire body, and set all our lives on fire—that is, cause real problems for us.
>
> In contrast, words that are inspired by wisdom from above are first of all pure, then peaceable, gentle, full of mercy.
>
> *adapted from James 3:3-8,17-18*

We can hurt others with words when we gossip or call others bad names. Instead of misusing words, James calls for us to use our words with the wisdom that comes from God, which results in bringing peace and harmony.

Understanding the Stories

Answer the following questions with your group.

1. In your own words, what is the folktale trying to teach?

_____

_____

2. What are the similarities between the folktale and James's ideas?

_____

_____

3. Think of your own metaphor for how rumors spread.

_____

_____

Moral Choices

As Christians, we are called to live moral lives. A moral life commits us to truth in deeds and words. All too often we make selfish and sinful choices that harm our relationships with God and others.

One sinful choice we can make is to steal: We can steal people's goods or cheat them. We can also steal with words when we steal others' good reputations by talking negatively about them.

Sinning Through Words

The eighth commandment, "You shall not bear false witness against your neighbor," is all about living truthfully. God is truth, and he wants us always to tell the truth. We must keep a balance between what we should say and what we should not say.

Sometimes we say things about someone else that we know are not true. This is called **slander** and is a sin against the eighth commandment. Sometimes we say things about someone else that may be true, but we say them only to harm that person's reputation. This is wrong and is called **detraction.** It is also a sin against the eighth commandment.

As persons with freedom to choose, we are responsible for the choices we make. When we sin, we are called to repent and to make reparation (to make up for what we've done) as far as we can.

The Positive Power of Words

1. Write about an experience when words had a good effect on you.

_____

_____

2. Write positive phrases that you like to hear.

_____

_____

Sin's Social Side

Sin does not just harm us as individuals and hurt our relationships with God. It has negative effects on society as a whole. The presence of sin helps explain why there are such things as war, violence, prejudice, crime, drug abuse, and unfair treatment of others.

Besides lying and using words to hurt others, there are other ways that our sinful actions can have negative effects on others. For example, when we are greedy, we want more than our share. When we act on our greed, we deprive others of their share. If ten cookies are given to ten children, and one child greedily takes five cookies, the other nine children are left with only about half a cookie each. One child's sin of greed has had a negative effect on the other children. This example shows how one person's sin can have a negative effect on society—on a small scale. Whole societies can be greedy, however, and then bad consequences can result on a large scale.

Exploring the Social Effects of Sin and of Doing Good

Work in small groups and look at newspapers. Find stories that show the effects of sin. Discuss the kinds of sins they show. Then find stories of people who are being peacemakers by their words or actions. Discuss the stories. Write what you have learned from the discussions.

_____

_____

 **Reading God's Word**

Blessed are the peacemakers,
for they will be called children of God.

Matthew 5:9

PRAYER

Jesus used words to teach and to heal. His words brought goodness and peace. Pray the following psalm, which is about how we should use our words.

Group One: *I will bless the LORD at all times;*
            praise shall be always in my mouth.

Group Two: *Keep your tongue from evil,*
            your lips from speaking lies.

Group One: *Turn from evil and do good;*
            seek peace and pursue it.

Group Two: *The LORD has eyes for the just*
            and ears for their cry.

            Psalm 34:2,14-16

Let Jesus come to you now. Sit quietly with him for a while. When you are ready, talk to him about using your words for good.

Take some time to think about the things Jesus has told you. Thank him for spending time with you.

Faith Summary

Christian life commits us to truth in deeds and words (following the eighth commandment). For example, we need to monitor what we say so that we don't cause harm to others. We need to recognize that sin does not just harm us as individuals. It has negative effects on others and on society as a whole. The presence of sin helps explain why there are such things as war, violence, prejudice, crime, drug abuse, and unfair treatment of others.

Words I Learned

detraction   slander

Ways of Being Like Jesus

We are like Jesus when we don't gossip about people.

With My Family

At a family dinner make a special place at the table for a family member who has done something good during the past week. You might do this by setting his or her place with fancy silverware, a special plate, a beautiful glass, or something else that is special.

PRAYER

Jesus, thank you for showing me ways to use words for the good.

My Response

Write one way that you will try to use words for a good purpose in the next week.

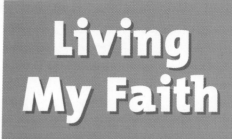
Living My Faith

Focus on Faith

God Calls Us to a Peaceable Life

In Chapter 3 of his letter, James describes the damage that can be done by an unbridled tongue. James calls the tongue "a restless evil, full of poison" that no one can tame. Just as a spark can set a forest ablaze, an uncontrolled tongue can create a forest fire of damage in human relationships. It is important to reflect on James when considering our role as parents. Does criticism of our children come more easily than praise? Do we find it easier to criticize our children's accomplishments than to build their self-esteem? In response to the unbridled tongue, James calls us to gain the wisdom that comes from God that is "peaceable, gentle, compliant, full of mercy."

Dinnertime Conversation Starter

Talk with your child about the effect on others of compliments, praise, and kind words. As a family, make an effort to say one positive thing to each other daily.

Hints for at Home

Take time to use words positively in your family by doing the following activity. Once a day throughout the week, each of you is to say something positive about a family member or to tell why that person is special to you. By the end of the week, each of you should have said something positive to each family member.

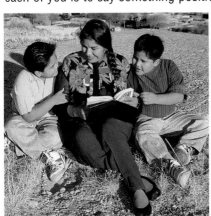

Our Catholic Heritage

Some sayings have long been part of the Catholic tradition. Others are newer and express ideas that are meaningful to us as Catholics:

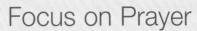

To God who is the best and greatest.—A MOTTO OF THE BENEDICTINES

Pray and work.—A MOTTO OF SAINT BENEDICT

All for the greater glory of God.—A MOTTO OF SAINT IGNATIUS OF LOYOLA

It is better to light one candle than to curse the darkness.—A MOTTO OF THE CHRISTOPHERS

(The Christophers is a nonprofit organization founded by Father James Keller in 1945 to spread a message of hope and understanding to people of all faiths.)

Focus on Prayer

Your child prayed a psalm about how we should use our words. Together as a family pray this psalm (Psalm 34:2, 14–16).

Growing in Holiness

What do you do to take care of your body? What are some ways you see people not taking care of their bodies? What are some things everyone should do to keep their bodies and minds healthy? Share your ideas with the group.

PRAYER

Jesus, please show me how to love and care for my body and spirit.

We Are Called to Act as Jesus Did

Through the sacraments we receive the grace to act in our lives as Jesus acted in his. When we act morally, we reflect Jesus, become his witnesses in the world, and participate in the plan of salvation. When we live morally, we show our love for Jesus and others.

We Are Called to Act Morally

We learn and live the moral life first and foremost in the domestic church, which is our family. Parents care for, love, and respect their children. Children, in turn, owe respect and obedience to their parents. As their parents grow older, children also need to take care of their parents in whatever ways they can. For example, some grown children have their parents live with them so they can help their parents with day-to-day living.

We can also act morally at school when we respect our teachers and follow rules. We can act morally with our friends when we try to include them and share with them.

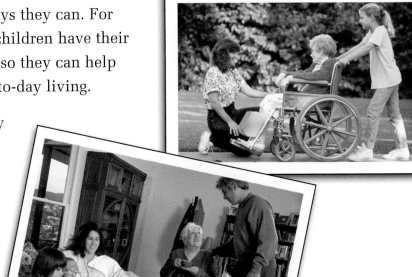

 Reading God's Word

For I, the LORD, am your God; and you shall make and keep yourselves holy, because I am holy.

Leviticus 11:44

Jesus as Teacher and Model of the Moral Life

In the Gospels Jesus both teaches us and shows us how to act morally. Read each of the following passages to learn how Jesus is telling us to act. Answer the questions.

Matthew 5:14–16

How does Jesus want us to act?

_____

_____

How can you act that way in your life?

_____

_____

Matthew 5:21–24

How does Jesus want us to act?

_____

_____

How can you act that way in your life?

_____

_____

Matthew 5:43–48

How does Jesus want us to act?

_____

_____

How can you act that way in your life?

_____

_____

Respecting Our Bodies

To live a moral life, we need to respect our bodies and ourselves. We can lose control in a number of ways. For example, if we abuse alcohol or drugs or if we dress immodestly, we then show a lack of respect for our bodies and ourselves.

As humans, we are sexual beings, male and female. Sexuality is given to us by God; it is part of every person, and it is good. **Chastity** is the practice that helps us unite our physical sexuality with our spiritual nature. It involves respecting our bodies and the bodies of others. United with our spiritual nature, our physical sexuality can be used rightly. Chastity makes us more complete human persons, able to give to others our whole life and love. All people, married and single, are called to practice chastity. When we act in a chaste manner, when we dress modestly, we are showing respect for our bodies. Jesus is the model for chastity.

Saint Paul explains the importance of chastity and respecting our bodies.

> Do you not know that your body is a temple of the holy Spirit within you, whom you have from God, and that you are not your own? For you have been purchased at a price. Therefore glorify God in your body.

1 Corinthians 6:19-20

Paul wants to emphasize the immense dignity of being human. He points out that because our bodies are temples of the Holy Spirit, our physical sexuality, used rightly, glorifies God.

Kateri Tekakwitha

Kateri Tekakwitha was born in 1656 in Auriesville, New York. She lost her parents to an outbreak of smallpox when she was only four. She herself was left with scars and suffered the loss of some of her eyesight. When priests visited her village, Tekakwitha heard the call of Jesus. She was baptized at the age of 20, despite the opposition of her family and others in her Mohawk tribe of the Iroquois nation. Many could not understand her decision and her refusal to follow the ways of the Mohawks, and they insulted her and made life difficult for her. But she had the courage to continue to live her faith.

Kateri Tekakwitha of the Iroquois,
Robert Lentz

She left her home to live in a settlement of Catholic villages in Canada. There she took a vow to remain a virgin, and she dedicated herself entirely to God. She lived a life of prayer and fasting, and she cared for poor and elderly people. After her death in 1680, many who prayed to her reported miracles.

In 1980 Tekakwitha was the first Native American to be declared Blessed—the step before sainthood. Her feast day is April 17.

 Sacred Site

A shrine at Auriesville, in northern New York State, honors the place where the Jesuit priest Isaac Jogues and his companions René Goupil and Jean de la Lande were martyred, as well as where Kateri Tekakwitha lived. The Auriesville shrine has statues of Saint Isaac Jogues and Tekakwitha, memorials on the sites of the martyrdoms, Stations of the Cross, and a retreat house.

PRAYER

Our bodies are part of the goodness of God's creation. Read what Saint Paul says about our bodies. Invite Jesus to be with you as you read.

> Do you not know
> that your body
> is a temple of the
> holy Spirit within you,
> whom you have from God,
> and that you are not your own?
> For you have been purchased at
> a price. Therefore glorify God
> in your body.
>
> *1 Corinthians 6:19-20*

Imagine that you are in a place that is sacred—in a quiet church, in the woods, or by some peaceful stream. It is so quiet that you don't want to speak out loud or make any noise. Feel yourself grow quiet.

Jesus is now next to you. Gently he tells you that you are more sacred than this place.

Reflect on what it means to you to be so special to Jesus.

Faith Summary

Jesus gives us grace that helps us make good moral choices and act on these choices in our everyday lives. Making good moral choices includes respecting our bodies and practicing the virtue of chastity. Chastity unites our physical sexuality with our spiritual nature. Chastity helps us to be complete human persons, able to give to others our whole life and love. All people, married or single, ordained or lay, are called to practice chastity.

Word I Learned

chastity

Ways of Being Like Jesus

Jesus chose to do God's will even when it was difficult. We are like Jesus when we follow God's will and make good moral choices even if it is hard to do so.

With My Family

With your family make a plan to get some exercise together. You might take a walk or a bike ride through your neighborhood or through a nearby woods or park.

 PRAYER

Jesus, thank you for giving me the sacraments and through them the grace to make good choices.

My Response

Write one thing you will do to take care of your body this week.

Kateri Tekakwitha of the Iroquois, Robert Lentz

Focus on Faith

Blessed Kateri Tekakwitha

Called the Lily of the Mohawks, Blessed Kateri Tekakwitha (1656–1680) was born in Auriesville, New York. She was baptized at the age of 20, although this provoked a great deal of anger in her tribe. Kateri took a vow of chastity and suffered from the insults of those who did not understand her dedication to Jesus Christ. She left her home for a settlement of Catholic villages in Canada. There she lived a life of prayer, fasting, and care for poor and elderly people. Kateri was the first Native American to be declared Blessed when Pope John Paul II beatified her on June 22, 1980. Kateri can serve as a model for us because she was a witness to the Catholic faith and to the virtue of chastity in the most difficult of circumstances.

Dinnertime Conversation Starter

Discuss with your child the help available when he or she encounters difficulty following Jesus. Assure him or her that you are always available for guidance.

Spirituality in Action

Talk about and then choose one very special thing each of you as a family member can do for every other member to show your love. Encourage each other to carry out the actions.

In Our Parish

Help the seniors in your parish take care of their bodies by starting a nutrition and exercise program for them.

Focus on Prayer

Your child is reflecting on the idea that our bodies are temples of the Holy Spirit. Talk with your family about things each family member can do to care for his or her body. You may want to talk about such things as nutrition, exercise, and hygiene.

The Way to Jesus

Who are your neighbors? What does it mean to be a good neighbor? What does a good neighbor do?

 PRAYER

Jesus, help me to be a good, loving neighbor.

Jesus Judges All

The Gospel of Matthew has a famous description of how Jesus will judge us at the end of time:

Last Judgment, Giotto di Bondone

> All the nations will be assembled before him [Jesus]. And he will separate them one from another, as a shepherd separates the sheep from the goats. He will place the sheep on his right and the goats on his left.
>
> Then the king [Jesus] will say to those on his right, "Come, you who are blessed by my Father. Inherit the kingdom prepared for you from the foundation of the world. For I was hungry and you gave me food, I was thirsty and you gave me drink, a stranger and you welcomed me, naked and you clothed me, ill and you cared for me, in prison and you visited me." Then the righteous will answer him and say, "Lord, when did we see you hungry and feed you, or thirsty and give you drink? When did we see you a stranger and welcome you, or naked and clothe you? When did we see you ill or in prison, and visit you?" And the king will say to them in reply, "Amen I say to you, whatever you did for one of these least brothers of mine, you did for me."
>
> Then he will say to those on the left, "Depart from me. . . . For I was hungry and you gave me no food, I was thirsty and you gave me no drink, a stranger and you gave me no welcome, naked and you gave me no clothing, ill and in prison, and you did not care for me." . . . And these will go off to eternal punishment, but the righteous to eternal life.

adapted from Matthew 25:32-46

The Meaning of Our Judgment

During our human life we can either accept or reject God's grace. When we die, we will be judged according to our works and faith. As a result of this particular judgment, a person may be united with God in heaven, may undergo a purification in **purgatory** before being united with God, or, because of his or her choices, may enter **hell**, which is total separation from God.

In the passage from Matthew, Jesus speaks of the final judgment that everyone will face before God. It describes how all people will need to answer to God for the decisions they have made in life. At the Last Judgment the Kingdom of God will come into its fullness, and the material universe itself will be transformed. God will then be "all in all."

It is God's intention that all people live in eternal glory with him. In Church teaching, death was not originally part of God's plan but entered the world through human sin. In death our souls are separated from our bodies, but the soul will be reunited with the body at the end of time.

The Last Judgment, Petrus Christus, 1452

We Pray for Those in Purgatory

Purgatory in Catholic belief is the continuation of the journey to achieve complete union with God—a continuation that occurs after death. The person has been saved and is a member of the Communion of Saints, but the union is still imperfect because of the effect of sin. Purgatory is the final step before complete union with God in heaven.

As believers we can help ourselves and those in purgatory on the final journey to God through **indulgences.** Indulgences are the help we receive to continue to say yes to God and to choose to live the way Jesus taught. Through prayer we believe that we can intercede with God for those who have died and ask for indulgences on their behalf so that they may be united with God.

To receive an indulgence, a person says a designated prayer such as the Rosary or takes part in a pilgrimage. A person can also receive indulgences for doing good works. The use of indulgences is a voluntary practice in the Church.

? Did You Know?

A Holy Year is a special time of joy and pardon. Holy Years occur every 25 years. During a Holy Year, people can earn special indulgences through prayers and visits to churches. Many people make pilgrimages to Rome or to local churches designated as places of pilgrimage.

Pope John Paul II in Saint Peter's Basilica beginning Holy Year celebrations

How to Treat Your Neighbor

Think about the ways of treating people that Jesus described in the Gospel story from Matthew. What are some ways that you can do these same types of things?

Add at least four ideas to the list below.

- You help to get your little sister ready for school because your mom is busy.

- You go out of your way to welcome new students in your class and include them in activities.

- You speak up for someone when others are saying negative things about him or her.

Ideas

Stained glass window
at Annunciation Chapel,
in Hevelee, Belgium,
Eugene Yoors

 Reading God's Word

For the Son of Man will come with his angels in his Father's glory, and then he will repay everyone according to his conduct.

Matthew 16:27

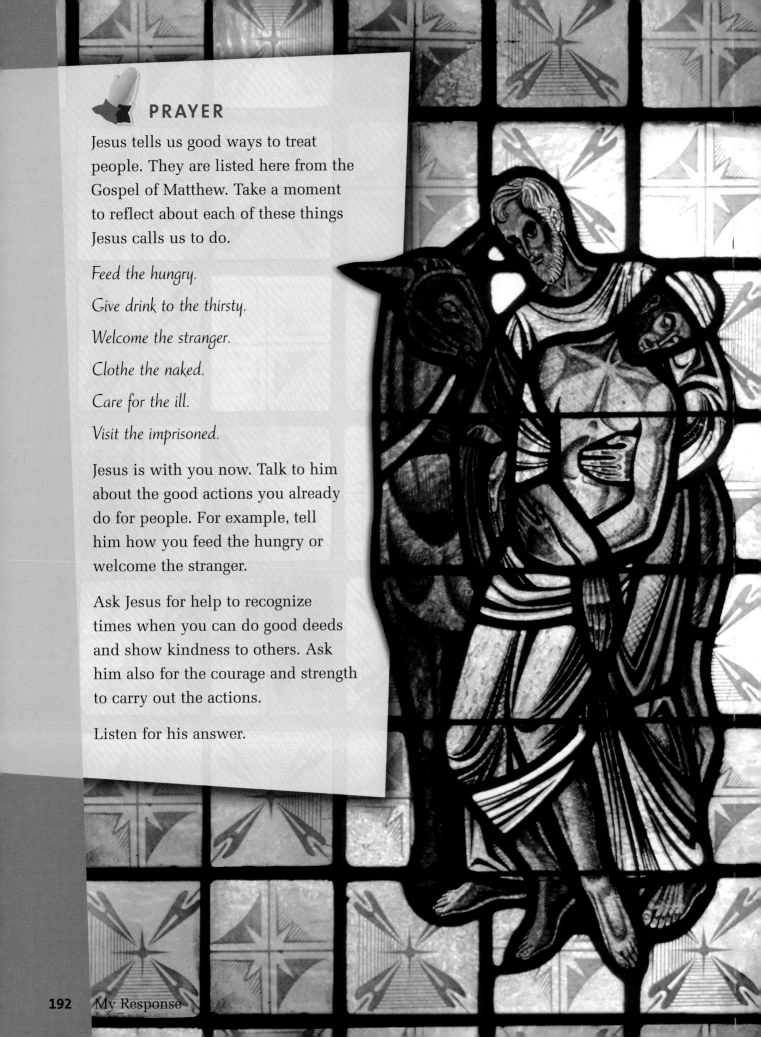

PRAYER

Jesus tells us good ways to treat people. They are listed here from the Gospel of Matthew. Take a moment to reflect about each of these things Jesus calls us to do.

Feed the hungry.

Give drink to the thirsty.

Welcome the stranger.

Clothe the naked.

Care for the ill.

Visit the imprisoned.

Jesus is with you now. Talk to him about the good actions you already do for people. For example, tell him how you feed the hungry or welcome the stranger.

Ask Jesus for help to recognize times when you can do good deeds and show kindness to others. Ask him also for the courage and strength to carry out the actions.

Listen for his answer.

Faith Summary

Jesus will judge each of us. We will be judged on whether we have lived a life of good deeds and of loving kindness to our neighbors. As a result of this judgment, each person will be united with God in heaven, undergo a purification in purgatory before being united with God, or, because of his or her choices, enter hell—total separation from God.

Words I Learned

hell   indulgence   purgatory

Ways of Being Like Jesus

Jesus befriended the outcast. You are like Jesus when you offer friendship and kindness to someone in your class who does not have many friends. You might invite this person to sit with you at lunch or join you in a game on the playground.

With My Family

Make dinner for a neighbor or parish member who is sick. Each family member can help in some way, for example, helping grocery shop, washing and chopping fruits and vegetables, cleaning up the kitchen, or delivering the meal. You might make a get-well card to include with the meal.

 PRAYER

Jesus, thank you for loving me and teaching me how to love you by acting with loving kindness toward other people.

My Response

Write a good deed you are going to do this week.

Focus on Faith

Responding to Tragedy

In the days after September 11, 2001, churches were filled with people. Around the world candles were lit. Impromptu shrines were filled with flowers. Prayers were offered for the dead and their suffering families. In tragic times our children naturally have questions about God and heaven. Treat their questions with respect. Be patient, knowing that you do not have all the answers. Pray with your children for all those caught up in tragedy.

Dinnertime Conversation Starter

Think of concrete ways that you as a family can be a source of help and comfort for those who suffer, especially those faced with tragic situations.

Hints for at Home

Find the name of an elderly person in your parish who is not able to leave home because of illness or some other reason. Take your child to visit this person. With your child you might prepare a bouquet of fresh flowers or a plate of homemade cookies to bring to this person. Try to make regular visits to this person to give him or her some company.

Our Catholic Heritage

The eucharistic fast has been a practice in the Church since the fifth century. At first it consisted of fasting from midnight on, including not drinking water or taking medicine. In 1964 the fast was reduced by Pope Paul VI to one hour, including all food and drink, but allowing for water and medicine. In 1973 the fast was reduced for the elderly and sick to 15 minutes.

Focus on Prayer

Your child is learning how to love God through loving other people—by responding to their physical and spiritual needs. With your child read Matthew 25:31–46, in which Jesus tells us how to treat other people. Afterward pray silently for God to help you recognize the needs of others and do good things for them.

Review

We have a new life in Jesus. In our new life we are called to be like Jesus, to make good choices and to act with loving kindness toward our neighbors.

 PRAYER

Jesus, help me make good choices and be a good friend to others.

Faith Summary

As Christians, we are called to lead moral lives in which God is central. We believe that we have a new life in Jesus and are called to follow his teachings and to be like him. With the grace and help of the Holy Spirit, we can make good choices that keep us in a close friendship with God and with others.

We are called to live moral lives, but all too often we make selfish and sinful choices that harm our relationships with God and others. Christian life commits us to truth in deeds and words. For example, we need to monitor what we say so that we don't cause harm to others—intentionally or unintentionally. We need to recognize that sin does not just harm us as individuals. It has negative effects on others and on society as a whole. The presence of sin helps explain why there are such things as war, violence, prejudice, crime, drug abuse, and unfair treatment of others.

Jesus is present to us in the sacraments. The sacraments give us grace to act in our lives as Jesus acted in his. They help us make good moral choices and act on the choices in our everyday lives. Making good moral choices includes respecting our bodies and being in control of ourselves. Chastity involves treating our own and others' sexuality with respect— whether we are young or old, married or single.

Jesus will judge each of us. We will be judged on whether we have lived a life of good deeds and of loving kindness to our neighbors. As a result of this judgment, each person will be united with God in heaven, undergo a purification in purgatory before being united with God, or, because of his or her choices, enter hell—total separation from God.

Important Words

Complete the crossword with words you've read and learned in this unit. Use the clues below.

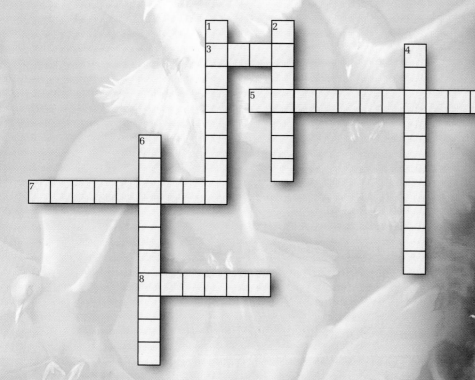

Across

3. Total separation from God

5. The help we receive to continue to say yes to God

7. Final preparation for complete union with God

8. Saint Paul says your body is this for the Holy Spirit.

Down

1. The practice that helps us unite our physical sexuality with our spiritual nature

2. Untrue things said about someone

4. The secret core inside of us where we can be alone with God and hear his voice; it helps us know if an action is right or wrong

6. Things said about someone to harm the person's reputation

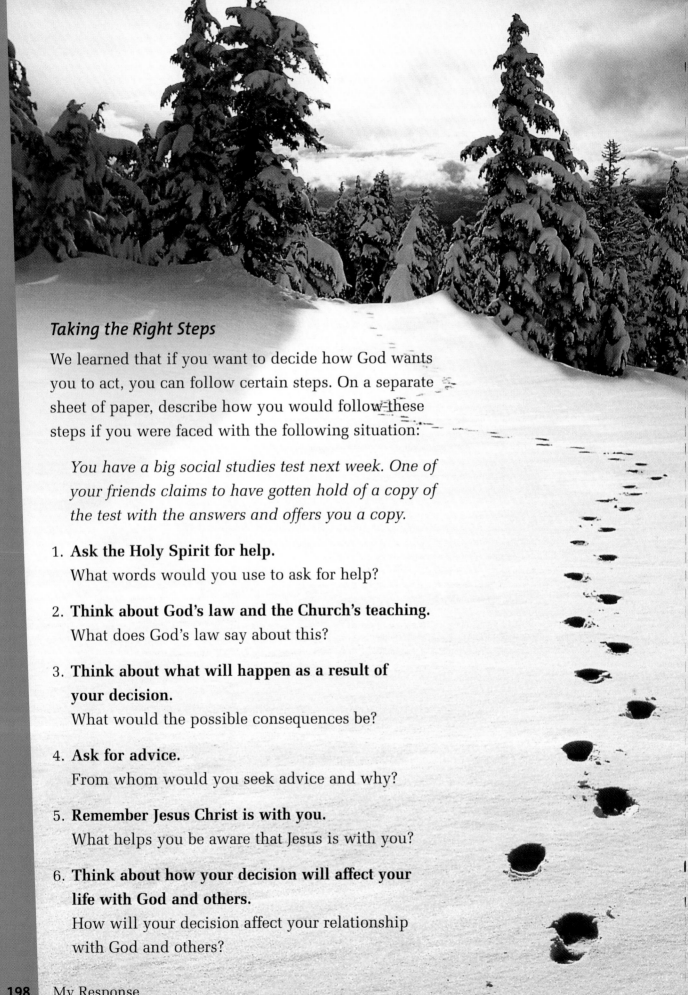

Taking the Right Steps

We learned that if you want to decide how God wants you to act, you can follow certain steps. On a separate sheet of paper, describe how you would follow these steps if you were faced with the following situation:

You have a big social studies test next week. One of your friends claims to have gotten hold of a copy of the test with the answers and offers you a copy.

1. **Ask the Holy Spirit for help.**
   What words would you use to ask for help?

2. **Think about God's law and the Church's teaching.**
   What does God's law say about this?

3. **Think about what will happen as a result of your decision.**
   What would the possible consequences be?

4. **Ask for advice.**
   From whom would you seek advice and why?

5. **Remember Jesus Christ is with you.**
   What helps you be aware that Jesus is with you?

6. **Think about how your decision will affect your life with God and others.**
   How will your decision affect your relationship with God and others?

 PRAYER SERVICE

Leader: Let us consider the choices we make in our lives. Let us pray to make choices that help us carry Jesus into the world. Let us live so that at our judgment we can tell Jesus that we spent our lives helping others.

Reader: A reading from the Book of Psalms. [Psalm 34:12–28]

The Word of the Lord.

All: Thanks be to God.

Leader: Let us make promises in response to God's call to carry Jesus into the world. The response is *We will help, O Lord.*

Leader: When we see someone in need of a friend,

All: We will help, O Lord.

Leader: When we see someone sick who needs company or sympathy,

All: We will help, O Lord.

Leader: When we can work to feed and clothe others,

All: We will help, O Lord.

Leader: When we can help to be peacemakers, even just by example or by comforting words,

All: We will help, O Lord.

Leader: Now let's pray the Sign of the Cross to show that we are dedicating ourselves to God and to being Jesus' witnesses in the world.

Living My Faith

Ways of Being Like Jesus

Jesus set an example by following God's greatest commandments— to love God above all and to love our neighbors as we love ourselves. He followed his Father's will and fulfilled his mission on earth. He also showed concern for others in all his actions in his public life. We are like Jesus when we keep God central in our lives, choose to follow his Ten Commandments and Jesus' teachings, and look for ways to help others.

With My Family

We can show our love for God by loving other people through our actions. With your family clean the house or apartment or yard of an elderly or sick member of your parish.

 PRAYER

Jesus, thank you for teaching me throughout this year how to be a good person, a faithful witness to your love and caring, someone who serves you through serving others.

My Response

This week set aside a time with Jesus when you can talk to him. Bring your questions, your ideas, your worries. Talk with Jesus about how you will put into practice what you have learned this year.

The Year in Our Church

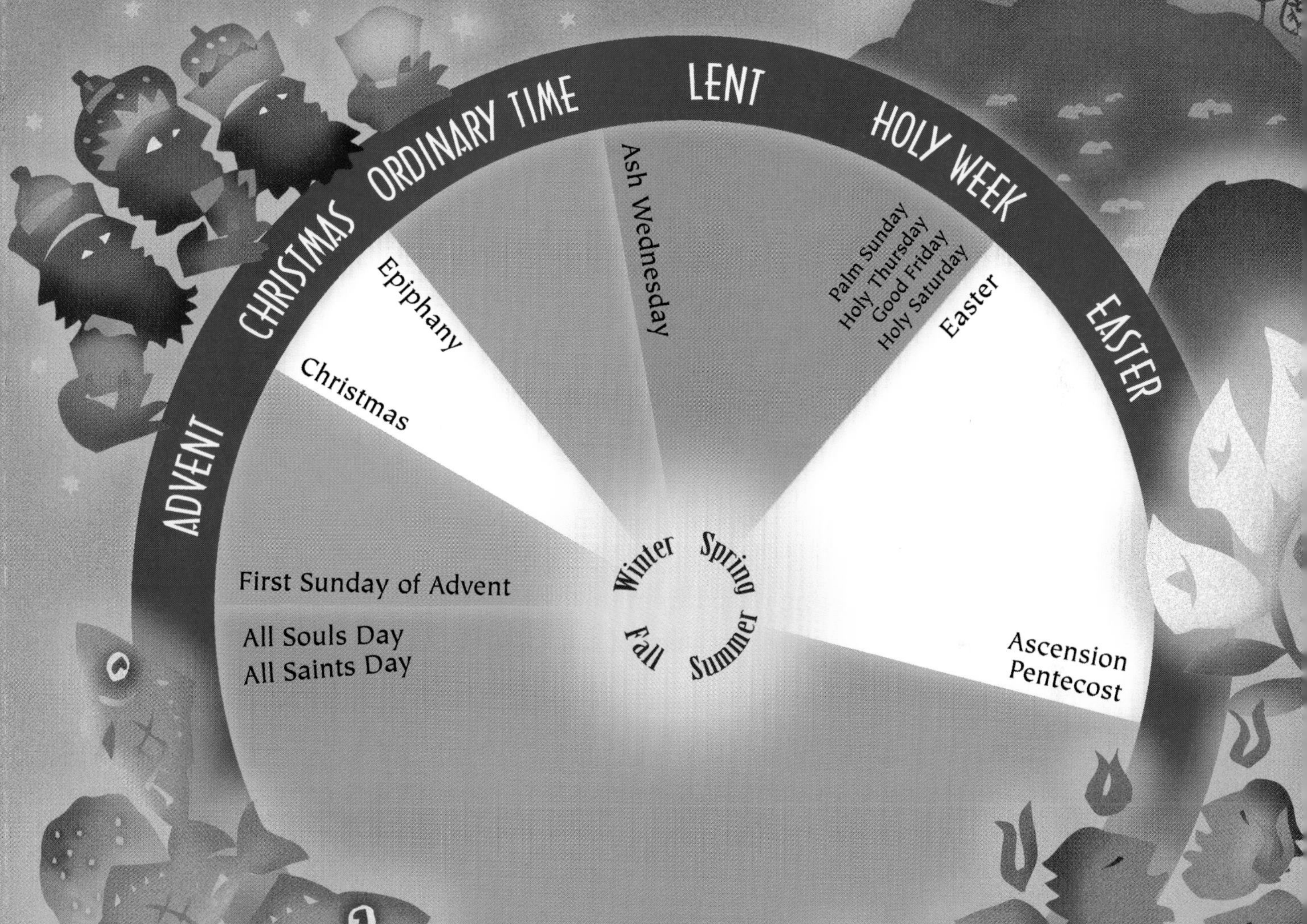

ORDINARY TIME

CHRISTMAS

LENT

HOLY WEEK

ADVENT

EASTER

Epiphany

Christmas

Ash Wednesday

Palm Sunday
Holy Thursday
Good Friday
Holy Saturday

Easter

First Sunday of Advent

All Souls Day
All Saints Day

Winter Spring

Fall Summer

Ascension
Pentecost

ORDINARY TIME

Liturgical Year

The liturgical calendar highlights the feast days and seasons of the Church year.

Liturgical Year

Advent marks the beginning of the Church year. It is a time of anticipation for Christmas and begins four Sundays before that feast.

The Christmas season includes the celebrations of Jesus' birth and his becoming known to the world, **Christmas** and **Epiphany.**

Lent is a season of conversion that begins on Ash Wednesday. It is a time of turning toward God in preparation for Easter.

During **Holy Week,** we recall the events surrounding the suffering and death of Jesus. Holy Week begins with Palm Sunday and ends on Holy Saturday.

Easter celebrates Jesus being raised from the dead. The Resurrection is the central mystery of the Christian faith.

The coming of the Holy Spirit is celebrated on **Pentecost.** With this feast the Easter season ends.

All Saints Day celebrates the holy persons in heaven. On **All Souls Day** we pray for those who have died but are still in purgatory.

The time set aside for celebrating our call to follow Jesus day by day as his disciples is Ordinary Time.

Advent

Advent is a time of anticipation. We are getting ready to celebrate the birth of Christ.

Jesus was born a long time ago. However, in the season of Advent, we live in the joyful expectation that his love will grow in each of us in a more complete way.

We prepare to celebrate Jesus' birth so that we will better understand what he means in our own lives.

PRAYER

Loving God, help me spend the season of Advent aware of your love, so I will be prepared to celebrate the birth of your son, Jesus.

Fresco painting depicting the condemnation of the Jews by order of King Nebuchadnezzar

Hope for the Future

Advent is a season that calls us to live every day with joyful hope for the future. This is not always easy for people who face great challenges. The Old Testament gives us a good example of how the Jewish people struggled to maintain hope when faced with a doubtful future.

In 586 B.C. the army of Nebuchadnezzar, king of the Babylonians, attacked and destroyed the city of Jerusalem. Many of the city's Jewish people were exiled to Babylon and forced to live in a hostile land.

The Jews formed their own community in Babylon and remained faithful to God, but as time went by they began to give up hope. Their defeat and the loss of their land made them start to doubt God's promise to protect them.

To encourage them, God sent the prophet Isaiah. Through this prophet God gave the people words of comfort and joy so they could live with a sense of hope for the future. The prophet said:

The spirit of the Lord GOD is upon me,
    because the LORD has anointed me;
He has sent me to bring glad tidings to the lowly,
    to heal the brokenhearted,
To proclaim liberty to the captives
    and release to the prisoners,
To announce a year of favor from the LORD
    and a day of vindication by our God.

Isaiah 61:1-2

Fulfillment in Jesus

The great events of the Old Testament help us understand what God would accomplish completely in Christ. The words of Isaiah are seen as finding their fulfillment in Jesus.

During Advent, the Church turns to the comforting and joyful words of Isaiah to help us live with a sense of hope for our future—a hope made possible by the birth of Jesus.

George Frideric Handel,
Balthasar Denner, 1727

Handel's *Messiah*

Every year during Advent, millions of people all over the world listen to George Frideric Handel's *Messiah*. This famous choral work is in three parts: (1) the prophecy and coming of the Messiah, (2) the redemption of humankind through the sacrifice of Jesus, (3) praise and thanksgiving to God. The work starts with these words from Isaiah:

Comfort ye, comfort ye my people, saith your God.
Speak ye comfortably to Jerusalem, and cry unto her,
    that her warfare is accomplished, that her
    iniquity is pardoned. . . .
The voice of him that crieth in the wilderness,
    Prepare ye the way of the LORD, make straight
    in the desert a highway for our God.

Isaiah 40:1-3 (King James Version)

PRAYER SERVICE

All: O God, we remember your promise to send us your Son. May the blessing of Christ come upon us, brightening our way and guiding us by his truth.

Leader: May the Light of Christ shine forth in each of us.

All: Amen.

Reader: A reading from the prophet Isaiah.
[Isaiah 61:1–2a,10–11]

The Word of the Lord.

All: Thanks be to God.

Group One: O Lord and Ruler of the House of Israel, you appeared to Moses in the flame of the burning bush and gave him the law on Sinai:

Group Two: Come, and redeem us with outstretched arms.

Group One: O Rising Dawn, Radiance of the Light Eternal and Sun of Justice:

Group Two: Come, and enlighten those who sit in darkness and in the shadow of death.

Group One: O Emmanuel, our King and Lawgiver, the Expected of the Nations and their Savior:

Group Two: Come, and save us, O Lord our God.

Leader: Let us pray in the words Jesus gave us.
Our Father . . .

Leader: Go forth to love and serve God and your neighbor, in the name of the Father, and of the Son, and of the Holy Spirit.

All: Amen.

Christmas and Epiphany

The birth of Jesus is even more exciting and important than other births because it was the birth of God's only Son, the Messiah, who had been promised to the people of God by the prophets in the Old Testament. We celebrate Christmas to remember that God became man in Jesus, while remaining divine.

 PRAYER

Loving God, help me welcome Jesus into my heart during the season of Christmas.

Epiphany

In the time following the birth of Jesus, many important things happened. The three Magi (astrologers) from the East came to Bethlehem to see the newborn king. On their way to Bethlehem, the Magi stopped in Jerusalem and met King Herod, who was the leader of the Jewish people.

King Herod felt worried about the birth of Jesus. Herod was afraid that Jesus would become a powerful leader who would threaten the king's own power. According to the Bible, Herod decided to kill the baby Jesus. Herod told the Magi, "After you find the baby, return here and tell me where I can find him, so I can worship him too." However, the Magi did not trust Herod and returned home without stopping in Jerusalem.

Herod was angry and decided on a plan to kill Jesus. However, an Angel of God appeared to Joseph in a dream and warned him to take Mary and Jesus and escape to Egypt. This event is called the Flight to Egypt. When it was safe, Joseph, Mary, and Jesus returned to Israel.

adapted from Matthew 2:1-15

The word *epiphany* means "to show or reveal." During the Christmas season, we celebrate the fact that, in Jesus Christ, God is revealed to us. On the feast of the Epiphany, we celebrate that day when Jesus was revealed to the whole world, represented by the Magi who came from distant lands. Like the Magi, we come to adore the newborn king and to go forth, carrying tidings of great joy to all those we meet.

Flight into Egypt, Gentile da Fabriano (detail from the altarpiece at right)

Adoration of the Magi, Gentile da Fabriano, 1423

A Gift for Jesus

The Magi gave gifts to Jesus to honor him. You can honor Jesus with a gift as well. You might give him the gift of a special prayer that you create for him, or you might do something kind or helpful for another person, knowing that when you serve others, you serve Jesus. On the lines provided, write your special prayer or the details of how you will be kind or helpful to another person in Jesus' honor.

_____

_____

_____

_____

_____

PRAYER SERVICE

Leader: Let us pray. Jesus, you came to us, our Savior, as the prophets said you would. We rejoice in your presence and pray to always follow your way. This we pray through you with the Father in the Holy Spirit.

Reader: A reading from the Gospel of Matthew. [Matthew 2:1–12]

The gospel of the Lord.

All: Praise to you, Lord Jesus Christ.

Group One: The people who lived in gloom have seen a great light;

Group Two: Upon those who walked in darkness a light has shone.

Group One: For a child, a son, is born to us.

Group Two: They name him God, Hero, Prince of Peace.
[adapted from Isaiah 9:1–5]

Leader: Let us pray the Lord's Prayer, the words Jesus taught us.

Leader: Jesus has come. As we go forth in his light, let us offer each other a sign of his peace.

Lent

During Lent, thousands of people all over the world prepare for their Baptisms on Holy Saturday. Throughout these 40 days the whole Church prepares and prays with them. For example, we read the Bible or go to Mass as often as possible. We repent of our sins and develop good habits. We also help those in need. By doing these things, we prepare to renew our own Baptism and to celebrate Jesus' death and resurrection.

Lent starts on Ash Wednesday and ends on Holy Thursday. Ash Wednesday is 40 days before Easter, not counting Sundays.

 PRAYER

Loving God, help me spend the season of Lent in prayer and sacrifice so that I will be ready to celebrate the death and resurrection of Jesus at Easter.

Jesus in the Wilderness

After Jesus was baptized by John the Baptist, the Holy Spirit led Jesus to the wilderness. In the wilderness Jesus spent 40 days fasting and praying in order for God to make him ready to begin preaching his message of redemption.

After Jesus had fasted for 40 days, he was very hungry. The devil came to him to test his strength. The devil would tempt Jesus three times. First, since the devil knew that Jesus had to be very hungry, the devil showed Jesus some large stones and said, "If you are the Son of God, command that these stones become loaves of bread." Jesus refused to be tempted.

Second, the devil took Jesus to the top of a high tower at the Temple in Jerusalem. There, the devil tried to trick him again. The devil wanted Jesus to jump from the tower so that God's angels could catch him. Again Jesus refused.

Third, the devil took Jesus to the top of a high mountain. He showed Jesus all of the kingdoms of the world. The devil told Jesus that he could be king of all the kingdoms if only he would worship the devil. Again, Jesus refused. Finally, Jesus told him, "Get away, Satan." The devil knew that he could not tempt Jesus and left. Then angels came and ministered to Jesus.

adapted from Matthew 4:1-11

The Temptation of Christ, Botticelli

Resisting Temptation

The temptation of Jesus contains an important lesson for us: We need to follow God's way and remember to resist temptation. Lent is a time of prayer and sacrifice in order to help us resist temptation and to prepare ourselves to celebrate the redemption offered to us by Jesus' death and resurrection. Just as Jesus prepared for his ministry by prayer and fasting, we pray and fast during Lent. We also provide for poor people during this time.

Making a Lenten Cross

During Lent we spend 40 days praying, reading the Bible, making sacrifices, and helping others. To help remember the special activities we do during Lent, make a Lenten Cross. Draw a large cross on a sheet of black construction paper. Then cut some small squares from colored construction paper. Use colors such as purple, pink, blue, yellow, and white.

Each week during Lent, review the things you have done that week to celebrate Lent. You might have said a special prayer, read the Bible, gone to Mass and communion, avoided buying candy, given money to charity, or avoided eating meat on Fridays. For each thing you have done, glue one of the colored squares on the cross. Try to cover the black cross completely with colored squares by Easter Sunday.

PRAYER SERVICE

Leader: In the name of the Father, and of the Son, and of the Holy Spirit.

All: Amen.

Leader: God, as we enter into the season of Lent, help us remember the 40 days and 40 nights Jesus spent fasting in the wilderness.

Reader: A reading from the Gospel of Matthew. [Matthew 4:1–11]

The gospel of the Lord.

All: Praise to you, Lord Jesus Christ.

Leader: Let us take time to reflect on the meaning of Lent for our lives. Lent is a time to remember that we are preparing for the celebration of Jesus' death and resurrection. Spend a few minutes talking with God about how you will observe this season.

Thank you for sending your only Son, Jesus, to help us turn from sin.

All: Help us use prayer and sacrifice to grow closer to you as we prepare for Easter.

Holy Week

Holy Week is a time for remembering. We remember all of the events leading to the death and resurrection of Jesus.

On Palm Sunday we remember Jesus' triumphant entrance into Jerusalem, and on Holy Thursday we recall how he gave himself to us in the Eucharist. On Good Friday we remember how Jesus suffered and died, and at the vigil Mass on Holy Saturday we celebrate his resurrection. Through his death and resurrection Jesus redeemed us from our sins.

 PRAYER

Faithful God, during Holy Week, help me remember that you sent your only Son, Jesus, to die for our sins so that we might be redeemed and live a new life.

Redemption Through Jesus

When Jesus was crucified, two criminals were crucified with him. No one knows the names of the criminals or what they had done. They might have been thieves or murderers. They were put on crosses to the left and to the right of Jesus.

As they hung on the crosses, one of the criminals cried out to Jesus, "Aren't you the Messiah? Then save yourself and us." But the other criminal interrupted the first criminal and said, "Have you no fear of God, seeing you are under the same sentence? We deserve it, after all. We are only paying the price for what we've done, but this man has done nothing wrong."

Then the second criminal turned to Jesus and said, "Jesus, remember me when you enter your kingdom." And Jesus replied, "I assure you: This day you will be with me in paradise."

adapted from Luke 23:39-43

Depiction of the Crucifixion, Anonymous

Even in the hour of his death, Jesus repeated his message of salvation to the good criminal. Even when he was suffering most, Jesus continued to heal. Because the criminal reached out to Jesus in faith and told Jesus that he believed Jesus' message, the criminal's sins were pardoned.

Jesus' message is the same for us as it was for the faithful criminal: If we believe in Jesus' message of salvation, we will be redeemed from our sins and find eternal life.

The Last Words of Jesus

The Gospel of Luke records some of the last words of Jesus while he was on the cross. These words show us that even in deep suffering Jesus stayed close to God and remained loving and forgiving.

Read Jesus' words and think about them. Write answers to the questions.

"Father, forgive them, they know not what they do." (Luke 23:34)

What do these words mean to you?

_____

_____

"Amen, I say to you, today you will be with me in Paradise."
(Luke 23:43)

What do these words mean to you?

_____

_____

_____

_____

"Father, into your hands I commend my spirit." (Luke 23:46)

What do these words mean to you?

_____

_____

_____

_____

PRAYER SERVICE

Leader: *As we observe Holy Week and Easter, let us remember God's message of salvation.*

Reader: *A reading from the Gospel of Luke.*

Reader: *Now one of the criminals hanging there spoke snidely to Jesus, saying,*

Group One: *Are you not the Messiah? Save yourself and us.*

Reader: *The other, however, reprimanding him, said in reply,*

Group Two: *Have you no fear of God, for you are subject to the same condemnation. And indeed, we have been condemned justly, for the sentence we received fits our crimes, but this man hasn't committed a crime.*

Reader: *Then he said,*

Group Two: *Jesus, remember me when you come into your kingdom.*

Reader: *Jesus replied to him,*

Group One: *Amen, I say to you, today you will be with me in Paradise.*
[adapted from Luke 23:39–43]

Reader: *The gospel of the Lord.*

All: *Praise to you, Lord Jesus Christ.*

Leader: *Let us pray. Jesus, thank you for always loving and forgiving, for healing us no matter what we have done.*

All: *In the name of the Father, and of the Son, and of the Holy Spirit. Amen.*

Leader: *Go in peace.*

Easter

Easter is the time when we remember the events in Jesus' life that are most important to our faith: his death on the cross, his resurrection, and his ascension into heaven. We remember these events each time we celebrate Mass.

The events of Holy Week and Easter are truly amazing. Jesus died for our sins, rose from the dead, and ascended into heaven. These events are difficult to explain. Not even all of the disciples believed that Jesus had risen from the dead, and some of them demanded proof. However, we can only believe in the Resurrection through faith.

PRAYER

Faithful God, help me have the faith to believe your promise to us.
You sent your only Son, Jesus, who died for our sins on the cross,
so that we might have eternal life.

Doubting Thomas,
Guercino,
Vatican Museums

Thomas Doubts Jesus

After Jesus was crucified, his body was placed in a tomb. However, on the third day his body was gone. At first, nobody understood what had happened. People felt confused. Then the risen Jesus appeared to many who believed in him. Mary Magdalene and the women who went to Jesus' tomb to prepare his body for burial saw him. So did Peter and many others.

The apostle Thomas, however, was not with the others when they saw Jesus. Later, when Thomas met the others, they excitedly told him the good news: Jesus had risen from the dead and had appeared to them.

Thomas felt surprised and suspicious. He said, "Unless I see the mark of the nails and put my finger into his side, I will not believe."

A week later, Thomas and the apostles were together in a locked room. Suddenly Jesus appeared to them. Everyone felt surprised because the door was locked. Jesus greeted everyone and then said to Thomas, "Put your finger here and see my hands, and bring your hand and put it in my side, and do not be unbelieving but believe."

Thomas answered Jesus, "My Lord and my God." Thomas's answer showed that he finally believed. Then Jesus said, "Have you come to believe because you have seen me? Blessed are those who have not seen but believe."

adapted from John 20:24-29

Believing God's Word

Jesus invited Thomas to touch his wounds on his hands and side. Thomas believed and was saved. Jesus makes the same offer to us. With the eyes of faith, we can see the risen Christ present in ourselves and others. Because of our faith, we believe God's Word and we obtain the salvation that Jesus won for us on the cross.

Seeing with the Eyes of Faith

When we see with the eyes of faith, we help people who are in need. Our parish community tries to help others. Through various parish ministries many people bring Holy Communion to people who can't leave their homes because of illness, and visit hospitals. They bring comfort to families that have lost loved ones, or they provide food and shelter for those in need.

You can help people in these ministries by making them cards of thanks and encouragement. On the front of each card, draw a happy-looking face and the words "You See With the Eyes of Faith." On the inside write a note thanking them for their service and encouraging them to continue helping others. When you are finished, your cards will be delivered to people in these ministries.

PRAYER SERVICE

Leader: *Jesus rose from the dead and ascended into heaven. Through love and service, may we deepen our faith in Jesus and his promise of eternal life.*

Reader: *A reading from the Gospel of John.*
[John 20:24–29]

The gospel of the Lord.

All: *Praise to you, Lord Jesus Christ.*

Leader: *Knowing that God hears our prayers, let us offer our prayers of petition. The response is Lord, hear our prayer.*

Leader: *For all Catholics, that they may be strengthened in their faith in Jesus and his promise of eternal life, let us pray to the Lord.*

All: *Lord, hear our prayer.*

Leader: *For those who struggle to believe, that their hearts may become open to Jesus and his saving Word, let us pray to the Lord.*

All: *Lord, hear our prayer.*

Leader: *Lord, hear these prayers that we speak and the prayers in our hearts. We pray this through Jesus, your Son, and the Holy Spirit.*

All: *Amen.*

Pentecost

God sent the Holy Spirit to Jesus' followers on Pentecost. The Holy Spirit gave them the strength and guidance they needed to do God's work. Because of the Holy Spirit, Christianity spread throughout the world. Today the Holy Spirit continues to guide Catholics as we live out our faith.

 PRAYER

Loving God, thank you for sending us the Holy Spirit that we might have the strength, courage, and guidance to understand and follow your will for us.

A New Follower in Christ

Philip was one of Jesus' early followers. One day an angel of the Lord spoke to Philip telling him to leave Jerusalem and head out toward the desert. As he traveled he came across a man from Ethiopia.

The Holy Spirit encouraged Philip to approach the man, who was reading the Scriptures. The man began asking Philip questions about the passage he was reading from Isaiah. He asked Philip to explain this Scripture passage:

> Like a sheep he was led to the slaughter,
> and as a lamb before its shearer is silent,
>> so he opened not his mouth.
> In [his] humiliation justice was denied him.
>> Who will tell of his posterity?
>>> For his life is taken from the earth.

Philip began talking to the Ethiopian about Jesus. He told him that just like the sheep in Isaiah, Jesus was an innocent victim. Very interested, the Ethiopian asked Philip to get into his chariot so that they could continue to talk as they traveled.

Philip talked more about Jesus. When they came to a stream, the man suddenly asked Philip to baptize him. Philip did so. Then the Holy Spirit took Philip away. The man resumed his travel back to Ethiopia rejoicing. Philip continued his journey spreading the good news of Jesus.

adapted from Acts of the Apostles 8:26-40

Saint Philip Baptizing the Ethiopian, Claude Lorrain, 1677

Following the Holy Spirit

The Holy Spirit led Philip to complete an important mission—talk to a person from another country about Jesus. Because Philip paid attention to the Holy Spirit, he accomplished a great thing—he proclaimed Jesus' message to a new people in another land. How excited Philip must have felt when he realized Jesus' message was spreading!

The Holy Spirit can lead us to do great things too. He can remind us to help others. He can help us remember to pray for people who are sick. He can help us work hard to be kind to our friends and our brothers and sisters. By being open to the Holy Spirit, we can find out how God wants us to live out our faith and show Jesus' love to others.

The Gifts of the Holy Spirit

As Catholics we believe that the Holy Spirit has given us seven special gifts. These are called the Gifts of the Holy Spirit.

Here is a list of the Gifts of the Holy Spirit. Beside each gift write an example of a way that you could show it in your life today. For instance, you might show the gift of counsel when you decide not to repeat a bad rumor that you overheard.

The Gifts of the Holy Spirit

Wisdom _____

_____

Understanding _____

_____

Counsel _____

_____

Fortitude _____

_____

Knowledge _____

_____

Piety _____

_____

Fear of the Lord _____

_____

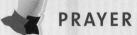

PRAYER SERVICE

Leader: Let us pray. God our Father, you have sent the Holy Spirit to guide and strengthen us as we follow you. May our hearts remain open to the Spirit. We pray this through Christ our Lord and with the Holy Spirit.

Reader: A reading from the Acts of the Apostles.
[Acts of the Apostles 2:1–4]

The Word of the Lord.

All: Thanks be to God.

Leader: Lord, send out your Spirit,
and renew the face of the earth.

All: Lord, send out your Spirit,
and renew the face of the earth.

Group One: Bless and praise the Lord our God.
God, you are great indeed!

Group Two: How many are your creations, Lord!
In wisdom you have made them all.

All: Lord, send out your Spirit, and renew the
face of the earth.

Group One: If you take away their breath, they die
and return to their dust.

Group Two: When you send forth your Spirit, they are given life
and you renew the face of the earth.

All: Lord, send out your Spirit, and renew the face
of the earth.
[adapted from Psalm 104:1,24,29,30]

Leader: Filled with the Spirit, we go forth to love and serve
the Lord. In the name of the Father, and of the Son,
and of the Holy Spirit.
Amen.

All Saints Day and All Souls Day

The Church is like a family. We need to stay in contact in order to remain united. The sacraments, especially the Eucharist, keep us united with God and also with one another. Two feast days—All Saints Day on November 1 and All Souls Day on November 2—celebrate the way that Christians remain connected and united.

 PRAYER

Faithful God, as we celebrate All Saints Day and All Souls Day, help me learn how to stay united with you and all those you have saved through prayer and the sacraments.

United in Christ

On All Saints Day and All Souls Day, we celebrate the Communion of Saints. The Communion of Saints includes all the members of the Church, living and dead, because we are all united in Christ.

Jesus used an image of a vine and its branches to explain the Communion of Saints. Vines were common where he lived. A vine is a plant that is very strong and can grow long distances from a single root. From this root grow branches and leaves that are nourished through the vine. When they are attached to the vine, they receive their needed nourishment and are very strong, but they wither and die for lack of nourishment when they are detached.

Jesus said, "I am the true vine, and my Father is the vine grower. He takes away every branch in me that does not bear fruit, and everyone that does he prunes so that it bears more fruit."

Jesus went on to say, "Remain in me, as I remain in you. Just as a branch cannot bear fruit on its own unless it remains on the vine, so neither can you unless you remain in me. I am the vine, you are the branches. Whoever remains in me and I in him will bear much fruit, because without me you can do nothing."

adapted from John 15:1-5

Jesus emphasizes that we need to stay in contact with him if we are to remain strong as Christians. Through prayer and celebration of the sacraments, our connection with Jesus is strengthened and nourished.

All Saints Day,
Giannicola di Paolo

The Communion of Saints

Jesus gave us the sacraments, which nourish our faith. The union of all those, living and dead, saved by Jesus is called the Communion of Saints.

By participating in the sacraments, and especially the Eucharist, we stay close to God and to all other Christians, both living and dead. In the Eucharist all Christians share a deep personal relationship with God. The Eucharist also creates a union among us, those who have died, and the saints living fully in God's presence in heaven.

On All Saints Day, we celebrate the Communion of Saints by praying with those who have died and are living in heaven. We celebrate our union with the saints and all who follow Jesus.

On All Souls Day we pray for those who have died but are still in purgatory being prepared to live in God's presence forever. We can help those in purgatory by praying for them.

Prayers for the Communion of Saints

Write a prayer for someone you know who is alive and needs prayers, and write a prayer for someone you know who has died.

_____

_____

_____

_____

_____

PRAYER SERVICE

Leader: Let us thank God for uniting us, his followers, in the Communion of Saints.

Reader: A reading from the Gospel of John.

[John 15:1–5]

The gospel of the Lord.

All: Praise to you, Lord Jesus Christ.

Leader: Let us pray that we will live our days united with Christ in God's vineyard.

Group One: O LORD of hosts, restore us;
    let your face shine upon us,
    that we may be saved.

Group Two: You brought a vine out of Egypt;
    you drove away the nations and planted it.

Group One: You cleared the ground;
    it took root and filled the land.

Group Two: The mountains were covered by its shadow,
    the cedars of God by its branches.

Group One: Turn again, LORD of hosts;
    look down from heaven and see;

Group Two: Attend to this vine,
    the shoot your right hand has planted.

All: LORD of hosts, restore us.

[Psalm 80:8–11,15–16,20]

Leader: In communion with the saints in heaven and on earth, let us pray the Lord's Prayer, the words Jesus taught us.

All: In the name of the Father, and of the Son, and of the Holy Spirit.

Prayers and Practices of Our Faith

Knowing and Praying Our Faith

Celebrating Our Faith

Living Our Faith

Songs of Our Faith

Understanding the Words of Our Faith

The Bible and You

God speaks to us in many ways. One way God speaks to us is through the Bible. The Bible is the most important book in Christian life because it is God's message, or revelation. The Bible is the story of God's promise to care for us, especially through his Son, Jesus. At Mass we hear readings from the Bible. We can also read the Bible on our own.

The Bible is not just one book; it is a collection of many books. The writings in the Bible were inspired by the Holy Spirit and written by many different authors.

The Bible is made up of two parts. The Old Testament contains 46 books that tell stories about the Jewish people and their faith in God before Jesus was born.

The New Testament contains 27 books that tell the story of Jesus' life, death, and resurrection and the experience of the early Christians. For Christians, the most important part of the New Testament is the four Gospels—Matthew, Mark, Luke, and John. The New Testament also contains letters written by leaders such as Saint Paul.

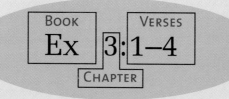

How can you find a passage in the Bible? Bible passages are identified by book, chapter, and verse—for example, Ex 3:1–4. The name of the book comes first and is in abbreviated form. Your Bible's table of contents will help you determine what the abbreviation means. In our example, *Ex* stands for *Exodus*. After the name of the book, there are two numbers. The first one identifies the chapter, which in our example is chapter three; it is followed by a colon. The second number or numbers identify the verses, which in our example are verses one to four.

BOOK · VERSES · Ex 3:1–4 · CHAPTER

Prayer and Forms of Prayer

God is always with us. He wants us to talk to him and to listen to him. In prayer we raise our hearts and minds to God. We are able to speak to and listen to God because, through the Holy Spirit, God teaches us how to pray.

We Pray in Many Ways

Because prayer is so important, the Church teaches us to pray often and in many ways. Sometimes we bless or adore God (prayer of blessing and adoration). Other times we ask God for something for ourselves (prayer of petition). Sometimes we pray for others (prayer of intercession). We also thank God in prayer (prayer of thanksgiving). Finally, we can also praise God (prayer of praise). We can pray alone or with others. We can pray silently or aloud. Praying with others is called communal prayer.

We Meditate and Contemplate

One way to pray is to meditate. To meditate is to think about God. We try to keep our attention and focus on God. In meditation we may use Scripture, prayer books, or icons, which are religious images, to help us concentrate and to spark the imagination.

Another way to pray is to contemplate. This means that we rest quietly in God's presence.

We Get Ready to Pray

We live in a very busy, noisy, and fast-paced world. Sometimes, because of this, our attention span can be short. In order to meditate or reflect, we need to prepare ourselves to pray.

We can get ready for meditation by getting our bodies into a comfortable position. Keeping our backs straight and both feet on the floor is a comfortable position. We can close our eyes, fold our hands comfortably in front of us, and slowly and silently take a deep breath and then let it out slowly. We can establish a rhythm by slowly counting to three while breathing in and slowly counting to three while breathing out. We can keep concentrating on our breathing. This will help us to quiet our thoughts.

We Avoid Distractions

If we become distracted by thinking about something, such as the day at school or a sports event, we can just go back to thinking about our breathing.

After a little practice we will be able to avoid distractions, pray with our imagination, and spend time with God or Jesus in our hearts.

Prayers to Take to Heart

We can pray with any words that come
to mind. Sometimes, when we find that
choosing our own words is difficult,
we can use traditional prayers.
Likewise, when we pray aloud with
others, we rely on traditional prayers
to unite our minds, hearts, and voices.
Memorizing traditional prayers such as
the following can be very helpful. When
we memorize prayers, we take them to heart,
meaning that we not only learn the words but
also try to understand and live them.

Lord's Prayer

Our Father, who art in heaven,
hallowed be thy name;
thy kingdom come;
thy will be done
on earth as it is in heaven.
Give us this day our daily bread;
and forgive us our trespasses
as we forgive those who trespass against us;
and lead us not into temptation,
but deliver us from evil.
Amen.

Hail Mary

Hail Mary, full of grace,
the Lord is with you.
Blessed are you among women,
and blessed is the fruit of your womb, Jesus.
Holy Mary, Mother of God,
pray for us sinners,
now and at the hour of our death.
Amen.

Morning Offering

My God, I offer you my prayers,
works, joys and sufferings of this day
in union with the holy sacrifice of the Mass throughout the world.
I offer them for all the intentions of your Son's Sacred Heart,
for the salvation of souls, reparation for sin,
and the reunion of Christians.
Amen.

Prayer Before Meals

Bless us, O Lord, and these your gifts
which we are about to receive from your goodness.
Through Christ our Lord.
Amen.

Prayer After Meals

We give you thanks
for all your gifts,
almighty God,
living and reigning
now and for ever.
Amen.

Act of Contrition

My God,
I am sorry for my sins with all my heart.
In choosing to do wrong
and failing to do good,
I have sinned against you
whom I should love above all things.
I firmly intend, with your help,
to do penance,
to sin no more,
and to avoid whatever leads me to sin.
Our Savior Jesus Christ
suffered and died for us.
In his name, my God, have mercy.

Apostles' Creed

I believe in God, the Father almighty,
    creator of heaven and earth.
I believe in Jesus Christ, his only Son, our Lord.
    He was conceived by the power of the Holy Spirit
        and born of the Virgin Mary.
    He suffered under Pontius Pilate,
        was crucified, died, and was buried.
    He descended to the dead.
    On the third day he arose again.
    He ascended into heaven,
        and is seated at the right hand of the Father.
    He will come again to judge the living and the dead.
I believe in the Holy Spirit,
    the holy catholic Church,
    the communion of saints,
    the forgiveness of sins,
    the resurrection of the body,
    and the life everlasting. Amen.

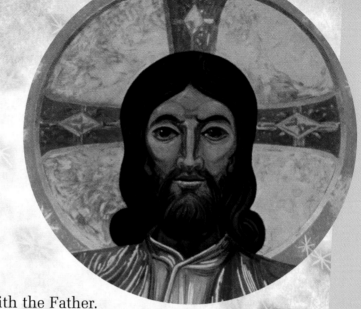

Nicene Creed

We believe in one God,
    the Father, the Almighty,
    maker of heaven and earth,
    of all that is seen and unseen.
We believe in one Lord, Jesus Christ,
    the only Son of God,
    eternally begotten of the Father,
    God from God, Light from Light,
    true God from true God,
    begotten, not made, one in Being with the Father.
    Through him all things were made.
    For us men and for our salvation
        he came down from heaven:
by the power of the Holy Spirit
    he was born of the Virgin Mary, and became man.
For our sake he was crucified under Pontius Pilate;
    he suffered, died, and was buried.
    On the third day he rose again
        in fulfillment of the Scriptures;
    he ascended into heaven
        and is seated at the right hand of the Father.
He will come again in glory to judge the living and the dead,
    and his kingdom will have no end.
We believe in the Holy Spirit, the Lord, the giver of life,
    who proceeds from the Father and the Son.
    With the Father and the Son he is worshiped and glorified.
    He has spoken through the Prophets.
    We believe in one holy catholic and apostolic Church.
    We acknowledge one baptism for the forgiveness of sins.
    We look for the resurrection of the dead,
        and the life of the world to come. Amen.

Act of Faith

O my God, I firmly believe that you are one God in three divine Persons, Father, Son, and Holy Spirit. I believe that your divine Son became man and died for our sins, and that he will come to judge the living and the dead. I believe these and all the truths which the holy Catholic Church teaches, because you have revealed them, who can neither deceive nor be deceived. Amen.

Act of Hope

O my God, relying on your infinite mercy and promises,
I hope to obtain pardon of my sins, the help of your grace,
and life everlasting, through the merits of Jesus Christ,
my Lord and Redeemer.
Amen.

Act of Love

O my God, I love you above all things with my whole heart and soul,
because you are all good and worthy of all my love.
I love my neighbor as myself for the love of you.
I forgive all who have injured me and
I ask pardon of those whom I have injured.
Amen.

Hail, Holy Queen

Hail, holy Queen, Mother of mercy,
hail, our life, our sweetness, and our hope.
To you we cry, the children of Eve;
to you we send up our sighs,
mourning and weeping in this land of exile.
Turn, then, most gracious advocate,
your eyes of mercy toward us;
lead us home at last
and show us the blessed fruit of your womb, Jesus:
O clement, O loving, O sweet Virgin Mary.

Prayer to the Holy Spirit

Come, Holy Spirit, fill the hearts of your faithful.
And kindle in them the fire of your love.
Send forth your Spirit and they shall be created.
And you will renew the face of the earth.

Lord,
by the light of the Holy Spirit
you have taught the hearts of your faithful.
In the same Spirit
help us to relish what is right
and always rejoice in your consolation.
We ask this through Christ our Lord.
Amen.

Prayer for Vocations

God, in Baptism you called me by name
and made me a member of your people, the Church.
Help all your people to know their vocation in life,
and to respond by living a life of holiness.
For your greater glory and for the service of your people,
raise up dedicated and generous leaders
who will serve as sisters, priests,
brothers, deacons, and lay ministers.

Send your Spirit to guide and strengthen me
that I may serve your people
following the example of your Son, Jesus Christ,
in whose name I offer this prayer.
Amen.

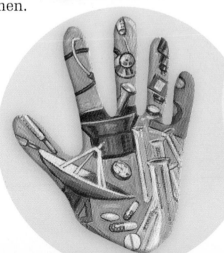

Knowing and Praying Our Faith   **243**

The Rosary

The Rosary helps us to pray to Jesus through Mary. When we pray the Rosary, we think about the special events, or mysteries, in the lives of Jesus and Mary.

The Rosary is made up of a string of beads and a crucifix. We hold the crucifix in our hands as we pray the Sign of the Cross. Then we pray the Apostles' Creed.

Between the crucifix and the medal of Mary, there is a single bead, followed by a set of three beads and another single bead. We pray the Lord's Prayer as we hold the first single bead and a Hail Mary at each bead in the set of three that follows. Then we pray the Glory Be to the Father. On the next single bead we think about the first mystery and pray the Lord's Prayer.

There are five sets of ten beads; each set is called a decade. We pray a Hail Mary on each bead of a decade as we reflect on a particular mystery in the lives of Jesus and Mary. The Glory Be to the Father is prayed at the end of each set. Between sets is a single bead on which we think about one of the mysteries and pray the Lord's Prayer.

We end by holding the crucifix in our hands as we pray the Sign of the Cross.

A 10-bead rosary and crucifix discovered at the site of St. Mary's City, Maryland, founded in the early 17th century by English settlers seeking religious freedom

Praying the Rosary

10. Think about the fourth mystery. Pray the Lord's Prayer.

9. Pray ten Hail Marys and one Glory Be to the Father.

11. Pray ten Hail Marys and one Glory Be to the Father.

8. Think about the third mystery. Pray the Lord's Prayer.

12. Think about the fifth mystery. Pray the Lord's Prayer.

7. Pray ten Hail Marys and one Glory Be to the Father.

6. Think about the second mystery. Pray the Lord's Prayer.

5. Pray ten Hail Marys and one Glory Be to the Father.

4. Think about the first mystery. Pray the Lord's Prayer.

13. Pray ten Hail Marys and one Glory Be to the Father.

3. Pray three Hail Marys and one Glory Be to the Father.

2. Pray the Lord's Prayer.

14. Pray the Sign of the Cross.

1. Pray the Sign of the Cross and the Apostles' Creed.

Mysteries of the Rosary

The Church has used three sets of mysteries for many years. In 2002 Pope John Paul II proposed a fourth set of mysteries—the Mysteries of Light, or Luminous Mysteries. According to his suggestion, the four sets of mysteries might be prayed on the following days: the Joyful Mysteries on Monday and Saturday, the Sorrowful Mysteries on Tuesday and Friday, the Glorious Mysteries on Wednesday and Sunday, and the Luminous Mysteries on Thursday.

The Joyful Mysteries

1. **The Annunciation**
   Mary learns that she has been chosen to be the mother of Jesus.

2. **The Visitation**
   Mary visits Elizabeth, who tells her that she will always be remembered.

3. **The Nativity**
   Jesus is born in a stable in Bethlehem.

4. **The Presentation**
   Mary and Joseph take the infant Jesus to the Temple to present him to God.

5. **The Finding of Jesus in the Temple**
   Jesus is found in the Temple, discussing his faith with the teachers.

The Mysteries of Light

1. **The Baptism of Jesus in the River Jordan**
   God proclaims that Jesus is his beloved Son.

2. **The Wedding Feast at Cana**
   At Mary's request, Jesus performs his first miracle.

3. **The Proclamation of the Kingdom of God**
   Jesus calls all to conversion and service to the kingdom.

4. **The Transfiguration of Jesus**
   Jesus is revealed in glory to Peter, James, and John.

5. **The Institution of the Eucharist**
   Jesus offers his Body and Blood at the Last Supper.

The Sorrowful Mysteries

1. **The Agony in the Garden**
   Jesus prays in the Garden of Gethsemane on the night before he dies.

2. **The Scourging at the Pillar**
   Jesus is beaten with whips.

3. **The Crowning With Thorns**
   Jesus is mocked and crowned with thorns.

4. **The Carrying of the Cross**
   Jesus carries the cross on which he will be crucified.

5. **The Crucifixion**
   Jesus is nailed to the cross and dies.

The Glorious Mysteries

1. **The Resurrection**
   God the Father raises Jesus from the dead.

2. **The Ascension**
   Jesus returns to his Father in heaven.

3. **The Coming of the Holy Spirit**
   The Holy Spirit comes to bring new life to the disciples.

4. **The Assumption of Mary**
   At the end of her life on earth, Mary is taken body and soul into heaven.

5. **The Coronation of Mary**
   Mary is crowned as Queen of Heaven and Earth.

Stations of the Cross

The fourteen Stations of the Cross represent events from Jesus' passion and death. At each station we use our senses and our imagination to reflect prayerfully upon Jesus' suffering, death, and resurrection.

1. Jesus Is Condemned to Death.

Pontius Pilate condemns Jesus to death.

2. Jesus Takes Up His Cross.

Jesus willingly accepts and patiently bears his cross.

3. Jesus Falls the First Time.

Weakened by torments and by loss of blood, Jesus falls beneath his cross.

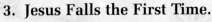

4. Jesus Meets His Sorrowful Mother.

Jesus meets his mother, Mary, who is filled with grief.

5. Simon of Cyrene Helps Jesus Carry the Cross.

Soldiers force Simon of Cyrene to carry the cross.

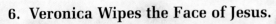

6. Veronica Wipes the Face of Jesus.

Veronica steps through the crowd to wipe the face of Jesus.

7. Jesus Falls a Second Time.

Jesus falls beneath the weight of the cross a second time.

8. Jesus Meets the Women of Jerusalem.
Jesus tells the women not to weep for him,
but for themselves and for their children.

9. Jesus Falls the Third Time.
Weakened almost to the point of death,
Jesus falls a third time.

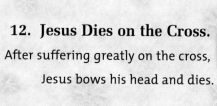

10. Jesus Is Stripped of His Garments.
The soldiers strip Jesus of his
garments, treating him as a
common criminal.

11. Jesus Is Nailed to the Cross.
Jesus' hands and feet are nailed to the cross.

12. Jesus Dies on the Cross.
After suffering greatly on the cross,
Jesus bows his head and dies.

13. Jesus Is Taken Down From the Cross.
The lifeless body of Jesus is tenderly placed in the arms
of Mary, his mother.

14. Jesus Is Laid in the Tomb.
Jesus' disciples place his body
in the tomb.

The closing prayer—sometimes included as a
fifteenth station—reflects on the Resurrection of Jesus.

The Seven Sacraments

Jesus touches our lives through the sacraments. Our celebrations of the sacraments are signs of Jesus' presence in our lives and a means for receiving his grace. The Church celebrates seven sacraments, which are divided into three categories.

Sacraments of Initiation

These sacraments lay the foundation of every Christian life.

Baptism

In Baptism we receive new life in Christ. Baptism takes away original sin and gives us a new birth in the Holy Spirit. Its sign is the pouring of water.

Confirmation

Confirmation seals our life of faith in Jesus. Its signs are the laying of hands on a person's head, most often by a bishop, and the anointing with oil. Like Baptism, Confirmation is received only once.

Eucharist

The Eucharist nourishes our life of faith. Its signs are the bread and wine we receive— the Body and Blood of Christ.

Sacraments of Healing

These sacraments celebrate the healing power of Jesus.

Penance

Through Penance we receive God's forgiveness. Forgiveness requires being sorry for our sins. In Penance we receive Jesus' healing grace through absolution by the priest. The signs of this sacrament are our confession of sins and the words of absolution.

Anointing of the Sick

This sacrament unites a sick person's suffering with that of Jesus and brings forgiveness of sins. Oil, a symbol of strength, is the sign of this sacrament. A person is anointed with oil and receives the laying on of hands from a priest.

Sacraments at the Service of Communion

These sacraments help members serve the community.

Holy Orders

In Holy Orders men are ordained as deacons, priests, or bishops. Deacons serve to remind us of our baptismal call to help others, and priests serve as spiritual leaders of their communities. Bishops carry on the teachings of the apostles. The signs of this sacrament are the laying on of hands and anointing with chrism by a bishop.

Matrimony

In Matrimony a baptized man and woman are united with each other as a sign of the unity between Jesus and his Church. Matrimony requires the consent of the couple, as expressed in the marriage promises. The couple and their wedding rings are the signs of this sacrament.

Celebrating the Lord's Day

Sunday is the day on which we celebrate the Resurrection of Jesus. Sunday is the Lord's Day. We gather for Mass, rest from work, and perform works of mercy. People all over the world gather at God's eucharistic table as brothers and sisters.

Order of the Mass

The Mass is the high point of the Christian life, and it always follows a set order.

Introductory Rites—preparing to celebrate the Eucharist

Entrance Procession
We gather as a community and praise God in song.

Sign of the Cross and Greeting
We pray the Sign of the Cross. The priest welcomes us.

Penitential Rite
We remember our sins and ask God for mercy.

Gloria
We praise God in song.

Opening Prayer
We ask God to hear our prayers.

Liturgy of the Word—hearing God's plan of salvation

First Reading
We listen to God's Word, usually from the Old Testament.

Responsorial Psalm
We respond to God's Word in song.

Second Reading
We listen to God's Word from the New Testament.

Alleluia or Gospel Acclamation
We sing "Alleluia!" (except during Lent) to praise God for the Good News.

Gospel
We stand and listen to the Gospel of the Lord.

Homily
The priest or the deacon explains God's Word.

Profession of Faith
We proclaim our faith through the Nicene Creed.

General Intercessions
We pray for our needs and the needs of others.

Liturgy of the Eucharist—celebrating Jesus' presence in the Eucharist

Preparation of the Altar and the Gifts

We bring gifts of bread and wine to the altar.

- **Prayer Over the Gifts**—The priest prays that God will accept our sacrifice.

Eucharistic Prayer

This prayer of thanksgiving is the center and high point of the entire celebration.

- **Preface**—We give thanks and praise to God.
- **Holy, Holy**—We sing an acclamation of praise.
- **Consecration**—The bread and wine become the Body and Blood of Jesus Christ.
- **Memorial Acclamation**—We proclaim the mystery of our faith.
- **Great Amen**—We affirm the words and actions of the eucharistic prayer.

Communion Rite

We prepare to receive the Body and Blood of Jesus Christ.

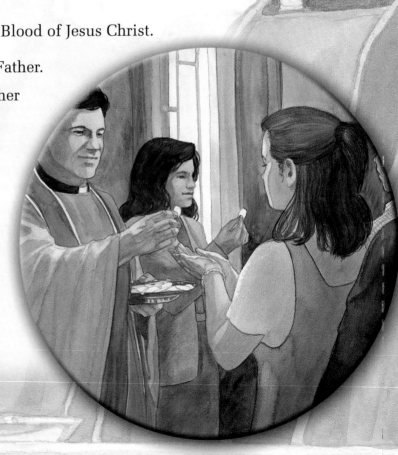

- **Lord's Prayer**—We pray the Our Father.
- **Sign of Peace**—We offer one another Christ's peace.
- **Breaking of the Bread and the Lamb of God**—We pray for forgiveness, mercy, and peace.
- **Communion**—We receive the Body and Blood of Jesus Christ.
- **Prayer After Communion**—We pray that the Eucharist will strengthen us to live as Jesus Christ did.

Concluding Rite—going forth to serve the Lord and others

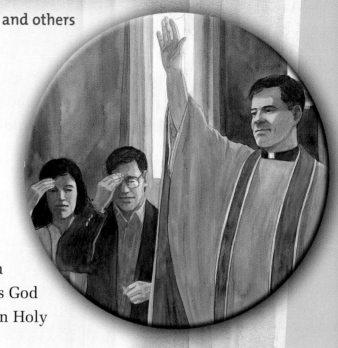

Blessing

We receive God's blessing.

Dismissal

We go in peace to love and
serve the Lord and one another.

Holy Days of Obligation

Holy Days of Obligation are the days other than
Sundays on which we celebrate the great things God
has done for us through Jesus and the saints. On Holy
Days of Obligation, Catholics attend Mass.

Six Holy Days of Obligation are celebrated in the United States.

January 1—Mary, Mother of God

Fortieth day after Easter—Ascension

August 15—Assumption of the Blessed Virgin Mary

November 1—All Saints

December 8—Immaculate Conception

December 25—Nativity of Our Lord Jesus Christ

Precepts of the Church

The Precepts of the Church describe the minimum effort we must
make in prayer and in living a moral life. Catholics are called to
move beyond the minimum by growing in love of God and love
of neighbor. They are as follows:

1. attendance at Mass on Sundays and Holy Days of Obligation

2. confession of serious sin at least once a year

3. reception of Holy Communion at least once a year
   during the Easter season

4. observance of the days of fast and abstinence

5. providing for the needs of the Church

An Examination of Conscience

An examination of conscience is the act of looking prayerfully into our hearts to ask how we have hurt our relationships with God and other people through our thoughts, words, and actions. We reflect on the Ten Commandments and the teachings of the Church. Questions such as the following will help us in our examination of conscience:

My Relationship With God

What steps am I taking to help me grow closer to God and to others? Do I turn to God often during the day, especially when I am tempted?

Do I participate at Mass with attention and devotion on Sundays and holy days? Do I pray often and read the Bible?

Do I use God's name and the names of Jesus, Mary, and the saints with love and reverence?

My Relationships With Family, Friends, and Neighbors

Have I set a bad example through my words or actions? Do I treat others fairly? Do I spread stories that hurt other people?

Am I loving to those in my family? Am I respectful of my neighbors, my friends, and those in authority?

Do I show respect for my body and for the bodies of others? Do I keep away from forms of entertainment that do not respect God's gift of sexuality?

Have I taken or damaged anything that did not belong to me? Have I cheated, copied homework, or lied?

Do I quarrel with others just so I can get my own way? Do I insult others to try to make them think they are less than I am? Do I hold grudges and try to hurt people who I think have hurt me?

How to Go to Confession

An examination of conscience is an important part of preparing for the Sacrament of Penance. The Sacrament of Penance includes the following steps:

1. The priest greets us and we pray the Sign of the Cross. He invites us to trust in God. He may read God's Word with us.

2. We confess our sins. The priest may help and counsel us.

3. The priest gives us a penance to perform. Penance is an act of kindness or prayers to pray, or both.

4. The priest asks us to express our sorrow, usually by reciting an Act of Contrition.

5. We receive absolution. The priest says, "I absolve you from your sins in the name of the Father, and of the Son, and of the Holy Spirit." We respond, "Amen."

6. The priest dismisses us by saying, "Go in peace." We go forth to perform the act of penance he has given us.

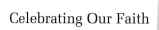

The Ten Commandments

As believers in Jesus Christ, we are called to a new life and are asked to make moral choices that keep us united with God. With the help and grace of the Holy Spirit, we can choose ways to act to keep us close to God, to help other people, and to be witnesses to Jesus in the world.

The Ten Commandments guide us in making choices that allow us to live as God wants us to live. The first three commandments tell us how to love God; the other seven show us how to love our neighbor.

1. I am the Lord your God: you shall not have strange gods before me.
2. You shall not take the name of the Lord your God in vain.
3. Remember to keep holy the Lord's Day.
4. Honor your father and your mother.
5. You shall not kill.
6. You shall not commit adultery.
7. You shall not steal.
8. You shall not bear false witness against your neighbor.
9. You shall not covet your neighbor's wife.
10. You shall not covet your neighbor's goods.

The Great Commandment

The Ten Commandments are fulfilled in Jesus' Great Commandment: "You shall love God with all your heart, with all your soul, with all your mind, and with all your strength. You shall love your neighbor as yourself."

adapted from Mark 12:30-31

The New Commandment

Before his death on the cross, Jesus gave his disciples a new commandment: "Love one another. As I have loved you, so you also should love one another."

John 13:34

The Beatitudes

The Beatitudes are the teachings of Jesus in the Sermon on the Mount (Matthew 5:1–10). The Beatitudes fulfill God's promises made to Abraham and his descendants and describe the rewards that will be theirs as loyal followers of Christ.

Blessed are the poor in spirit,
  for theirs is the kingdom of heaven.

Blessed are they who mourn,
  for they will be comforted.

Blessed are the meek,
  for they will inherit the land.

Blessed are they who hunger and thirst for
  righteousness, for they will be satisfied.

Blessed are the merciful,
  for they will be shown mercy.

Blessed are the clean of heart,
  for they will see God.

Blessed are the peacemakers,
  for they will be called children of God.

Blessed are they who are persecuted for
    the sake of righteousness,
  for theirs is the kingdom of heaven.

Making Good Choices

Our conscience is the inner voice that helps us to know the law God has placed in our hearts. Our conscience helps us to judge the moral qualities of our own actions. It guides us to do good and avoid evil.

The Holy Spirit can help us to form a good conscience. We form our conscience by studying the teachings of the Church and following the guidance of our parents and pastoral leaders.

Christian freedom upholds the dignity of every human being. It does not mean that we have the right to do whatever we please. We can live in true freedom if we cooperate with the Holy Spirit, who gives us the virtue of prudence. This virtue helps us to recognize what is good in every situation and to make correct choices. The Holy Spirit gives us the gifts of wisdom and understanding to help us make the right choices in life in relationship to God and others. The gift of counsel helps us to reflect on making correct choices in life.

The Ten Commandments help us to make moral choices that are pleasing to God. We have the grace of the sacraments, the teachings of the Church, and the good example of saints and fellow Christians to help us make good choices.

Making moral choices involves the following steps:

1. Ask the Holy Spirit for help.

2. Think about God's law and the teachings of the Church.

3. Think about what will happen as a result of your choice. (Ask yourself, Will the consequences be pleasing to God? Will my choice hurt someone else?)

4. Seek advice from someone you respect and remember that Jesus is with you.

5. Ask yourself how your choice will affect your relationship with God and others.

Making moral choices takes into consideration the object of the choice, our intention in making the choice, and the circumstances in which the choice is made. It is never right to make an evil choice in the hope of gaining something good.

Virtues

Virtues are gifts from God that lead us to live in a close relationship with him. Virtues are like habits. They need to be practiced; they can be lost if they are neglected. The three most important virtues are called *theological* virtues because they come from God and lead to God. The *cardinal* virtues are human virtues, acquired by education and good actions. *Cardinal* comes from the Latin word for *hinge* (*cardo*), meaning "that on which other things depend."

Theological Virtues

faith   hope   charity

Cardinal Virtues

prudence   justice   fortitude   temperance

Gifts of the Holy Spirit

The Holy Spirit makes it possible for us to do what God asks of us by giving us these many gifts.

wisdom	understanding	counsel
fortitude	knowledge	piety
fear of the Lord		

Fruits of the Holy Spirit

The Fruits of the Holy Spirit are signs of the Holy Spirit's action in our lives.

love	joy	peace
patience	kindness	generosity
faithfulness	gentleness	self-control

Church tradition also includes **goodness, modesty,** and **chastity** as Fruits of the Holy Spirit.

Works of Mercy

The Corporal and Spiritual Works of Mercy are actions we can perform that extend God's compassion and mercy to those in need.

Corporal Works of Mercy

The Corporal Works of Mercy are these kind acts by which we help our neighbors with their material and physical needs.

feed the hungry

clothe the naked

bury the dead

shelter the homeless

visit the sick and imprisoned

give alms to the poor

Spiritual Works of Mercy

The Spiritual Works of Mercy are acts of compassion by which we help our neighbors with their emotional and spiritual needs.

instruct

console

forgive

advise

comfort

bear wrongs patiently

Showing Our Love for the World

In the story of the Good Samaritan (Luke 10:29–37), Jesus makes clear our responsibility to care for those in need. The Catholic Church teaches this responsibility in the following themes of Catholic Social Teaching.

Life and Dignity of the Human Person

All human life is sacred, and all people must be respected and valued over material goods. We are called to ask whether our actions as a society respect or threaten the life and dignity of the human person.

Call to Family, Community, and Participation

Participation in family and community is central to our faith and to a healthy society. Families must be supported so that people can participate in society, build a community spirit, and promote the well-being of all, especially the poor and vulnerable.

Rights and Responsibilities

Every person has a right to life as well as a right to those things required for human decency. As Catholics, we have a responsibility to protect these basic human rights in order to achieve a healthy society.

Option for the Poor and Vulnerable

In our world many people are very rich while at the same time many are extremely poor. As Catholics, we are called to pay special attention to the needs of the poor by defending and promoting their dignity and by meeting their immediate material needs.

The Dignity of Work and the Rights of Workers

The basic rights of workers must be respected: the right to productive work, fair wages, and private property; and the right to organize, join unions, and pursue economic opportunity. Catholics believe that the economy is meant to serve people and that work is not merely a way to make a living but is an important way in which we participate in God's creation.

Solidarity

Because God is our Father, we are all brothers and sisters with the responsibility to care for one another. Solidarity is the attitude that leads Christians to share spiritual and material goods. Solidarity unites rich and poor, weak and strong, and helps to create a society that recognizes that we all depend upon one another.

Care for God's Creation

God is the creator of all people and all things, and he wants us to enjoy his creation. The responsibility to care for all God has made is a requirement of our faith.

Song of Love

Chorus

Thank you Je - sus for help -ing me to see.

Thank you God for the heart you've giv - en me.

Thank you Spir - it for com -ing to me, and for show - ing me how to sing your song of love.

(to Verse 1)

2 A G **2**
your song of love. (to Verses 2 and 3)

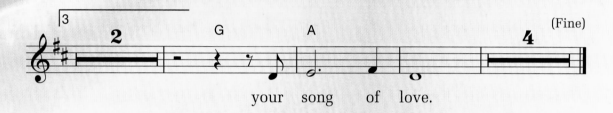

3 G A **4** (Fine)
your song of love.

Verse 1

Bm G A D
I saw some-one lone-ly by the road,

Em A G D
Some-one my age sad-ly all a - lone.

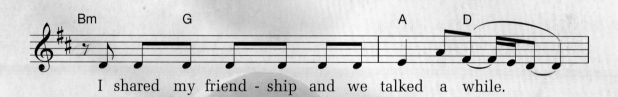

Bm G A D
I shared my friend - ship and we talked a while.

Em A G A D (to Chorus)
I gave a hand, Je - sus gave back a smile.

continued

Song of Love *(continued)*

Verse 2

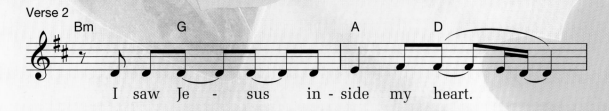

I saw Je - sus in - side my heart.

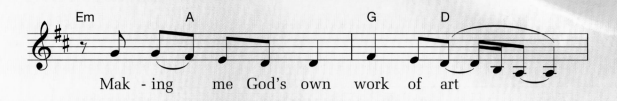

Mak - ing me God's own work of art

If I spread my joy in life each day

I can show my love for God's world in ev -'ry way.

Verse 3

I saw Je-sus in friends and fam-i-ly

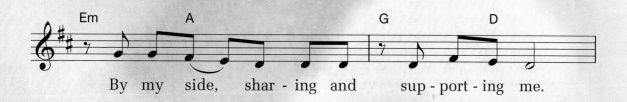

By my side, shar-ing and sup-port-ing me.

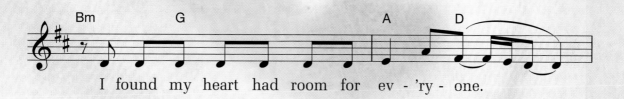

I found my heart had room for ev-'ry-one.

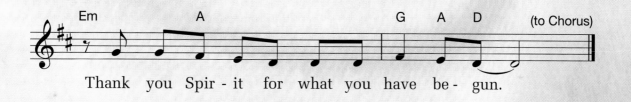

(to Chorus)

Thank you Spir-it for what you have be-gun.

Sing Out, Earth and Skies

Verses

D   G   D

1. Come, O God of all the earth:
2. Come, O God of wind and flame:
3. Come, O God of flash - ing light:
4. Come, O God of snow and rain:
5. Come, O Jus - tice, Come, O Peace:

Dm   Am   Dm

1. Come to us, O Right - eous One;
2. Fill the earth with right - eous - ness;
3. Twin - kling star and burn - ing sun;
4. Show - er down up - on the earth;
5. Come and shape our hearts a - new;

D   G   D

1. Come, and bring our love to birth:
2. Teach us all to sing your name:
3. God of day and God of night:
4. Come, O God of joy and pain:
5. Come and make op - pres - sion cease:

Dm   Am   Dm

1. In the glo - ry of your Son.
2. May our lives your love con - fess.
3. In your light we are all one.
4. God of sor - row, God of mirth.
5. Bring us all to life in you.

Refrain

Sing   out,   earth   and   skies!

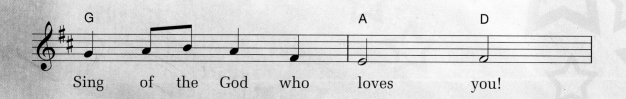

Sing   of   the   God   who   loves   you!

Raise   your   joy - ful   cries!

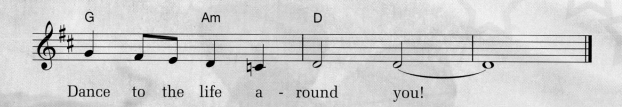

Dance   to   the   life   a - round   you!

"Sing Out, Earth and Skies" by Marty Haugen. © by GIA Publications, Inc.
All rights reserved. Reprinted by permission.

Let the Children Come to Me

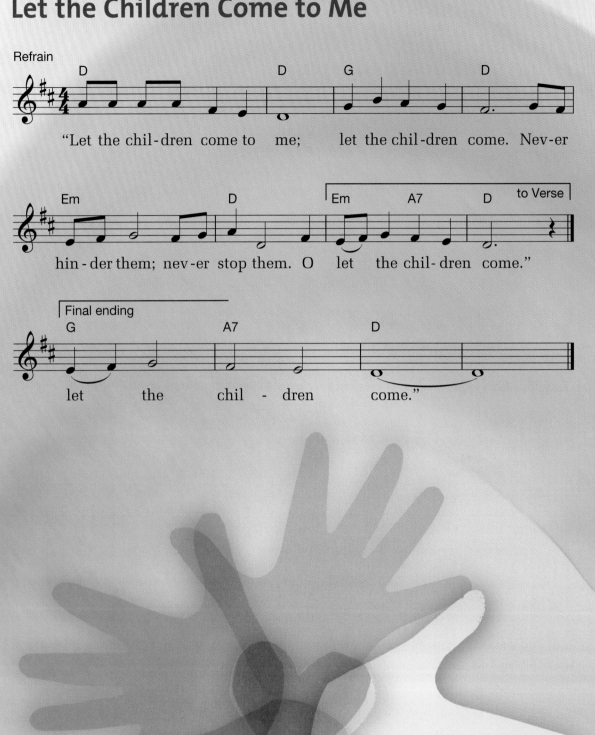

Prayers and Practices of Our Faith

Verses

G

1. Peo - ple were bring - ing chil - dren,
2. "If you seek the king - dom,
3. Then the Lord em - braced them,

D

Em

1. Just to see the Lord. And when the dis - ci - ples
2. Lis - ten to what I say: Un - less you be - come like
3. Held them in his care. With love he be - stowed his

D   G

D

1. stopped them, This is what they heard:
2. chil - dren, You can - not know the way."
3. bless - ing, With love he spoke this prayer:

A7   A7   (to Refrain)

When Jesus the Healer

1. When Je - sus the heal - er passed through Gal - i - lee,
2. A par - a - lyzed man was let down through a roof,
3. The death of his daugh - ter caused Jai - rus to weep.
4. When blind Bar - ti - mae - us cried out to the Lord,
5. The lep - ers were healed and the de - mons cast out.

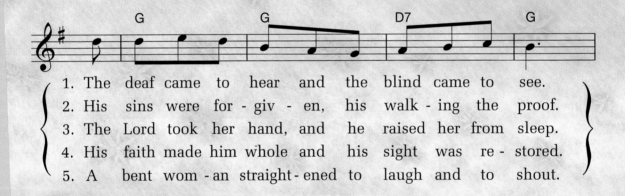

Heal us, heal us to - day.

1. The deaf came to hear and the blind came to see.
2. His sins were for - giv - en, his walk - ing the proof.
3. The Lord took her hand, and he raised her from sleep.
4. His faith made him whole and his sight was re - stored.
5. A bent wom - an straight - ened to laugh and to shout.

Heal us, Lord Je - sus.

Immaculate Mary

Verses

1. Im - mac - u - late Mar - y, your prais - es we sing;
2. To you by an an - gel, the Lord God made known
3. The an - gels re - joiced when you brought forth God's Son;
4. Your child is the Sav - ior, all hope lies in him:
5. In glo - ry for e - ver now close to your Son,

1. You reign now in splen - dor with Je - sus our King.
2. The grace of the Spi - rit, the gift of the Son.
3. Your joy is the joy of all a - ges to come.
4. He gives us new life and re - deems us from sin.
5. All a - ges will praise you for all God has done.

Refrain

A - ve, A - ve, A - ve, Ma - ri - a.

A - ve, A - ve, Ma - ri - a.

Jesus, Bread of Life

Refrain

Je - sus, Je - sus: Bread of Life.

Je - sus, Je - sus: sav - ing cup.

Je - sus, Je - sus, live in us. We be-

lieve, O God, we be - lieve.

1. "I am the bread which comes from heav - en.
2. "Come now to me, all who are thirst - y.
3. "Be not a - fraid; do not be trou - bled.
4. "A - bide in me; keep my com - mand - ments.

G   C   G   D   A   (to Refrain)

1. Those who eat will nev - er die."
2. Come and drink with faith in me."
3. Trust in God and trust in me."
4. Learn to love as I have loved you."

Make Me a Channel of Your Peace

Verses 1 and 2

1. Make me a chan - nel of your peace.
2. Make me a chan - nel of your peace.

1. Where there is ha - tred, let me bring your love.
2. Where there's de - spair in life, let me bring hope.

1. Where there is in - ju - ry, your par - don, Lord,
2. Where there is dark - ness, on - ly light,

1. And where there's doubt, true faith in you.
2. And where there's sad - ness, ev - er joy.

Verse 3

3. Oh, Mas - ter, grant that I may nev - er seek

3. So much to be con - soled as to con - sole.

3. To be un-der-stood as to un-der-stand.

3. To be loved as to love with all my soul.

Verse 4

4. Make me a chan-nel of your peace.

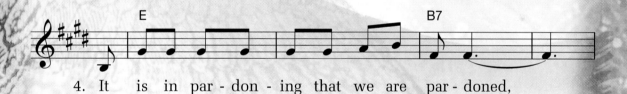

4. It is in par-don-ing that we are par-doned,

4. in giv-ing of our-selves that we re-ceive,

4. and in dy-ing that we're born to e-ter-nal life.

Prayer of Peace

1. Peace be - fore us, peace be - hind us,
2. Love be - fore us, love be - hind us,
3. Light be - fore us, light be - hind us,
4. Christ be - fore us, Christ be - hind us,

1. peace un - der our feet.
2. love un - der our feet.
3. light un - der our feet.
4. Christ un - der our feet.

1. Peace with - in us, peace o - ver us,
2. Love with - in us, love o - ver us,
3. Light with - in us, light o - ver us,
4. Christ with - in us, Christ o - ver us,

1. let all a - round us be peace.
2. let all a - round us be love.
3. let all a - round us be light.
4. let all a - round us be Christ.

Glossary

A

Abba an informal word for *father* in Aramaic, the language Jesus spoke. It is like "dad" in English. When Jesus spoke to God the Father, he called him "Abba." [Abba]

absolution the forgiveness we receive from God through the priest in the Sacrament of Penance [absolución]

Advent the four weeks before Christmas. It is a time of joyful preparation for the celebration of the Incarnation, Jesus' birth as our savior, and a time for anticipating the coming of Jesus Christ at the end of time. [Adviento]

Advocate Jesus' name for the Holy Spirit. The Holy Spirit comforts us, speaks for us in difficult times, and makes Jesus present to us. [Abogado]

All Saints Day November 1, the day on which the Church honors all who have died and now live with God as saints in heaven. This group includes those who are officially recognized as saints as well as many unknown people who after a good life have died and now live in God's presence. The feast celebrates our union with those who have gone before us and points to our ultimate goal of union with God. [Día de Todos los Santos]

All Souls Day November 2, the day on which the Church prays that all friends of God who have died may rest in peace. Those who have died may need purification in purgatory before living fully in God's presence. Our prayers and good works can help them in this process. Along with All Saints Day, this feast reminds us that all who love God, living and dead, are united in living communion with Jesus Christ and with one another. [Día de Difuntos]

altar the table in the church on which the priest celebrates Mass, where the sacrifice of Christ on the cross is made present in the Sacrament of the Eucharist. The altar represents two aspects of the mystery of the Eucharist. It is the place where Jesus Christ offers himself for our sins and where he gives us himself as our food for eternal life. [altar]

ambo a raised stand from which a person reads the Word of God during Mass [ambón]

ambo

Amen the Hebrew word used to conclude Jewish and Christian prayers. It means "This is true," "So be it," or "Let it be so." We end prayers with "Amen" to show that we mean what we have just said. [Amén]

angel a spiritual creature who worships God in heaven. Angels serve God as messengers. They tell us of his plans for our salvation. [ángel]

Annunciation the announcement to Mary by the angel Gabriel that God had chosen her to be the mother of Jesus. When Mary agreed, the Son of God became human in her. The feast of the Annunciation is celebrated on March 25, nine months before Christmas. [Anunciación]

Anointing of the Sick one of the seven sacraments. In this sacrament a sick person has holy oil applied and receives the strength, peace, and courage to overcome the difficulties associated with illness. Through this sacrament, Jesus brings the sick person spiritual healing and forgiveness of sins. If it is God's will, healing of the body is given as well. [unción de los enfermos]

apostle one of twelve special men who accompanied Jesus in his ministry and were witnesses to the Resurrection. *Apostle* means "one sent." These were the people sent to preach the gospel to the whole world. [apóstol]

Apostles' Creed a statement of Christian belief that developed out of a creed used in Baptism in Rome. The Apostles' Creed lists simple statements of belief in God the Father, Jesus Christ the Son, and the Holy Spirit. The profession of faith used in Baptism today is based on it. [Credo de los Apóstoles]

apostolic one of the four Marks of the Church. The Church is apostolic because it continues to hand on the teaching of the apostles through their successors, the bishops, in union with the successor of Saint Peter, the pope. [apostólico]

Ark of the Covenant a portable box in which were placed the tablets of the Ten Commandments. The Ark was the most important item in the shrine that was carried through the desert and then placed in the holiest part of the Temple in Jerusalem. Two angels are depicted on the cover of the Ark of the Covenant. The wings of the angels curve upward, representing the place where God came close to Israel and revealed his will. [Arca de la Alianza]

Ark of the Covenant

Ascension the entry of Jesus into God's presence in heaven. In the Acts of the Apostles, it is written that Jesus, after his Resurrection, spent 40 days on earth, instructing his followers. He then returned to his Father in heaven. [Ascensión]

Ash Wednesday the first day of Lent, on which we receive ashes on our foreheads. The ashes remind us to prepare for Easter by repenting and showing sorrow for the choices we make that offend God and hurt our relationships with others. [Miércoles de Ceniza]

assembly the people of God when they are gathered together to worship him [asamblea]

Assumption Mary's being taken, body and soul, into heaven. Mary had a special relationship with her son, Jesus, from the very beginning, when she conceived him. Catholics believe that because of this relationship, she enjoys a special participation in Jesus' Resurrection and has been taken into heaven where she now lives with him. We celebrate this event in the Feast of the Assumption on August 15. [Asunción]

Assumption

B

Baptism the first of the seven sacraments. Baptism frees us from original sin and is necessary for salvation. Baptism gives us new life in Jesus Christ through the Holy Spirit. The celebration of Baptism consists of immersing a person in water while declaring that the person is baptized in the name of the Father, the Son, and the Holy Spirit. [bautismo]

Beatitudes the teachings of Jesus in the Sermon on the Mount in Matthew's Gospel. The Beatitudes are eight ways of living the Christian life. They are the fulfillment of the commandments given to Moses. These teachings present the way to true happiness. [Bienaventuranzas]

Bible the collection of books containing the truths of God's revelation to us. These writings were inspired by the Holy Spirit and written by human beings. The Bible is made up of the 46 books in the Old Testament and 27 books in the New Testament. [Biblia]

bishop a man who has received the fullness of Holy Orders. As a successor to the original apostles, he takes care of the Church and is a principal teacher in it. [obispo]

Blessed Sacrament the bread that has been consecrated by the priest at Mass. It is kept in the tabernacle to adore and to be taken to the sick. [Santísimo Sacramento]

blessing a prayer that calls for God's power and care upon some person, place, thing, or special activity [bendición]

Body and Blood of Christ the bread and wine that has been consecrated by the priest at Mass. In the Sacrament of the Eucharist, all of the risen Lord Jesus Christ—body, blood, soul, and divinity—is present under the appearances of bread and wine. [Cuerpo y Sangre de Cristo]

C

canonize to declare that a Christian who has died is already in heaven and may be looked to as a model of Christian life who may intercede for us as a saint [canonizar]

capital sins those sins that can lead us to more serious sin. They are pride, covetousness, envy, anger, gluttony, lust, and sloth. [pecados capitales]

catechumen a person being formed in the Christian life through instruction and by the example of the parish community. Through conversion and maturity of faith, a catechumen is preparing to be welcomed into the Church at Easter through the Sacraments of Baptism, Confirmation, and Eucharist. [catecúmeno]

catholic one of the four Marks of the Church. The Church is catholic because Jesus is fully present in it and because Jesus has given the Church to the whole world. It is universal. [católico]

character a permanent spiritual mark. Character shows that a person has a new relationship with Jesus and a special standing in the Church. Baptism, Confirmation, and Holy Orders each have a specific permanent character and therefore may be received only once. [carácter]

charity a virtue given to us by God that helps us love God above all things and our neighbor as ourselves [caridad]

chastity the integration of our physical sexuality with our spiritual nature. Chastity helps us to be completely human, able to give to others our whole life and love. All people, married and single, are called to practice chastity. [castidad]

Chosen People the people set apart by God to have a special relationship with him. God first formed a Chosen People when he made a covenant, or solemn agreement, with Abraham. He reaffirmed the covenant through Moses at Mount Sinai. The covenant is fulfilled in Jesus and his Church. [Pueblo Elegido]

chrism a perfumed oil, consecrated by a bishop, that is used in the Sacraments of Baptism, Confirmation, and Holy Orders. Anointing with chrism signifies the call of the baptized to the threefold ministry of priest, prophet, and king. [crisma]

Christ a title that means "anointed with oil." It is from a Greek word that means the same thing as the Hebrew word *Messiah*, or "anointed." It is the name given to Jesus after the Resurrection when he completed his mission as priest, prophet, and king. [Cristo]

Christian the name given to all those who have been anointed through the gift of the Holy Spirit in Baptism and have become followers of Jesus Christ [cristiano]

Christmas the feast of the birth of Jesus (December 25) [Navidad]

Church the people of God throughout the whole world, or diocese (the local Church), or the assembly of those called together to worship God. The Church is one, holy, catholic, and apostolic. [Iglesia]

clergy those men who are set apart as sacred ministers to serve the Church through Holy Orders [clero]

commandment a standard, or rule, for living as God wants us to live. Jesus summarized all of the commandments into two: love God and love your neighbor. [mandamiento]

communal prayer the worship of God together with others. The Liturgy of the Hours and the Mass are the main forms of communal prayer. [oración común]

Communion of Saints the unity of all, dead or living, who have been saved in Jesus Christ. The Communion of Saints is based on our one faith, and it is nourished by our participation in the Eucharist. [Comunión de los Santos]

confession the act of telling our sins to a priest in the Sacrament of Penance. The sacrament itself is sometimes referred to as "Confession." [confesión]

Confirmation the sacrament that completes the grace we receive in Baptism. It seals, or confirms, this grace through the seven gifts of the Holy Spirit that we receive as part of Confirmation. This sacrament also makes us better able to participate in the worship and apostolic life of the Church. [confirmación]

conscience the inner voice that helps each of us to judge the morality of our own actions. It guides us to follow God's law by doing good and avoiding evil. [consciencia]

consecration the making of a thing or a person to be special to God through a prayer or blessing. At Mass the words of the priest are a consecration that makes Jesus Christ's Body and Blood present in the bread and wine. People or objects set apart for God in a special way are also consecrated. For example, churches and altars are consecrated for use in liturgy, and bishops are consecrated as they receive the fullness of the Sacrament of Holy Orders. [consagración]

contrition the sorrow we feel when we know that we have sinned, followed by the decision not to sin again. Perfect contrition arises from a love that loves God above all else. Imperfect contrition arises on other motives. Contrition is the most important act of the penitent preparing to celebrate the Sacrament of Penance. [contrición]

conversion a radical or serious change of the whole life, away from sin and toward God. The call to change of heart is a key part of the preaching of Jesus. Throughout our entire lives, Jesus calls us to change in this way. [conversión]

Corporal Works of Mercy kind acts by which we help our neighbors with their everyday, material needs. Corporal Works of Mercy include feeding the hungry, finding a home for the homeless, clothing the naked, visiting the sick and those in prison, giving alms to the poor, and burying the dead. [obras corporales de misericordia]

counsel one of the seven Gifts of the Holy Spirit. Counsel helps us to make correct choices in life through reflection, discernment, consulting, and the advising of others. [consejo]

covenant a solemn agreement between people or between people and God. God made covenants with humanity through agreements with Noah, Abraham, and Moses. These covenants offered salvation. God's new and final covenant was established through Jesus' life, death, and resurrection. *Testament* is another word for *covenant*. [alianza]

creation God's act of making everything that exists outside himself. Creation is everything that exists. God said that all of creation is good. [creación]

Creator God, who made everything that is and whom we can come to know through everything he created [Creador]

creed a brief summary of what people believe. The word *creed* comes from the Latin *credo*, "I believe." The Nicene Creed is the most important summary of Christian beliefs. [credo]

crozier the staff carried by a bishop that shows he cares for us in the same way that a shepherd cares for his sheep. It also reminds us that he represents Jesus, the Good Shepherd. [báculo]

Corporal Works of Mercy

Understanding the Words of Our Faith   **285**

culture the collection of knowledge, belief, and behavior of a particular group of people. Culture expresses the shared attitudes, values, goals, and social practices of the group. In order to take root in a culture, the gospel must be adapted to live in that culture as well as transform it. [cultura]

D

deacon a man ordained through the Sacrament of Holy Orders to the ministry of service in the Church. Deacons help the bishop and priests by serving in the various charitable practices of the Church. They also help by proclaiming the gospel and preaching and by assisting at the Liturgy of the Eucharist. Deacons also celebrate Baptism, bless marriages, and preside at funerals. [diácono]

detraction the act of talking about the faults and sins of another person to someone who has no reason to hear this and cannot help the person. Detraction damages the reputation of another person without any intent to help that person. [detracción]

diocese the members of the Church in a particular area, united in faith and the sacraments, and gathered under the leadership of a bishop [diócesis]

disciple a person who has accepted Jesus' message and tries to live as he did, sharing his mission, his suffering, and his joys [discípulo]

Doctor of the Church, Theresa of Avila

discrimination the act of mistreating other people because of how they look or act, or just because they are different [discriminación]

Divine Providence the guidance of God over all he has created. Divine Providence exercises care for all creation and guides it toward its final perfection. [Divina Providencia]

Doctor of the Church a man or a woman recognized as a model teacher of the Christian faith [Doctor de la Iglesia]

domestic church the Christian home, which is a community of grace and prayer and a school of human virtues and Christian charity [iglesia doméstica]

E

Easter the celebration of the bodily raising of Jesus Christ from the dead. Easter is the festival of our redemption and the central Christian feast, the one from which other feasts arise. [Pascua]

Easter Vigil the celebration of the first and greatest Christian feast, the Resurrection of Jesus. It occurs on the first Saturday evening after the first full moon of spring. During this night watch before Easter morning, catechumens are baptized, confirmed, and receive Eucharist for the first time. [Vigilia Pascual]

Eastern Catholic Churches a group of churches that developed in the East (in countries such as Lebanon) that are in union with the Roman Catholic Church but have their own liturgical, theological, and administrative traditions. They show the truly catholic nature of the Church, which takes root in many cultures. [Iglesias Católicas Orientales]

Emmanuel a Hebrew name from the Old Testament that means "God with us." In Matthew's Gospel, Jesus is called Emmanuel. [Emanuel]

encyclical a letter written by the pope and sent to the whole Church and sometimes to the whole world. It expresses Church teaching on some specific and important issue. [encíclica]

envy a feeling of resentment or sadness because someone has a quality, a talent, or a possession that we want. Envy is one of the seven capital sins, and it is contrary to the tenth commandment. [envidia]

Epiphany the day on which we celebrate the visit of the Magi to Jesus after his birth. This is the day that Jesus was revealed as the savior of the whole world. [Epifanía]

Epiphany

epistle a letter written by Saint Paul or another leader to a group of Christians in the early Church. Twenty-one of the twenty-seven books of the New Testament are epistles. The second reading at Mass on Sundays and holy days is always from one of these books. [epistola]

eternal life the never-ending life after death with God, granted to those who die as God's friends, with the grace of God alive in them [vida eterna]

Eucharist the sacrament in which we give thanks to God for giving us the bread and wine that become the Body and Blood of Jesus Christ. This sacrament brings us into union with Jesus Christ and his saving death and resurrection. [Eucaristía]

Eucharistic liturgy the public worship, held by the Church, in which bread and wine is consecrated to become the Body and Blood of Jesus Christ. The Sunday celebration of the Eucharistic liturgy is at the heart of Church life. [liturgia eucarística]

evangelization the proclamation, or declaring by word and by example, of the good news about the salvation we have received in Jesus Christ. Evangelization is a sharing of our faith with others, both those who do not know Jesus and those who are called to follow Jesus more closely. [evangelización]

examination of conscience the act of prayerfully thinking about what we have said or done in light of what the gospel asks of us. We also think about how our actions may have hurt our relationship with God or others. An examination of conscience is an important part of our preparing to celebrate the Sacrament of Penance. [examen de conciencia]

Exile
by order
of King
Nebuchadnezzar

Exile the period in the history of Israel between the destruction of Jerusalem in 587 B.C. and the return to Jerusalem in 537 B.C. During this time, many of the Jewish people were forced to live in Babylon, far from home. [exilio]

Exodus God's liberation of the Hebrew people from slavery in Egypt and his leading them to the Promised Land [Éxodo]

F

faith a gift of God that helps us to believe in him. We profess our faith in the creed, celebrate it in the sacraments, live by it through our good conduct of loving God and our neighbor, and express it in prayer. [fe]

fasting limiting the amount we eat for a period of time to express sorrow for sin and to make ourselves more aware of God's action in our lives. Adults 18 years old and older fast on Ash Wednesday and Good Friday. The practice is also encouraged as a private devotion at other times of penitence. [ayuno]

fear of the Lord one of the seven Gifts of the Holy Spirit. This gift leads us to a sense of wonder and awe in the presence of God because we recognize his greatness. [temor de Dios]

forgiveness the willingness to be kind to those who have hurt us but have then shown that they are sorry. In the Lord's Prayer, we pray that since God will forgive us for our sins, we are able to forgive those who have hurt us. [perdón]

fortitude the strength to choose to do the right thing even when that is difficult. Fortitude is one of the four central human virtues, called the Cardinal Virtues, by which we guide our conduct through faith and the use of reason. It is also one of the Gifts of the Holy Spirit. [fortaleza]

free will the ability to choose to do good because God has made us like him. Our free will is what makes us truly human. Our exercise of free will to do good increases our freedom. Using free will to choose sin makes us slaves to sin. [libre albedrío]

Fruits of the Holy Spirit the demonstration through our actions that God is alive in us. Saint Paul lists the Fruits of the Holy Spirit in Galatians 5:22–23: love, joy, peace, patience, kindness, generosity, faithfulness, gentleness, and self-control. Church tradition has added goodness, modesty, and chastity to make a total of twelve. [frutos del Espíritu Santo]

G

genuflect to show respect in church by touching a knee to the ground, especially before the Blessed Sacrament in the tabernacle [genuflexión, hacer la]

Gifts of the Holy Spirit the permanent willingness, given to us by the Holy Spirit, that makes it possible for us to do what God asks of us. The Gifts of the Holy Spirit are drawn from Isaiah 11:1–3. They include wisdom, understanding, counsel, fortitude, knowledge, and fear of the Lord. Church tradition has added piety to make a total of seven. [dones del Espíritu Santo]

God the Father, Son, and Holy Spirit, one God in three distinct persons. God created all that exists. He is the source of salvation, and he is truth and love. [Dios]

godparent a witness to Baptism who assumes the responsibility for helping the baptized person along the road of Christian life [padrino/madrina de bautismo]

gospel the good news of God's mercy and love that we experience by hearing the story of Jesus' life, death, and resurrection. The story is passed on in the teaching ministry of the Church as the source of all truth and right living. It is presented to us in four books in the New Testament, the Gospels of Matthew, Mark, Luke, and John. [Evangelio]

grace the gift of God, given to us without our meriting it. Sanctifying grace fills us with his life and makes it possible for us always to be his friends. Grace is the Holy Spirit alive in us, helping us to live our Christian vocation. Grace helps us to live as God wants us to. [gracia]

Great Commandment Jesus' commandment that we are to love both God and our neighbor as we love ourselves. Jesus tells us that this commandment sums up everything taught in the Old Testament. [El Mandamiento Mayor]

H

heaven union with God the Father, Son, and Holy Spirit in life and love that never ends. Heaven is a state of complete happiness and the goal of the deepest wishes of the human heart. [cielo]

Hebrews the descendants of Abraham, Isaac, and Jacob, who were enslaved in Egypt. God helped Moses lead these people out of slavery. [hebreos]

hell a life of total separation from God forever. In his infinite love for us, God can only desire our salvation. Hell is the result of the free choice of a person to reject God's love and forgiveness once and for all. [infierno]

holiness the fullness of Christian life and love. All people are called to holiness, which is made possible by cooperating with God's grace to do his will. As we do God's will, we are transformed more and more into the image of the Son, Jesus Christ. [santidad]

holy one of the four Marks of the Church. It is the kind of life we live when we share in the life of God, who is all holiness. The Church is holy because it is united with Jesus Christ. [santa]

Holy Communion the consecrated bread and wine that we receive at Mass, which is the Body and Blood of Jesus Christ. It brings us into union with Jesus and his saving death and resurrection. [Sagrada Comunión]

Holy Days of Obligation the principal feast days, other than Sundays, of the Church. On Holy Days of Obligation, we celebrate the great things that God has done for us through Jesus and the Saints. Catholics are obliged to participate in the Eucharist on these days, just as we are on Sundays. [días de precepto]

Holy Family the family of Jesus as he grew up in Nazareth. It included Jesus; his mother, Mary; and his foster father, Joseph. [Sagrada Familia]

Holy of Holies the holiest part of the Temple in Jerusalem. The high priest entered this part of the Temple once a year to address God and ask God's forgiveness for the sins of the people. [Sanctasanctórum]

Holy Orders the sacrament through which the mission given by Jesus to his apostles continues in the Church. The sacrament has three degrees: deacon, priest, and bishop. Through the laying on of hands in the Sacrament of Holy Orders, men receive a permanent sacramental mark that calls them to minister to the Church. [orden sagrado]

Holy Spirit the third person of the Trinity, who is sent to us as our helper and, through Baptism and Confirmation, fills us with God's life. Together with the Father and the Son, the Holy Spirit brings the divine plan of salvation to completion. [Espíritu Santo]

holy water water that has been blessed and is used as a sacramental to remind us of our Baptism [agua bendita]

Holy Week the celebration of the events surrounding Jesus' suffering, death, resurrection, and establishment of the Eucharist. Holy Week commemorates Jesus' triumphal entry into Jerusalem on Palm Sunday, the gift of himself in the Eucharist on Holy Thursday, his death on Good Friday, and his resurrection at the Easter Vigil on Holy Saturday. [Semana Santa]

Holy Week celebration

homily the explanation by a bishop, a priest, or a deacon of the Word of God in the liturgy. The homily relates the Word of God to our life as Christians today. [homilía]

hope the confidence that God will always be with us, make us happy now and forever, and help us to live so that we will be with him forever [esperanza]

I

Incarnation the Son of God, Jesus, being born as a full human being in order to save us. The Son of God, the second person of the Trinity, is both true God and true man. [Encarnación]

indulgence a lessening of the punishment due for sins that have been forgiven. Indulgences move us toward our final purification, when we will live with God forever. [indulgencia]

inspired influenced by the Holy Spirit. The human authors of Scripture were influenced by the Holy Spirit. The creative inspiration of the Holy Spirit makes sure that the Scripture is taught according to the truth God wants us to know for our salvation. [inspirado]

interpretation explanation of the words of Scripture, combining human knowledge and the teaching office of the Church under the guidance of the Holy Spirit [interpretación]

Islam the third great religion, along with Judaism and Christianity, professing belief in one God. *Islam* means "submission" to that one God. [islamismo]

Israelites the descendants of Abraham, Isaac, and Jacob. God changed Jacob's name to "Israel," and Jacob's twelve sons and their children became the leaders of the twelve tribes of Israel. (*See* Hebrews.) [israelitas]

J

Jesus the Son of God, who was born of the Virgin Mary and who died and was raised from the dead for our salvation. He returned to God and will come again to judge the living and the dead. His name means "God saves." [Jesús]

Jews the name given to the Hebrew people, from the time of the exile to the present. The name means "the people who live in the territory of Judah," the area of Palestine surrounding Jerusalem. [judíos]

Joseph the foster father of Jesus, who was engaged to Mary when the angel announced that Mary would have a child through the power of the Holy Spirit. In the Old Testament, Joseph was the son of Jacob who was sold into slavery in Egypt by his brothers and then saved them from starvation when famine came. [José]

Judaism the name of the religion of Jesus and all of the people of Israel after they returned from exile in Babylon and built the second Temple [judaísmo]

justice the virtue that guides us to give to God and others what is due them. Justice is one of the four central human virtues, called the Cardinal Virtues, by which we guide our Christian life. [justicia]

K

Kingdom of God God's rule over us, announced in the gospel and present in the Eucharist. The beginning of the Kingdom here on earth is mysteriously present in the Church, and it will come in completeness at the end of time. [Reino de Dios]

knowledge one of the seven Gifts of the Holy Spirit. This gift helps us to know what God asks of us and how we should respond. [conocimiento]

L

laity those who have been made members of Christ in Baptism and who participate in the priestly, prophetic, and kingly functions of Christ in his mission to the whole world. The laity is distinct from the clergy, whose members are set apart as ministers to serve the Church. [laicado]

Joseph

Last Supper the last meal Jesus ate with his disciples on the night before he died. At the Last Supper, Jesus took bread and wine, blessed it, and said that it was his Body and Blood. Jesus' death and resurrection, which we celebrate in the Eucharist, was anticipated in this meal. [Última Cena]

Last Supper

Lectionary the official book that contains all of the Scripture readings used in the Liturgy of the Word [Leccionario]

Lent the 40 days before Easter (not counting Sundays) during which we prepare, through prayer, fasting, and giving aid to the poor, to change our lives and live the gospel more completely [Cuaresma]

liturgical year the celebrations throughout the year of all of the mysteries of Jesus' birth, life, death, and resurrection. The celebration of Easter is at the heart of the liturgical year. The other feasts celebrated throughout the year make up the basic rhythm of the Christian's life of prayer. [Año Litúrgico]

liturgy the public prayer of the Church that celebrates the wonderful things God has done for us in Jesus Christ, our high priest, and the way in which he continues the work of our salvation. The original meaning of *liturgy* was "a public work or service done for the people." [liturgia]

Liturgy of the Eucharist the second half of the Mass, in which the bread and wine are blessed and become the Body and Blood of Jesus Christ, which we then receive in Holy Communion [Liturgia de la Eucaristía]

Liturgy of the Hours the public prayer of the Church to praise God and sanctify the day. It includes an office of readings before sunrise, morning prayer at dawn, evening prayer at sunset, and prayer before going to bed. The chanting of psalms makes up a major portion of each of these services. [Liturgia de las Horas]

Liturgy of the Word the first half of the Mass, in which we listen to God's Word from the Bible and consider what it means for us today. The Liturgy of the Word can also be a public prayer and proclamation of God's Word that is not followed by the Liturgy of the Eucharist. [Liturgia de la Palabra]

M

Magisterium the living, teaching office of the Church. This office, through the bishops and with the pope, provides an authentic interpretation of the Word of God. It ensures faithfulness to the teaching of the Apostles in matters of faith and morals. [Magisterio]

Magnificat Mary's song of praise to God for the great things he has done for her and planned for us through Jesus [Magníficat]

Marks of the Church the four most important aspects of the Church found in the Nicene Creed. According to the Nicene Creed, the Church is one, holy, catholic, and apostolic. [calificados de la Iglesia]

Mary the mother of Jesus. She is called blessed and "full of grace" because God chose her to be the mother of the Son of God, the second person of the Trinity. [María]

Mary, Queen of Heaven

Mass the most important sacramental celebration of the Church, established by Jesus at the Last Supper as a remembrance of his death and resurrection. At Mass we listen to God's Word from the Bible and receive Jesus Christ in the bread and wine that has been blessed to become his Body and Blood. [Misa]

Matrimony a solemn agreement between a woman and a man to be partners for life, both for their own good and for bringing up children. Marriage is a sacrament when the agreement is properly made between baptized Christians. [matrimonio]

memorial a remembrance of events that have taken place in the past. We recall these events because they continue to affect us because they are part of God's saving plan for us. Every time we remember these events, we make God's saving action present. [conmemoración]

Messiah a title that means "anointed with oil." It is from a Hebrew word that means the same thing as the Greek word *Christ*. "Messiah" is the title that was given to Jesus after the Resurrection, when he had completed his mission as priest, prophet, and king. [Mesías]

ministry service or work done for others. Ministry is done by bishops, priests, and deacons, who are all ordained to ministry in the celebration of the sacraments. All those baptized are called to a variety of ministries in the liturgy and in service to the needs of others. [ministerio]

miracle signs or acts of wonder that cannot be explained by natural causes but are works of God. In the Gospels, Jesus works miracles as a sign that the Kingdom of God is present in his ministry. [milagro]

mission the work of Jesus Christ that is continued in the Church through the Holy Spirit. The mission of the Church is to proclaim salvation in Jesus' life, death, and resurrection. [misión]

monastery a place where men or women live out their solemn vows of poverty, chastity, and obedience in a stable community life. They spend their days in public prayer, work, and meditation. [monasterio]

moral choice a choice to do what is right or not do what is wrong. We make moral choices because they are what we believe God wants and because we have the freedom to choose what is right and avoid what is wrong. [opción moral]

moral law a rule for living that has been established by God and people in authority who are concerned about the good of all. Moral laws are based on God's direction to us to do what is right and avoid what is wrong. Some moral laws are "written" in the human heart and can be known through our own reasoning. Other moral laws have been revealed to us by God in the Old Testament and in the new law given by Jesus. [ley moral]

mortal sin a serious decision to turn away from God by doing something that we know is wrong. For a sin to be mortal it must be a very serious offense, the person must know how serious the sin is, and freely chose to do it anyway. [pecado mortal]

Muslim a follower of the religion of Islam. *Muslim* means "one who submits to God." [musulmán]

mystery a religious truth that we can know only through God's revelation and that we cannot fully understand. Our faith is a mystery that we profess in the creed and celebrate in the liturgy and sacraments. [misterio]

Mystical Body of Christ the members of the Church formed into a spiritual body and bound together by the life communicated by Jesus Christ through the sacraments. Christ is the center and source of the life of this body. In it, we are all are united. Each member of the body receives from Christ gifts fitting for him or her. [Cuerpo Místico de Cristo]

N

natural law the moral law that is "written" in the human heart. We can know natural law through our own reason because the Creator has placed the knowledge of it in our hearts. It can provide the solid foundation on which we can make rules to guide our choices in life. Natural law forms the basis of our fundamental rights and duties and is the foundation for the work of the Holy Spirit in guiding our moral choices. [ley natural]

New Testament the 27 books of the second part of the Bible which tell of the teaching, ministry, and saving events of the life of Jesus. The four Gospels present Jesus' life, death, and resurrection. The Acts of the Apostles tells the story of the message of salvation as it spread through the growth of the Church. Various letters instruct us in how to live as followers of Jesus Christ. The Book of Revelation offers encouragement to Christians living through persecution. [Nuevo Testamento]

New Testament

Nicene Creed the summary of Christian beliefs developed by the bishops at the first two councils of the Church, held in A.D. 325 and 381. It is the creed shared by most Christians, in the East and in the West. [Credo de Nicea]

O

obedience the act of willingly following what God asks us to do for our salvation. The fourth commandment requires children to obey their parents, and all people are required to obey civil authority when it acts for the good of all. To imitate the obedience of Jesus, members of religious communities make a special vow of obedience. [obediencia]

oil of catechumens the oil blessed by the bishop during Holy Week and used to anoint catechumens. This anointing strengthens them on their path to initiation into the Church. Infants are anointed with this oil right before they are baptized. [óleo de los catecúmenos]

oil of the sick the oil blessed by the bishop during Holy Week and used in the Sacrament of Anointing of the Sick, which brings spiritual and, if it is God's will, physical healing as well [óleo de los enfermos]

Old Testament the first 46 books of the Bible, which tell of God's covenant with the people of Israel and his plan for the salvation of all people. The first five books are known as the Torah. The Old Testament is fulfilled in the New Testament, but God's covenant presented in the Old Testament has permanent value and has never been revoked. [Antiguo Testamento]

one one of the four Marks of the Church. The Church is one because of its source in the one God and because of its founder, Jesus Christ. Jesus, through his death on the cross, united all to God in one body. Within the unity of the Church, there is great diversity because of the variety of the gifts given to its members. [una]

ordination the rite of the Sacrament of Holy Orders, by which a bishop gives to men, through the laying on of hands, the ability to minister to the Church as bishops, priests, and deacons [ordinación]

original sin the consequence of the disobedience of the first human beings. They disobeyed God and chose to follow their own will rather than God's will. As a result, human beings lost the original blessing God had intended and became subject to sin and death. In Baptism we are restored to life with God through Jesus Christ although we still experience the effects of original sin. [pecado original]

P

Palm Sunday the celebration of Jesus' triumphant entry into Jerusalem on the Sunday before Easter. It begins a week-long commemoration of the saving events of Holy Week. [Domingo de Ramos]

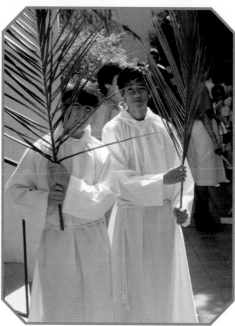

Palm Sunday

parable one of the simple stories that Jesus told to show us what the Kingdom of God is like. Parables present images drawn from everyday life. These images show us the radical choice we make when we respond to the invitation to enter the Kingdom of God. [parábola]

parish a stable community of believers in Jesus Christ who meet regularly in a specific area to worship God under the leadership of a pastor [parroquia]

Paschal Mystery the work of salvation accomplished by Jesus Christ through his passion, death, and resurrection. The Paschal Mystery is celebrated in the liturgy of the Church, and its saving effects are experienced by us in the sacraments. [Misterio Pascual]

Passover the Jewish festival that commemorates the delivery of the Hebrew people from slavery in Egypt. In the Eucharist we celebrate our passover from death to life through Jesus' death and resurrection. [Pascua Judía]

Passover plate

pastor a priest who is responsible for the spiritual care of the members of a parish community. It is the job of the pastor to see that the Word of God is preached, the faith is taught, and sacraments are celebrated. [pastor]

penance the turning away from sin with a desire to change our life and more closely live the way God wants us to live.

We express our penance externally by praying, fasting, and helping the poor. This is also the name of the action that the priest asks us take or the prayers that he asks us to pray after he absolves us in the Sacrament of Penance. (*See* Sacrament of Penance.) [penitencia]

Pentecost

Pentecost the 50th day after Jesus was raised from the dead. On this day the Holy Spirit was sent from heaven, and the Church was born. It is also the Jewish feast that celebrated the giving of the Ten Commandments on Mount Sinai 50 days after the Exodus. [Pentecostés]

People of God another name for the Church. In the same way that the people of Israel were God's people through the Covenant he made with them, the Church is a priestly, prophetic, and royal people through the new and eternal Covenant with Jesus Christ. [Pueblo de Dios]

personal prayer the kind of prayer that rises up in us in everyday life. We pray with others in the liturgy, but in addition we can listen and respond to God through personal prayer every moment of our lives. [oración personal]

personal sin a sin we choose to commit, whether serious (mortal) or less serious (venial). Although the consequences of original sin leave us with a tendency to sin, God's grace, especially through the sacraments, helps us to choose good over sin. [pecado personal]

petition a request to God asking him to fulfill a need. When we share in God's saving love, we understand that every need is one that we can ask God to help us with through petition. [petición]

piety one of the seven Gifts of the Holy Spirit. It calls us to be faithful in our relationships both with God and with others. Piety helps us to love God and to behave responsibly and with generosity and affection toward others. [piedad]

pope the bishop of Rome, successor of Saint Peter, and leader of the Roman Catholic Church. Because he has the authority to act in the name of Christ, the pope is called the Vicar of Christ. The pope and all of the bishops together make up the living, teaching office of the Church, the Magisterium. [Papa]

praise the expression of our response to God, not only for what he does, but simply because he is. In the Eucharist the whole Church joins with Jesus Christ in expressing praise and thanksgiving to the Father. [alabanza]

prayer the raising of our hearts and minds to God. We are able to speak to and listen to God in prayer because he teaches us how to pray. [oración]

Precepts of the Church those positive requirements that the pastoral authority of the Church has determined are necessary to provide a minimum effort in prayer and the moral life. The Precepts of the Church ensure that all Catholics move beyond the minimum by growing in love of God and love of neighbor. [preceptos de la Iglesia]

presbyter a word that originally meant "an elder or trusted advisor to the bishop." From this word comes the English word *priest*, one of the three degrees of the Sacrament of Holy Orders. All the priests of a diocese under the bishop form the presbyterate. [presbítero]

pride a false image of ourselves that goes beyond what we deserve as God's creation. Pride puts us in competition with God. It is one of the seven capital sins. [soberbia]

priest a man who has accepted God's special call to serve the Church by guiding it and building it up through the ministry of the Word and the celebration of the sacraments [sacerdote]

priesthood all the people of God who have been given a share of the one mission of Christ through the Sacraments of Baptism and Confirmation. The ministerial priesthood, which is made up of those men who have been ordained bishops and priests in Holy Orders, is essentially different from the priesthood of all the faithful because its work is to build up and guide the Church in the name of Christ. [sacerdocio]

Promised Land the land first promised by God to Abraham. It was to this land that God told Moses to lead the Chosen People after they were freed from slavery in Egypt and received the Ten Commandments at Mount Sinai. [Tierra Prometida]

prophet one called to speak for God and call the people to be faithful to the covenant. A major section of the Old Testament presents, in eighteen books, the messages and actions of the prophets. [profeta]

the prophet Isaiah

prudence the virtue that directs us toward the good and helps us to choose the correct means to achieve that good. When we act with prudence, we carefully and thoughtfully consider our actions. Prudence is one of the cardinal moral virtues that guide our conscience and influence us to live according to the law of Christ. [prudencia]

psalm a prayer in the form of a poem, written to be sung in public worship. Each psalm expresses an aspect of the depth of human prayer. Over several centuries 150 psalms were assembled into the Book of Psalms in the Old Testament. Psalms were used in worship in the Temple in Jerusalem, and they have been used in the public worship of the Church since its beginning. [salmo]

purgatory a state of final cleansing after death of all of our human imperfections to prepare us to enter into the joy of God's presence in heaven [purgatorio]

R

racism the opinion that race determines human traits and capacities and that a particular race has an inherent, or inborn, superiority. Discrimination based on a person's race is a violation of human dignity and a sin against justice. [racismo]

Real Presence the way in which the risen Jesus Christ is present in the Eucharist under the form of bread and wine. Jesus Christ's presence is called real because in the Eucharist his body and blood, soul and divinity, are wholly and entirely present. [Presencia Real]

reconciliation the renewal of friendship after that friendship has been broken by some action or lack of action. In the Sacrament of Penance, through God's mercy and forgiveness, we are reconciled with God, the Church, and others. [reconciliación]

Redeemer Jesus Christ, whose life, sacrificial death on the cross, and resurrection from the dead set us free from the slavery of sin and bring us redemption [Redentor]

redemption our being set free from the slavery of sin through the life, sacrificial death on the cross, and resurrection from the dead of Jesus Christ [redención]

reform to put an end to a wrong by introducing a better or changed course of action. The prophets called people to reform their lives by returning to being faithful to their covenant with God. [reformarse]

religious life a state of life recognized by the Church. In the religious life, men and women freely respond to a call to follow Jesus by living the vows of poverty, chastity, and obedience in community with others. [vida religiosa]

repentance our turning away from sin, with a desire to change our lives and live more closely as God wants us to live. We express our penance externally by prayer, fasting, and helping the poor. [arrepentimiento]

Resurrection the bodily raising of Jesus Christ from the dead on the third day after his death on the cross. The Resurrection is the crowning truth of our faith. [Resurrección]

Revelation God's communication of himself to us through the words and deeds he has used throughout history to show us the mystery of his plan for our salvation. This Revelation reaches its completion in his sending of his Son, Jesus Christ. [revelación]

rite one of the many forms followed in celebrating liturgy in the Church. A rite may differ according to the culture or country where it is celebrated. *Rite* also means the special form for celebrating each sacrament. [rito]

Rosary a prayer in honor of the Blessed Virgin Mary. When we pray the Rosary, we meditate on the mysteries of Jesus Christ's life while praying the Hail Mary on five sets of ten beads and the Lord's Prayer on the beads in between. In the Latin Church, praying the Rosary became a way for ordinary people to reflect on the mysteries of Christ's life. [Rosario]

S

Sabbath the seventh day, when God rested after finishing the work of creation. The third commandment requires us to keep the Sabbath holy. For Christians the Sabbath became Sunday because it was the day Jesus rose from the dead and the new creation in Jesus Christ began. [Sabat]

sacrament one of seven ways through which God's life enters our lives through the work of the Holy Spirit.

oils used in sacraments

Jesus gave us three sacraments that bring us into the Church: Baptism, Confirmation, and the Eucharist. He gave us two sacraments that bring us healing: Penance and Anointing of the Sick. He also gave us two sacraments that help members serve the community: Matrimony and Holy Orders. [sacramento]

Sacrament of Penance the sacrament in which we celebrate God's forgiveness of sin and our reconciliation with God and the Church. Penance includes sorrow for the sins we have committed, confession of sins, absolution by the priest, and doing the penance that shows our willingness to amend our ways. [sacramento de la penitencia]

sacramental an object, a prayer, or a blessing given by the Church to help us grow in our spiritual life [sacramental]

Sacraments at the Service of Communion the Sacraments of Holy Orders and Matrimony. These two sacraments contribute to the personal salvation of individuals by giving them a way to serve others. [sacramentos al servicio de la comunidad]

Sacraments of Healing the Sacraments of Penance and Anointing of the Sick, by which the Church continues the healing ministry of Jesus for soul and body [sacramentos de curación]

Sacraments of Initiation the sacraments that are the foundation of our Christian life. We are born anew in Baptism, strengthened by Confirmation, and receive in the Eucharist the food of eternal life. By means of these sacraments, we receive an increasing measure of divine life and advance toward the perfection of charity. [sacramentos de iniciación]

sacrifice a ritual offering of animals or produce made to God by the priest in the Temple in Jerusalem. Sacrifice was a sign of the people's adoration of God, giving thanks to God, or asking for his forgiveness. Sacrifice also showed union with God. The great high priest, Christ, accomplished our redemption through the perfect sacrifice of his death on the cross. [sacrificio]

Sacrifice of the Mass the sacrifice of Jesus on the cross, which is remembered and mysteriously made present in the Eucharist. It is offered in reparation for the sins of the living and the dead and to obtain spiritual or temporal blessings from God. [Sacrificio de la Misa]

saint a holy person who has died united with God. The Church has said that this person is now with God forever in heaven. [santo]

salvation the gift, which God alone can give, of forgiveness of sin and the restoration of friendship with him [salvación]

sanctifying grace the gift of God, given to us without our earning it, that unites us with the life of the Trinity and heals our human nature, wounded by sin. Sanctifying grace continues the work of making us holy that began at our Baptism. [gracia santificante]

Savior Jesus, the Son of God, who became human to forgive our sins and restore our friendship with God. *Jesus* means "God saves." [Salvador]

scriptorium the room in a monastery in which books were copied by hand. Often, beautiful art was created on the page to illustrate the story. [scriptorium]

Scriptures the holy writings of Jews and Christians collected in the Old and New Testaments of the Bible [Sagrada Escritura]

seraphim the heavenly beings who worship before the throne of God. One of them purified the lips of Isaiah with a burning coal so that he could speak for God. [seraphines]

Sermon on the Mount the words of Jesus, written in Chapters 5 through 7 of the Gospel of Matthew, in which Jesus reveals how he has fulfilled God's law given to Moses. The Sermon on the Mount begins with the eight Beatitudes and includes the Lord's Prayer. [Sermón de la Montaña]

Sermon on the Mount

sexism a prejudice or discrimination based on sex, especially discrimination against women. Sexism leads to behaviors and attitudes that foster a view of social roles based only on sex. [sexismo]

sin a deliberate thought, word, deed, or failure to act that offends God and hurts our relationships with other people. Some sin is mortal and needs to be confessed in the Sacrament of Penance. Other sin is venial, or less serious. [pecado]

slander a false statement that harms the reputation of someone and makes other people think bad of that person. Slander is an offense against the eighth commandment. [calumnia]

sloth a carelessness of heart that leads a person to ignore his or her development as a person, especially spiritual development and a relationship with God. Sloth is one of the seven capital sins, and it is contrary to the first commandment. [pereza]

solidarity the attitude of strength and unity that leads to the sharing of spiritual and material goods. Solidarity unites rich and poor, weak and strong, to create a society in which all give what they can and receive what they need. The idea of solidarity is based on the common origin of all humanity. [solidaridad]

Son of God the title revealed by Jesus that indicates his unique relationship to God the Father. The revelation of Jesus' divine sonship is the main dramatic development of the story of Jesus of Nazareth as it unfolds in the Gospels. [Hijo de Dios]

soul the part of us that makes us human and an image of God. Body and soul together form one unique human nature. The soul is responsible for our consciousness and for our freedom. The soul does not die and is reunited with the body in the final resurrection. [alma]

Spiritual Works of Mercy the kind acts through which we help our neighbors meet the needs that are more than material. The Spiritual Works of Mercy include instructing, advising, consoling, comforting, forgiving, and bearing wrongs with patience. [obras espirituales de misericordia]

Stations of the Cross a tool for meditating on the final hours of Jesus' life, from his condemnation by Pilate to his death and burial. We do this by moving to representations of 14 incidents, each one based on the traditional sites in Jerusalem where these incidents took place. [Estaciones del Vía Crucis]

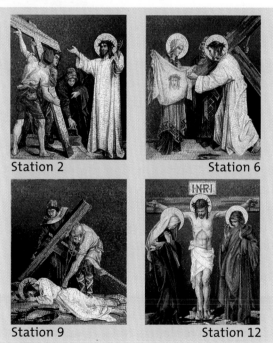

Station 2   Station 6

Station 9   Station 12

stewardship the careful and responsible management of something entrusted to one's care, especially the goods of creation, which are intended for the whole human race. The sixth precept of the Church makes clear our part in this stewardship by requiring us to provide for the material needs of the Church according to our abilities. [mayordomía]

Understanding the Words of Our Faith   **301**

T

tabernacle the container in which the Blessed Sacrament is kept so that Holy Communion can be taken to the sick and the dying. *Tabernacle* is also the name of the tent sanctuary in which the Israelites kept the Ark of the Covenant from the time of the Exodus to the construction of Solomon's temple. [sagrario]

Model of Tabernacle tent sanctuary, Israel

temperance the cardinal virtue that helps us to control our attraction to pleasure so that our natural desires are kept within proper limits. This moral virtue helps us choose to use created goods in moderation. [templanza]

Temple the house of worship of God, first built by Solomon. The Temple provided a place for the priests to offer sacrifice, to adore and give thanks to God, and to ask for forgiveness. It was destroyed and rebuilt. The second Temple was also destroyed, this time by the Romans in A.D. 70, and was never rebuilt. Part of the outer wall of the Temple mount remains to this day in Jerusalem. [Templo]

temptation an attraction, from outside us or inside us, that can lead us to disobey God's commands. Everyone is tempted, but the Holy Spirit helps us to resist temptation and choose to do good. [tentación]

Ten Commandments the ten rules given by God to Moses on Mount Sinai that sum up God's law and show us what is required to love God and our neighbor. By following the Ten Commandments, the Hebrews accepted their covenant with God. [Diez Mandamientos]

Theological Virtues those virtues given us by God and not by human effort. They are faith, hope, and charity. [virtudes teologales]

Torah the Hebrew word for "instruction" or "law." It is also the name of the first five books of the Old Testament: Genesis, Exodus, Leviticus, Numbers, and Deuteronomy. [Torá]

Torah

transubstantiation the unique change of the bread and wine in the Eucharist into the body and blood of the risen Jesus Christ, while retaining its physical appearance as bread and wine [transubstanciación]

trespasses unlawful acts committed against the property or rights of another person or acts that physically harm a person [ofensas]

Trinity the mystery of the existence of God in three persons, the Father, the Son, and the Holy Spirit. Each person is God, whole and entire. Each is distinct only in the relationship of each to the others. [Trinidad]

U

understanding one of the seven Gifts of the Holy Spirit. This gift helps us make the right choices in life and in our relationships with God and others. [entendimiento]

universal Church the entire Church as it exists throughout the world. The people of every diocese, along with their bishops and the pope, make up the universal Church. [Iglesia universal]

V

venial sin a choice we make that weakens our relationship with God or other people. Venial sin wounds and lessens the divine life in us. If we make no effort to do better, venial sin can lead to more serious sin. Through our participation in the Eucharist, venial sin is forgiven, strengthening our relationship with God and others. [pecado venial]

Trinity

viaticum the Eucharist that a dying person receives. It is spiritual food for the last journey we make as Christians, the journey through death to eternal life. [viático]

Vicar of Christ the title given to the pope who, as the successor of Saint Peter, has the authority to act in Christ's place. A vicar is someone who stands in for and acts for another. [Vicario de Cristo]

virtue an attitude or way of acting that enables us do good [virtud]

Visitation Mary's visit to Elizabeth to share the good news that Mary is to be the mother of Jesus. Elizabeth's greeting of Mary forms part of the Hail Mary. During this visit, Mary sings the Magnificat, her praise of God. [Visitación]

vocation the call each of us has in life to be the person God wants each to be and the way we each serve the Church and the Kingdom of God. Each of us can live out his or her vocation as a layperson, as a member of a religious community, or as a member of the clergy. [vocación]

vow a deliberate and free promise made to God by people who want especially to dedicate their lives to God. The vows give witness now to the kingdom that is to come. [voto]

Vulgate the Latin translation of the Bible by Saint Jerome from the Hebrew and Greek it was originally written in. Most Christians of Saint Jerome's day no longer spoke Hebrew or Greek. The common language, or vulgate, was Latin. [Vulgata]

illumination from a 7th century calfskin Vulgate

W

wisdom one of the seven Gifts of the Holy Spirit. Wisdom helps us to understand the purpose and plan of God and to live in a way that helps to bring about this plan. It begins in wonder and awe at God's greatness. [sabiduría]

Wisdom Literature the Old Testament books of Job, Proverbs, Ecclesiastes, the Song of Songs, Wisdom, and Sirach. The purpose of these books is to give instruction on ways to live and how to understand and cope with the problems of life. [Libros Sapienciales]

witness the passing on to others, by our words and by our actions, the faith that we have been given. Every Christian has the duty to give witness to the good news about Jesus Christ that he or she has come to know. [testimonio]

worship the adoration and honor given to God in public prayer [culto]

Y

Yahweh the name of God in Hebrew, which God told Moses from the burning bush. *Yahweh* means "I am who am" or "I cause to be all that is." [Yavé]

worship

Glosario

A

Abba vocablo familiar que significa "padre" en arameo, idioma que hablaba Jesús. Viene a ser como "papá" en español. Al hablar con Dios Padre, Jesús le decía *Abba*. [Abba]

Abogado nombre dado por Jesús al Espíritu Santo. El Espíritu Santo nos conforta, nos habla en tiempos difíciles, y nos manifiesta la presencia de Jesús. [Advocate]

absolución perdón que recibimos de Dios por intermedio del sacerdote en el sacramento de la penitencia [absolution]

Adviento las cuatro semanas antes de la Navidad. Es una época de jubilosa preparación para la celebración de la Encarnación, el nacimiento de Jesús como salvador nuestro, y la espera de la venida de Jesucristo en el fin de los tiempos. [Advent]

agua bendita agua que ha sido bendecida y que se usa como sacramental para recordarnos de nuestro bautismo [holy water]

alabanza la expresión de nuestra respuesta a Dios no sólo por lo que hace sino por quién es. En la Eucaristía, la Iglesia entera se une a Jesucristo para alabar y dar gracias al Padre. [praise]

alianza pacto solemne que hacen las personas entre sí o que hacen las personas con Dios. Dios hizo alianzas con la humanidad mediante los pactos hechos con Noé, Abraham y Moisés. Estas alianzas ofrecían salvación. La nueva y final alianza de Dios fue pactada mediante la vida, muerte y resurrección de Jesús. *Testamento* es sinónimo de *alianza*. [covenant]

alma parte de la persona que la hace humana e imagen de Dios. Juntos, el cuerpo y el alma forman una naturaleza humana única. El alma es responsable de nuestra conciencia y de nuestra libertad. El alma no muere y es reunida con el cuerpo en la resurrección final. [soul]

altar mesa que tienen las iglesias en la que el sacerdote celebra la Misa. En la Misa, el sacrificio de Cristo en la cruz se hace presente en el sacramento de la Eucaristía. El altar representa dos aspectos del misterio de la Eucaristía: en primer lugar, es el sitio donde Jesucristo se ofrece a sí mismo por nuestros pecados; y, en segundo, es el sitio donde Él se da a nosotros como alimento de vida eterna. [altar]

ambón plataforma elevada desde donde una persona lee la Palabra de Dios durante la Misa. [ambo]

Amén vocablo hebreo usado al final de las oraciones judías y cristianas que quiere decir "es verdad", "así es", o "así sea". Al terminar nuestras oraciones, decimos *Amén* para dar a entender que lo que acabamos de decir va en serio. [Amen]

ángel criatura espiritual que adora a Dios en el cielo. Los ángeles sirven a Dios como mensajeros y nos cuentan los planes que Él tiene para nuestra salvación. [angel]

Año Litúrgico las celebraciones en el transcurso del año de todos los misterios del nacimiento, vida, muerte, y resurrección de Jesús. La Pascua es la celebración central del Año Litúrgico. Las otras fiestas celebradas a lo largo del año constituyen el ritmo básico de la vida de oración del cristiano. [liturgical year]

Antiguo Testamento los 46 primeros libros de la Biblia que hablan de la alianza de Dios con el pueblo de Israel y su plan de salvación para todas las gentes. Los cinco primeros libros se conocen como el Torá. El Antiguo Testamento se cumple en el Nuevo Testamento, pero la alianza de Dios presentada en la escritura del Antiguo Testamento sigue teniendo un valor permanente y nunca ha sido revocada. [Old Testament]

Anunciación anuncio traído a María por el ángel Gabriel de que Dios la había elegido para ser madre de Jesús. Al aceptar María, el Hijo de Dios se hizo hombre dentro de ella. La fiesta de la Anunciación se celebra el 25 de marzo, nueve meses antes de la Navidad. [Annunciation]

apóstol uno de doce hombres singulares que acompañaron a Jesús en su ministerio y fueron testigos de su Resurrección. *Apóstol* quiere decir "enviado". Los apóstoles fueron los enviados a predicar el Evangelio al mundo entero. [apostle]

apostólica uno de los cuatro calificados de la Iglesia. La Iglesia es apostólica porque sigue transmitiendo las enseñanzas de los apóstoles a través de sus sucesores, los obispos, en unión con el sucesor de San Pedro, el Papa. [apostolic]

Arca de la Alianza caja portátil donde se guardaban las tablas de los Diez Mandamientos. El Arca, objeto más importante del santuario, fue transportada por todo el desierto y luego colocada en la parte más sagrada del Templo de Jerusalén. Sobre la tapa del Arca de la Alianza se encontraban dos ángeles cuyas alas se curvaban hacia arriba, representando el sitio donde Dios se acercó a Israel y le reveló Su Voluntad. [Ark of the Covenant]

arrepentimiento el apartarnos del pecado con el deseo de cambiar nuestra vida y acercarnos más a la forma de vida que Dios quiere que vivamos. Expresamos externamente nuestra penitencia mediante la oración, el ayuno, y ayudando a los pobres. [repentance]

asamblea pueblo de Dios congregado para rendirle culto [assembly]

Ascensión entrada de Jesús a la gloria divina junto al Padre. En los Hechos de los Apóstoles, se escribe que, después de la Resurrección, Jesús estuvo 40 días en la Tierra instruyendo a sus seguidores, y luego volvió al cielo junto a su Padre. [Ascension]

Asunción La llevada de María al cielo en cuerpo y alma. Desde el momento mismo en que María concibió a su hijo, Jesús, fue muy especial la relación que hubo entre ellos. Los católicos creen que, a raíz de esta relación, ella goza de una participación especial en la resurrección de Jesús y ha sido llevada al cielo, donde ahora vive con Él. Este acontecimiento se celebra el 15 de agosto, Día de la Asunción. [Assumption]

ayuno limitar la cantidad de alimento que comemos por un tiempo determinado para expresar arrepentimiento por nuestros pecados y hacernos más conscientes de la acción de Dios en nuestras vidas. Los adultos, de dieciocho años o más, ayunan el Miércoles de Ceniza y Viernes Santo. Se fomenta también esta práctica como devoción privada en otras ocasiones de penitencia. [fasting]

B

báculo cayado o vara que lleva el obispo. Al llevar este cayado, el obispo muestra que vela por nosotros de la misma forma en que el pastor cuida sus ovejas. También nos recuerda que él representa a Jesús, el Buen Pastor. [crozier]

bautismo el primero de los siete sacramentos. El bautismo nos libera del pecado original y es necesario para la salvación. El bautismo nos da una vida nueva en Jesucristo por medio del Espíritu Santo. La celebración del bautismo consiste en sumergir en agua a la persona diciendo que es bautizado ". . . en el nombre del Padre, del Hijo, y del Espíritu Santo". [Baptism]

bendición oración que invoca el poder y amparo de Dios para una persona, lugar, cosa, o una actividad específica [blessing]

Biblia la colección de libros que contienen las verdades de la revelación hecha a nosotros por Dios. Estos libros fueron inspirados por el Espíritu Santo y escritos por seres humanos. La Biblia se compone de 46 libros del Antiguo Testamento y 27 del Nuevo Testamento. [Bible]

Bienaventuranzas enseñanzas de Jesús en el Sermón de la Montaña del Evangelio de San Mateo. Las Bienaventuranzas son ocho formas de llevar una vida cristiana; y son la culminación de los mandamientos dados a través de Moisés. Estas enseñanzas nos presentan el camino a la verdadera felicidad. [Beatitudes]

C

calificados de la Iglesia las cuatro características más importantes de la Iglesia que se hallan en el Credo de Nicea. Según este credo, la Iglesia es una, santa, católica y apostólica. [Marks of the Church]

calumnia afirmación falsa que daña la reputación de una persona y hace que otros piensen mal de esa persona. La calumnia va en contra del octavo mandamiento. [slander]

canonizar declaración hecha por la Iglesia de que un cristiano difunto está ya en el cielo y puede servir de ejemplo de vida cristiana e interceder por nosotros como santo [canonize]

carácter señal espiritual permanente. El carácter muestra que la persona ha entablado una nueva relación con Jesús y ha llegado a un nivel especial en la Iglesia. El bautismo, la confirmación y el orden sagrado imprimen un carácter permanente; y, por eso, sólo pueden ser recibidos una sola vez. [character]

caridad virtud dada a nosotros por Dios. La caridad nos permite amar a Dios sobre todas las cosas y al prójimo como a nosotros mismos. [charity]

castidad la integración de nuestra sexualidad física con nuestra naturaleza espiritual. La castidad permite que seamos completamente humanos, capaces de dar a otros por entero nuestra vida y amor. Todos, ya sean casados o solteros, somos llamados a observar la castidad. [chastity]

catecúmeno persona que está recibiendo formación cristiana mediante instrucción y mediante el ejemplo de la comunidad. Por medio de la conversión y madurez de fe, el catecúmeno se prepara para ser recibido en el seno de la Iglesia en la Pascua a través de los sacramentos del bautismo, confirmación y Eucaristía. [catechumen]

católica uno de los calificados de la Iglesia. La Iglesia es católica porque Jesús está totalmente presente en ella y porque Jesús la ha dado al mundo entero. Es universal. [catholic]

cielo unión con Dios Padre, Hijo y Espíritu Santo en vida y amor que nunca acaba. El cielo es el estado de felicidad completa y es la meta de los deseos más profundos del corazón humano. [heaven]

clero varones elegidos ministros sagrados para servir a la Iglesia a través del orden sagrado [clergy]

Comunión de los Santos unidad de todos los que se han salvado en Jesucristo, vivos o muertos. La Comunión de los Santos se basa en nuestra fe única y se nutre de nuestra participación en la Eucaristía. [Communion of Saints]

conciencia voz interior que nos ayuda a cada uno a conocer la ley de Dios para que cada persona pueda juzgar las cualidades morales de sus acciones. La conciencia nos guía a hacer el bien y evitar el mal. [conscience]

confesión acto de contar nuestros pecados al sacerdote en el sacramento de la penitencia. Al sacramento mismo se le suele llamar "confesión". [confession]

confirmación sacramento que da plenitud a la gracia que recibimos en el bautismo. La confirmación sella, o confirma, esta gracia a través de los siete dones del Espíritu Santo que recibimos como parte de la confirmación. Este sacramento también nos hace más capaces de participar en el culto y en la vida apostólica de la Iglesia. [Confirmation]

conmemoración recuerdo de sucesos ocurridos en el pasado. Recordamos estos sucesos porque nos siguen afectando en el presente ya que son parte del plan de salvación que Dios tiene para nosotros. Cada vez que recordamos estos acontecimientos, hacemos presente la acción redentora de Dios. [memorial]

conocimiento uno de los siete dones del Espíritu Santo. Este don nos permite saber lo que Dios nos pide y cómo debemos responder. [knowledge]

consagración el hacer a una cosa o persona especial ante los ojos de Dios por medio de una oración o bendición. En la Misa, las palabras del sacerdote son una consagración que hace que el Cuerpo y Sangre de Cristo se hagan presentes en el pan y el vino. Las personas y objetos dedicados a Dios de forma especial también son consagrados. Por ejemplo, las iglesias y altares son consagrados para su uso en la liturgia. Del mismo modo, los obispos son consagrados al recibir la integridad del sacramento del orden sagrado. [consecration]

consejo uno de los siete dones del Espíritu Santo. El consejo nos ayuda a reflexionar sobre cómo tomar decisiones apropiadas en la vida, a través de la reflexión, el discernimiento, la consulta, y el consejo de otros. [counsel]

contrición pesar que sentimos cuando sabemos que hemos pecado, seguido por la decisión de no volver a pecar. Contrición perfecta brota de un amor que ama a Dios sobre todas las cosas. Contrición imperfecta está basada en otros motivos. La contrición es el acto más importante del penitente que se prepara a celebrar el sacramento de la penitencia. [contrition]

conversión cambio radical, o cambio serio y extremo, de nuestra vida total, que nos aparta del pecado y nos dirige a Dios. Este llamado a cambiar de vida es parte fundamental de las enseñanzas de Jesús. A lo largo de nuestra vida, Jesús nos llama a cambiar de esta forma. [conversion]

creación El acto en que Dios hace todo lo que existe fuera de Él. La creación es todo lo que existe. Dios dijo que todo lo creado es bueno. [creation]

Creador Dios, quien hizo todo lo que es y a quien podemos llegar a conocer a través de todo lo que Él creó [Creator]

credo breve resumen de lo que la gente cree. *Credo* proviene del verbo latino *credo,* que significa "creo". El Credo de Nicea es el resumen más importante de lo que creemos como cristianos. [creed]

Credo de los Apóstoles declaración de la creencia cristiana, originada de un credo usado en los bautismos en Roma. El Credo de los Apóstoles enumera sencillas declaraciones de la creencia en Dios Padre, su Hijo Jesucristo, y el Espíritu Santo. La profesión de fe usada actualmente en el bautismo se basa en este credo. [Apostles' Creed]

Credo de Nicea resumen de las creencias cristianas desarrolladas por los obispos en los dos primeros concilios de la Iglesia, llevados a cabo en 325 y 381 d. de C. Éste es el credo que comparten todos los cristianos, de oriente y occidente. [Nicene Creed]

crisma óleo perfumado que se utiliza en los sacramentos del bautismo, confirmación y orden sagrado. La unción con el crisma significa el llamado a los bautizados al triple ministerio de sacerdote, profeta y rey. [chrism]

cristiano nombre dado a todos los que han sido ungidos por medio del don del Espíritu Santo en el bautismo y se han convertido en seguidores de Jesucristo [Christian]

Cristo título que quiere decir "ungido". Proviene de una palabra griega que quiere decir lo mismo que el vocablo hebreo *Mesías* o "ungido". Cristo es el nombre que se le da a Jesús después de su Resurrección tras haber cumplido su misión como sacerdote, profeta y rey. [Christ]

Cuaresma los cuarenta días antes de la Pascua (sin contar domingos), durante los cuales nos preparamos, por medio de la oración, el ayuno y ayudando a los pobres, a cambiar nuestras vidas y a vivir el Evangelio más plenamente [Lent]

Cuerpo Místico de Cristo miembros de la Iglesia que forman un cuerpo espiritual y están unidos por la vida comunicada por Jesucristo a través de los sacramentos. Cristo es el centro y la fuente de la vida de este cuerpo en el cual todos estamos unidos. Cada miembro de este cuerpo recibe de Cristo dones que más conviene a esa persona. [Mystical Body of Christ]

Cuerpo y Sangre de Cristo pan y vino que han sido consagrados por el sacerdote en la Misa. En el sacramento de la Eucaristía, Nuestro Señor Jesucristo—todo cuerpo, sangre, alma, y divinidad—está presente en forma de pan y vino.
[Body and Blood of Christ]

culto adoración y honor que se le rinde a Dios en oración pública [worship]

cultura conjunto de conocimientos, creencias y conductas de un determinado grupo de personas. La cultura expresa las actitudes, valores, objetivos y prácticas sociales que tiene el grupo en común. Para que el Evangelio se arraigue en una cultura, debe ser adaptado para vivir en esa cultura y transformarla. [culture]

D

detracción el hablar de las faltas y pecados de alguien a otro que no tiene por qué enterarse de ello y que no puede ayudar a esa persona. La detracción daña la reputación de una persona sin que se tenga intención alguna de ayudarla. [detraction]

Día de Difuntos el 2 de noviembre, día en que la Iglesia ora por el eterno descanso de todos los que han muerto estando en amistad con Dios. Algunos de éstos necesitan purificación en el purgatorio antes de pasar a vivir en presencia total de Dios; y con nuestras plegarias y buenas obras les ayudamos en este proceso. Junto al Día de Todos los Santos, esta fiesta nos recuerda que todos los que aman a Dios, vivos o muertos, están unidos en comunión viva con Jesucristo y entre sí. [All Souls Day]

Día de Todos los Santos el 1 de noviembre, día en que la Iglesia conmemora a todos los muertos que pasaron a ser santos y ahora viven con Dios en el cielo. Entre éstos figuran aquéllos que han sido declarados santos de forma oficial por la Iglesia así como muchos otros desconocidos que han muerto tras haber llevado una vida recta y ahora viven en presencia de Dios. Esta fiesta celebra nuestra unión con aquéllos que se han ido antes que nosotros y nos señala nuestra meta final de unión con Dios. [All Saints Day]

diácono varón ordenado mediante el sacramento del orden sagrado al ministerio de servicio en la Iglesia. Los diáconos asisten al obispo y a los sacerdotes sirviendo en las distintas prácticas caritativas de la Iglesia. También dan su asistencia proclamando el Evangelio y predicando y ayudando en la liturgia de la Eucaristía. Los diáconos, además, celebran bautismos, bendicen matrimonios y presiden funerales. [deacon]

días de precepto principales días de fiesta de la Iglesia, exceptuando los domingos. En los días de precepto celebramos las grandes cosas que Dios ha hecho por nosotros a través de Jesucristo y los Santos. Es obligación de los católicos participar de la Eucaristía en estos días, al igual que lo es los domingos. [Holy Days of Obligation]

Diez Mandamientos diez reglas que Dios dio a Moisés en el Monte Sinaí que resumen la ley de Dios y nos muestran lo que hay que hacer para amar a Dios y al prójimo. Al seguir los Diez Mandamientos, los hebreos aceptaron su alianza con Dios. [Ten Commandments]

diócesis miembros de la Iglesia de una zona determinada, unidos en la fe y los sacramentos y congregados bajo la guía de un obispo [diocese]

Dios Padre, Hijo y Espíritu Santo: un solo Dios en tres personas distintas. Dios creó todo lo que es; Él es la fuente de la salvación y es verdad y amor. [God]

discípulo persona que ha aceptado el mensaje de Jesús y trata de vivir de la misma forma en que Él vivió, compartiendo su misión, su sufrimiento y sus alegrías [disciple]

discriminación acto de tratar mal a otros en razón de su apariencia o comportamiento, o sencillamente porque son distintos a nosotros [discrimination]

Divina Providencia guía que da Dios a todo lo creado por Él. La Divina Providencia vela por toda la creación y la guía hacia su perfección final. [Divine Providence]

Doctor de la Iglesia persona declarada como maestro ejemplar de la fe cristiana [Doctor of the Church]

Domingo de Ramos celebración de la entrada triunfal de Jesús en Jerusalén que se hace el domingo antes de la Pascua. Esta celebración inicia una semana de conmemoración de los eventos de salvación de la Semana Santa. [Palm Sunday]

dones del Espíritu Santo voluntad permanente dada a nosotros por el Espíritu Santo que nos permite hacer lo que Dios nos pide. Los dones del Espíritu Santo se encuentran en Isaías 11:1–3 y son: sabiduría, entendimiento, consejo, fortaleza, conocimiento, y temor de Dios. La tradición de la Iglesia ha agregado piedad, lo cual hace un total de siete. [Gifts of the Holy Spirit]

E

Emanuel nombre hebreo del Antiguo Testamento que significa "Dios con nosotros". En el Evangelio de San Mateo, se le llama Emanuel a Jesús. [Emmanuel]

Encarnación acto por el que el Hijo de Dios, Jesús, se hace plenamente hombre para salvarnos. El Hijo de Dios, segunda persona de la Trinidad, es tanto Dios verdadero como hombre verdadero. [Incarnation]

encíclica carta escrita por el Papa y enviada a toda la Iglesia y a veces a todo el mundo. Expresa la doctrina de la Iglesia sobre un determinado e importante asunto. [encyclical]

entendimiento uno de los siete dones del Espíritu Santo. Este don nos ayuda a tomar decisiones apropiadas en la vida, y en nuestra relación con Dios, y los demás. [understanding]

envidia sentimiento de resentimiento o tristeza debido a que alguien tiene una cualidad, talento o pertenencia que deseamos. La envidia es uno de los siete pecados capitales y va en contra del décimo mandamiento. [envy]

Epifanía día en que se celebra la visita de los Reyes Magos a Jesús recién nacido. Éste es el día en que se reveló a Jesús como salvador del mundo entero. [Epiphany]

epístola carta escrita por San Pablo u otro líder espiritual a un grupo de cristianos en los primeros tiempos de la Iglesia. Veintiuno de los veintisiete libros del Nuevo Testamento son Epístolas. En la Misa de los domingos y días santos, la segunda lectura se hace siempre de uno de estos libros. [epistle]

esperanza confianza de que Dios estará siempre con nosotros, nos dará felicidad ahora y siempre, y nos ayudará a vivir de forma que vivamos con Él para siempre [hope]

Espíritu Santo tercera persona de la Trinidad, que es enviada a nosotros para asistirnos y, mediante el bautismo y la confirmación, nos llena de la vida de Dios. Junto con el Padre y el Hijo, el Espíritu Santo da plenitud al plan divino de salvación. [Holy Spirit]

Estaciones del Vía Crucis forma de meditar las horas finales de la vida de Jesús, desde su condena a muerte por Pilatos hasta su muerte y sepultura. Consiste en recorrer representaciones de catorce incidentes distintos, cada uno de ellos basado en los sitios tradicionales de Jerusalén donde tuvieron lugar estos incidentes. [Stations of the Cross]

Eucaristía sacramento en el cual damos gracias a Dios por habernos dado a Jesucristo en el pan y el vino que se convierten en el Cuerpo y Sangre de Jesús. Este sacramento nos hace entrar en unión con Jesús y su muerte y resurrección redentoras. [Eucharist]

Evangelio buena nueva de la misericordia y amor de Dios que experimentamos al oír la historia de la vida, muerte y resurrección de Jesús. Esta historia es transmitida en el ministerio de enseñanza de la Iglesia como fuente de toda verdad y de vida recta. Se nos presenta en el Nuevo Testamento en cuatro libros: los Evangelios de San Mateo, San Marcos, San Lucas, y San Juan. [gospel]

evangelización proclamación, o declaración por medio de la palabra y el ejemplo, de la buena nueva de la salvación que hemos recibido en Jesucristo. Evangelizar es compartir nuestra fe con los demás, tanto con aquéllos que no conocen a Jesús como aquéllos que son llamados a seguir a Jesús más de cerca. [evangelization]

examen de conciencia acto de reflexionar en oración sobre aquello que hemos dicho o hecho considerando lo que el Evangelio pide de nosotros. Es también pensar acerca de cómo nuestras acciones pudieron haber dañado nuestra amistad con Dios y con otras personas. El examen de conciencia es una parte importante de la preparación para la celebración del sacramento de la penitencia. [examination of conscience]

exilio período de la historia de Israel comprendido entre la destrucción de Jerusalén en 587 a. de C. y el regreso a Jerusalén en 537 a. de C. Durante este tiempo, muchos de los judíos fueron obligados a vivir en Babilonia, lejos de su tierra. [Exile]

Éxodo liberación del pueblo hebreo de la esclavitud de Egipto dada por Dios y el haberlos guiado a la Tierra Prometida [Exodus]

F

fe don de Dios que nos llama a creer en Él. Profesamos nuestra fe en el credo; la celebramos en los sacramentos; vivimos según ella mediante nuestra buena conducta de amar a Dios y al prójimo; y la expresamos en la oración. [faith]

fortaleza fuerza que nos ayuda a obrar bien aun cuando sea difícil hacerlo. La fortaleza es una de las cuatro virtudes humanas centrales, llamadas virtudes cardinales, por las cuales guiamos nuestra conducta mediante el uso de la razón y la fe. Es también uno de los dones del Espíritu Santo. [fortitude]

frutos del Espíritu Santo forma en que actuamos porque Dios está vivo en nosotros. San Pablo enumera los frutos del Espíritu Santo en Gálatas 5:22–23: amor, gozo, paz, paciencia, benignidad, generosidad, fe, mansedumbre, y continencia. La tradición eclesial ha agregado bondad, modestia, y castidad, lo que hace un total de doce. [Fruits of the Holy Spirit]

G

genuflexión, hacer la forma de mostrar respeto en la iglesia doblando una rodilla y haciéndola tocar el suelo, sobre todo cuando estamos ante el Santísimo Sacramento que está en el sagrario [genuflect]

gracia don de Dios que se nos da gratuitamente. La gracia sanctificante nos llena de su vida y permite que seamos siempre amigos suyos. La gracia es el Espíritu Santo que habita en nosotros, ayudándonos a vivir nuestra vocación cristiana. La gracia también nos ayuda a vivir de la forma en que Dios quiere que vivamos. [grace]

gracia santificante don de Dios, dado a nosotros gratuitamente, que nos une con la vida de la Trinidad y sana nuestra naturaleza humana que ha sido herida por el pecado. La gracia santificante continúa la obra de nuestra santificación que se inició con nuestro bautismo. [sanctifying grace]

H

hebreos descendientes de Abraham, Isaac y Jacob que fueron esclavizados en Egipto. Dios ayudó a Moisés a liberar a este pueblo de la esclavitud. [Hebrews]

Hijo de Dios título revelado por Jesús que indica su relación única con Dios Padre. La revelación de Jesús como Hijo de Dios es el principal suceso de la historia de Jesús de Nazaret según la relatan los Evangelios. [Son of God]

homilía explicación de la Palabra de Dios en la liturgia hecha por el obispo, sacerdote o diácono. La homilía explica de qué forma se relaciona hoy la Palabra de Dios con nuestras vidas de cristianos. [homily]

I

Iglesia pueblo de Dios congregado en todo el mundo, la diócesis, o la Iglesia local, o la asamblea de los convocados a rendirle culto a Dios. La Iglesia es una, santa, católica, y apostólica. [Church]

iglesia doméstica el hogar cristiano, el cual es una comunidad de gracia y oración y una escuela de virtudes humanas y caridad cristiana [domestic church]

Iglesia universal toda la Iglesia tal como existe en el mundo entero. La gente de cada diócesis, junto con sus obispos y el Papa, forman la Iglesia universal. [universal Church]

Iglesias Católicas Orientales grupo de iglesias que se desarrollaron en el oriente (en países como el Líbano) que están en unión con la Iglesia Católica Romana pero tienen tradiciones litúrgicas, teológicas, y administrativas propias. Éstas muestran la verdadera naturaleza católica de la Iglesia, que se arraiga en numerosas culturas distintas. [Eastern Catholic Churches]

indulgencia reducción del castigo debido a pecados que han sido perdonados. Nos conduce hacia nuestra purificación final, cuando habremos de vivir con Dios para siempre. [indulgence]

infierno vida total y eternamente apartada de Dios. En su infinito amor hacia nosotros, Dios sólo puede desear nuestra salvación. El infierno es el resultado de la libre elección de la persona de rechazar el amor y perdón Dios de forma definitiva. [hell]

inspirado asistencia del Espíritu Santo a los autores humanos de la Sagrada Escritura. La inspiración del Espíritu Santo asegura que la Sagrada Escritura enseñe la verdad que Dios quiere que conozcamos para nuestra salvación. [inspired]

interpretación explicación de las palabras de la Sagrada Escritura, que combina el conocimiento humano con el oficio de enseñanza de la Iglesia bajo la guía del Espíritu Santo [interpretation]

islamismo La tercera gran religión, con judaísmo y el cristianismo, que profesa creencia en un solo Dios. *Islam* quiere decir "sumisión" a ese Dios único. [Islam]

israelitas descendientes de Abraham, Isaac y Jacob. Dios cambió el nombre de Jacob a "Israel"; y los doce hijos de Jacob junto con los hijos de estos hijos se convirtieron en jefes de las doce tribus de Israel. (*Véase* hebreos.) [Israelites]

J

Jesús hijo de Dios, que nació de la Virgen María y murió y fue resucitado de entre los muertos para nuestra salvación. Jesús volvió a Dios y vendrá de nuevo a juzgar a vivos y a muertos. Su nombre significa "Dios salva". [Jesus]

José padre adoptivo de Jesús, que estaba desposado con María cuando el ángel anunció que ella tendría un hijo por obra del poder del Espíritu Santo. En el Antiguo Testamento, José era el hijo de Jacob que fue vendido como esclavo en Egipto por sus hermanos y que luego los salvó de morir de hambre cuando hubo escasez de comida en la región. [Joseph]

judaísmo nombre de la religión de Jesús y de todo el pueblo de Israel después de su regreso del exilio en Babilonia y la construcción del segundo Templo [Judaism]

judíos nombre dado al pueblo hebreo, desde el tiempo del exilio al presente. Este nombre quiere decir "pueblo del territorio de Judea", zona de Palestina en torno a Jerusalén. [Jews]

justicia deseo firme y poderoso de dar a Dios y a los demás lo que les corresponde. Es una de las cuatro virtudes humanas centrales, llamadas virtudes cardinales, por las cuales guiamos nuestra vida cristiana. [justice]

L

laicado los que se han convertido en miembros de Cristo en el bautismo y que participan en las funciones sacerdotales, proféticas y regias de Cristo en su misión destinada al mundo entero. El laicado es distinto al clero, cuyos miembros están dedicados a servir a la Iglesia como ministros suyos. [laity]

Leccionario libro oficial que contiene todas las lecturas de la Sagrada Escritura utilizadas en la Liturgia de la Palabra [Lectionary]

ley moral regla de vida establecida por Dios y por personas de autoridad que se preocupan por el bien de todos. Las leyes morales se basan en la directiva que nos dio Dios de hacer lo que está bien y evitar lo que está mal. Algunas leyes morales están escritas en el corazón de la persona y se pueden conocer por medio de la razón. Otras nos han sido reveladas por Dios en el Antiguo Testamento y en la nueva ley dada por Jesús. [moral law]

ley natural ley moral que está escrita en el corazón de la persona. Podemos conocer la ley natural mediante la razón porque el Creador ha puesto en nuestros corazones el conocimiento de ella. Esta ley puede brindarnos una base sólida sobre la cual podemos crear las reglas para guiar nuestras decisiones en la vida. La ley natural representa la base de nuestros derechos y deberes fundamentales y es el cimiento de la obra del Espíritu Santo al guiar nuestras opciones morales. [natural law]

libre albedrío capacidad de optar por hacer el bien porque Dios nos ha hecho semejantes a Él. Nuestro libre albedrío es lo que nos hace verdaderamente humanos. Al ejercer nuestro libre albedrío para hacer el bien, nuestra libertad aumenta; pero, si lo usamos para elegir el pecado, nos hace esclavos de ese pecado. [free will]

Libros Sapienciales libros siguientes del Antiguo Testamento: Job, Proverbios, Eclesiastés, Cantar de los Cantares, Sabiduría y Eclesiástico. Su objetivo es instruir acerca de cómo vivir y cómo entender y sobrellevar los problemas de la vida. [Wisdom Literature]

liturgia oración pública de la Iglesia que celebra las maravillas que Dios ha hecho por nosotros en Jesucristo, nuestro Sumo Sacerdote, y cómo Él continúa la obra de nuestra salvación. El sentido original de *liturgia* era "obra pública o servicio prestado al pueblo". [liturgy]

Liturgia de la Eucaristía la segunda de las dos partes de la Misa. En esta parte, se bendice el pan y el vino, que se convierten en Cuerpo y Sangre de Jesucristo, que luego recibimos en la Sagrada Comunión. [Liturgy of the Eucharist]

Liturgia de la Palabra la primera de las dos partes de la Misa. Durante esta parte, oímos la Palabra de Dios en la Biblia y reflexionamos sobre lo que significa hoy para nosotros. La Liturgia de la Palabra también puede ser una oración pública y proclamación de la Palabra de Dios que no va seguida de la Liturgia de la Eucaristía. [Liturgy of the Word]

Liturgia de las Horas oración pública de la Iglesia para alabar a Dios y santificar el día. Consiste de: un Oficio de Lecturas antes del alba, los Laudes al amanecer, las Vísperas al anochecer, y una oración antes de acostarse. La recitación de los salmos conforma la mayor parte de cada uno de estos oficios. [Liturgy of the Hours]

liturgia eucarística culto público rendido por la Iglesia en el cual se consagran el pan y el vino para que se conviertan en Cuerpo y Sangre de Jesucristo. La celebración dominical de la liturgia eucarística es el eje central de la vida eclesial. [Eucharistic liturgy]

M

Magisterio oficio de enseñanza viviente de la Iglesia. Este oficio, a través de los obispos y junto con el Papa, ofrece una interpretación auténtica de la Palabra de Dios. Su objetivo es mantenerse fiel a las enseñanzas de los apóstoles en cuestiones de fe y moral. [Magisterium]

Magníficat canto de María de alabanza a Dios. Ella lo alaba por las grandes cosas que ha hecho por ella y los grandes planes que ha hecho para nosotros a través de Jesús. [Magnificat]

mandamiento norma, o regla, para vivir de la forma en que Dios quiere que vivamos. Jesús resumió todos los mandamientos en dos: amar a Dios y amar al prójimo. [commandment]

El Mandamiento Mayor enseñanza esencial de Jesús de amar a Dios y al prójimo como a nosotros mismos. Jesús nos dice que su mandamiento resume todo lo enseñado en el Antiguo Testamento. [Great Commandment]

María madre de Jesús. Se le dice bendita y "llena de gracia" porque Dios la eligió para ser madre de su Hijo, segunda persona de la Trinidad. [Mary]

matrimonio contrato solemne entre un varón y una mujer para ser compañeros por toda la vida, tanto para su bien propio como para procrear hijos. El matrimonio es un sacramento cuando el contrato se hace de forma apropiada entre cristianos bautizados. [matrimony]

mayordomía administración cuidadosa y responsable de algo que ha sido confiado a nuestro cuidado, en particular los bienes de la creación, que han sido destinados a toda la raza humana. El sexto precepto de la Iglesia deja clara nuestra participación en la administración al exigirnos que suplamos las necesidades materiales de la Iglesia según nuestras capacidades. [stewardship]

Mesías título que quiere decir "ungido". Proviene de un vocablo hebreo que significa lo mismo que la palabra griega *Cristo*, que es el título dado a Jesús después de su resurrección, cuando ya había terminado su misión como sacerdote, profeta, y rey. [Messiah]

Miércoles de Ceniza primer día de Cuaresma, en el que se nos coloca ceniza en la frente para que nos acordemos de que, para prepararnos para la Pascua, debemos mostrar arrepentimiento por decisiones que hemos tomado que ofenden a Dios y dañan nuestra relación con los demás [Ash Wednesday]

milagro señales o actos maravillosos que no pueden ser explicados por causas naturales pero que son obras de Dios. En los Evangelios, Jesús obra milagros como señal de que el Reino de Dios está presente en su ministerio. [miracle]

ministerio servicio, u obra, que se hace a otros. Lo hacen los obispos, sacerdotes y diáconos ordenados al ministerio en la celebración de los sacramentos. Todos los bautizados son llamados a una variedad de ministerios en la liturgia y en el servicio a las necesidades de los demás. [ministry]

Misa la celebración sacramental más importante de la Iglesia. La celebración de la Misa fue instituida por Jesús en la Última Cena para que fuera un recordatorio de su muerte y resurrección. En la Misa, oímos la Palabra de Dios en la Biblia y recibimos a Jesucristo en el pan y el vino que han sido consagrados para convertirse en su Cuerpo y Sangre. [Mass]

misión obra de Jesucristo que continúa en la Iglesia a través del Espíritu Santo. La misión de la Iglesia es proclamar la salvación en la vida, muerte, y resurrección de Jesús. [mission]

misterio verdad religiosa que sólo podemos conocer por revelación de Dios y que no podemos comprender totalmente. Nuestra fe es un misterio que profesamos en el credo y que celebramos en la liturgia y los sacramentos. [mystery]

Misterio Pascual obra de salvación realizada por Jesucristo mediante su pasión, muerte y resurrección. El Misterio Pascual se celebra en la liturgia de la Iglesia. En los sacramentos experimentamos sus efectos redentores. [Paschal Mystery]

monasterio lugar donde residen varones o mujeres cumpliendo sus votos de pobreza, castidad y obediencia en una vida de comunidad estable. Éstos pasan sus días en oración pública, trabajo, y meditación. [monastery]

musulmán seguidor de la religión islámica. *Musulmán* quiere decir "que se somete a Dios". [Muslim]

N

Navidad fiesta del nacimiento de Jesús (el 25 de diciembre) [Christmas]

Nuevo Testamento los 27 libros de la segunda parte de la Biblia, que relatan las enseñanzas, ministerio, y acontecimientos de salvación de la vida de Jesús. El Nuevo Testamento se compone de: cuatro Evangelios, que presentan la vida, muerte, y resurrección de Jesús; los Hechos de los Apóstoles, que narran la historia del mensaje de salvación al irse extendiendo con el crecimiento de la Iglesia; varias cartas que nos instruyen sobre cómo vivir como seguidores de Jesucristo; y el Libro del Apocalipsis, que da ánimo a los cristianos que sufren persecución. [New Testament]

O

obediencia acto de seguir por voluntad propia lo que Dios nos pide que hagamos para nuestra salvación. Según el cuarto mandamiento, los niños deben obedecer a sus padres; y todas las personas deben obedecer a la autoridad civil cuando obra en beneficio de todos. Imitando la obediencia de Jesús, los miembros de las comunidades religiosas hacen un voto especial de obediencia. [obedience]

obispo varón que ha recibido el orden sagrado en su totalidad. Como sucesor de los primeros apóstoles, el obispo vela por la Iglesia y es un educador importante dentro de la misma. [bishop]

obras corporales de misericordia buenas acciones con las que ayudamos a nuestro prójimo a cubrir sus necesidades materiales cotidianas. Las obras corporales de misericordia son: dar de comer al hambriento, dar techo al que no lo tiene, vestir al desnudo, visitar a los enfermos y a los presos, dar limosna a los pobres y enterrar a los muertos. [Corporal Works of Mercy]

obras espirituales de misericordia acciones caritativas mediante las cuales socorremos al prójimo en sus necesidades que van más allá de lo material. Las obras espirituales de misericordia son: instruir, aconsejar, consolar, confortar, perdonar y sufrir con paciencia las flaquezas ajenas. [Spiritual Works of Mercy]

ofensas actos contrarios a la ley cometidos contra la propiedad o los derechos de otra persona, o actos que físicamente lastiman a esa persona [trespasses]

óleo de los catecúmenos óleo bendecido por el obispo durante la Semana Santa y usado para ungir a los catecúmenos. Esta unción los afianza en su camino de iniciación en la Iglesia. Los bebés son ungidos con este óleo momentos antes de ser bautizados. [oil of catechumens]

óleo de los enfermos óleo bendecido por el obispo durante la Semana Santa y usado en el sacramento de la unción de los enfermos, la cual brinda sanación espiritual y, si Dios quiere, sanación física también [oil of the sick]

opción moral el elegir hacer lo que está bien o no hacer lo que está mal. Elegimos opciones morales porque son lo que creemos que Dios quiere y porque tenemos la libertad de escoger lo que está bien y evitar lo que está mal. [moral choice]

oración el levantar el corazón y la mente a Dios. Podemos hablar y escuchar a Dios porque Él nos enseña a orar. [prayer]

oración común culto a Dios que se rinde junto con otras personas. La Liturgia de las Horas y la Misa son las principales formas de oración común. [communal prayer]

oración personal tipo de oración que surge en nosotros en la vida cotidiana. Oramos junto con otras personas en la liturgia; pero, además, cada momento de nuestra vida es una ocasión de escuchar y responder a Dios a través de la oración personal. [personal prayer]

orden sagrado sacramento mediante el cual la misión, o deber, dado por Jesús a sus apóstoles continúa en la Iglesia. Tiene tres grados: diácono, sacerdote, y obispo. Mediante la imposición de manos en el sacramento del orden sagrado, los varones reciben una marca o carácter sacramental permanente que los llama a servir a la Iglesia como ministros suyos. [Holy Orders]

ordenación rito del sacramento del orden sagrado, mediante el cual el obispo da a los varones a través de la imposición de manos la capacidad de servir en el ministerio a la Iglesia como obispos, sacerdotes, y diáconos [ordination]

P

padrino/madrina de bautismo testigo de bautismo que asume la responsabilidad de ayudar al bautizado a seguir el camino de la vida cristiana [godparent]

Papa el obispo de Roma, sucesor de San Pedro, y cabeza de la Iglesia Católica Romana. Como tiene autoridad de actuar en nombre de Cristo, al Papa se le llama Vicario de Cristo. El Papa junto a todos los obispos conforma el oficio de enseñanza viviente de la Iglesia: el Magisterio. [pope]

parábola una de las sencillas narraciones que Jesús contaba que nos muestran cómo es el Reino de Dios. Las parábolas nos presentan imágenes, o escenas, tomadas de la vida cotidiana. Estas imágenes nos muestran la decisión radical, o seria, que tomamos cuando respondemos a la invitación de entrar en el Reino de Dios. [parable]

parroquia comunidad de creyentes en Jesucristo que se reúne regularmente en una zona determinada para rendirle culto a Dios bajo la guía de un pastor [parish]

Pascua celebración de la resurrección corporal de Jesucristo de entre los muertos. La Pascua festeja nuestra redención y es la fiesta cristiana central de las que se originan otras fiestas. [Easter]

Pascua judía festival judío que conmemora la liberación del pueblo hebreo de la esclavitud de Egipto. *Pascua* viene de una palabra hebrea que significa "tránsito" o "pasaje". En la Eucaristía, celebramos nuestro "tránsito" de la muerte a la vida a través de la muerte y resurrección de Jesús. [Passover]

pastor sacerdote responsable del cuidado espiritual de los miembros de una comunidad parroquial. El deber del sacerdote es velar por que se predique la Palabra de Dios, se enseñe la fe, y se celebren los sacramentos. [pastor]

pecado pensamiento, palabra, acción, o falta de acción deliberados que ofenden a Dios y dañan nuestra relación con otras personas. Algunos pecados son mortales y deben ser confesados en el sacramento de la penitencia. Otros son veniales, o menos graves. [sin]

pecado mortal decisión grave de apartarnos de Dios haciendo algo que sabemos que está mal. Para que un pecado sea mortal, debe ser una falta muy grave, la persona debe saber lo grave que es el pecado, y, a pesar de ello, decidir libremente cometerlo. [mortal sin]

pecado original consecuencia de la desobediencia de los primeros seres humanos, que desobedecieron a Dios y decidieron seguir su propia voluntad y no la de Dios. A raíz de esto, los seres humanos perdieron la bendición original que Dios les había destinado y se sometieron al pecado y la muerte. En el bautismo, se nos restaura la vida con Dios a través de Jesucristo, aunque aún seguimos sufriendo los efectos del pecado original. [original sin]

pecado personal pecado que decidimos cometer. Puede ser grave (mortal) o menos grave (venial). Aunque las consecuencias del pecado original nos dejan con una tendencia al pecado, la gracia de Dios, sobre todo a través de los sacramentos, nos ayuda a elegir el bien sobre el mal. [personal sin]

pecado venial decisión que tomamos que debilita nuestra relación con Dios y los demás. El pecado venial hiere y reduce la vida divina que hay en nosotros. Si no nos esforzamos por superarnos, el pecado venial puede llevarnos a pecados más graves. Nuestra participación en la Eucaristía perdona los pecados veniales y fortalece nuestra relación con Dios y los demás. [venial sin]

pecados capitales aquellos pecados que pueden llevarnos a cometer pecados más graves. Los pecados capitales son: soberbia, avaricia, envidia, ira, gula, lujuria y pereza. [capital sins]

penitencia el apartarnos del pecado con el deseo de cambiar nuestras vidas y acercarnos más a la forma de vida que Dios quiere que vivamos. Expresamos externamente nuestra penitencia mediante la oración, el ayuno, y ayudando a los pobres. También se le llama penitencia a la acción que el sacerdote nos pide hacer o a las oraciones que nos pide rezar después de que él nos absuelve en el sacramento de la penitencia. (*Véase* sacramento de la penitencia.) [penance]

Pentecostés el 50º día después de la resurrección de Jesús. En este día, el Espíritu Santo fue enviado del cielo y nació la Iglesia. También es el día de la fiesta judía que celebraba el recibimiento de los Diez Mandamientos en el Monte Sinaí 50 días después del Éxodo. [Pentecost]

perdón voluntad de ser benignos con una persona que nos ha hecho daño pero que después dice que está arrepentida. En la oración del Padrenuestro, rogamos que, al igual que Dios siempre nos ha de perdonar nuestros pecados, nosotros también sepamos perdonar a los que nos han hecho daño. [forgiveness]

pereza dejadez de corazón que lleva a una persona a no hacer caso de su desarrollo como persona, en particular de su desarrollo espiritual y de su relación con Dios. La pereza es uno de los siete pecados capitales, y va en contra del primer mandamiento. [sloth]

petición el pedir a Dios lo que necesitamos porque Él nos ha creado y quiere darnos lo que necesitamos. Cuando participamos del amor redentor de Dios, entendemos que para cada una de nuestras necesidades podemos pedirle a Dios que nos ayude mediante una petición. [petition]

piedad uno de los siete dones del Espíritu Santo. Nos llama a ser fieles en nuestras relaciones con Dios y los demás. Nos ayuda a amar a Dios y a comportarnos de una manera responsable y con generosidad y afecto en nuestra relación con los demás. [piety]

preceptos de la Iglesia aquellos requisitos positivos que la autoridad pastoral de la Iglesia ha determinado ser necesarios. Estos requisitos representan el esfuerzo mínimo que debemos hacer en la oración y en la vida moral. Los preceptos de la Iglesia se aseguran de que todos los católicos progresemos más allá del mínimo, creciendo en amor a Dios y en amor al prójimo. [Precepts of the Church]

presbítero palabra que originalmente quería decir "anciano" o "consejero de confianza del obispo". De esta palabra deriva el vocablo inglés *priest*, o "sacerdote" en español, uno de los tres grados del sacramento del orden sagrado. Todos los sacerdotes de una diócesis que están bajo la guía de un obispo forman el presbiterado. [presbyter]

Presencia Real modo en que Cristo resucitado está presente en la Eucaristía en forma de pan y vino. Se le llama "real" a la presencia de Jesucristo porque en la Eucaristía su cuerpo y sangre, alma y divinidad, están total y enteramente presentes. [Real Presence]

profeta persona llamada a hablar por Dios y a llamar a la gente a ser fiel a la alianza. Una sección importante del Antiguo Testamento presenta en dieciocho libros los mensajes y acciones de los profetas. [prophet]

prudencia virtud que nos orienta al bien. También nos ayuda a escoger los medios apropiados para alcanzar ese bien. Cuando actuamos con prudencia consideramos nuestros acciones con cuidado. La prudencia es una de las virtudes cardinales morales que guía nuestra conciencia e influye en nosotros para que vivamos según la ley de Cristo. [prudence]

Pueblo de Dios otro de los nombres de la Iglesia. Al igual que el pueblo de Israel era el pueblo de Dios debido a la alianza que Él hizo con ellos, la Iglesia es un pueblo sacerdotal, profético y regio gracias a la nueva y eterna alianza en Jesucristo. [people of God]

Pueblo Elegido pueblo escogido por Dios para que mantuviera con Él una relación especial. La primera vez que Dios formó un Pueblo Elegido fue cuando hizo una alianza, o pacto solemne, con Abraham. Más tarde, Él reafirmó esa alianza a través de Moisés en el Monte Sinaí. Esta alianza ha alcanzado su plenitud en Jesús y su Iglesia. [Chosen People]

purgatorio estado que viene después de la muerte de purificación final de todas las imperfecciones humanas antes de entrar a gozar la presencia de Dios en el cielo [purgatory]

R

racismo creencia de que la raza determina rasgos y capacidades humanas y que existe una superioridad inherente, o innata, de una raza determinada. La discriminación en razón de la raza de una persona es una violación de la dignidad humana y un pecado contra la justicia. [racism]

reconciliación reanudar la amistad que se había roto por alguna acción o falta de acción. En el sacramento de la penitencia, mediante la misericordia y perdón de Dios, nos reconciliamos con Él, la Iglesia y los demás. [reconciliation]

redención el liberarnos de la esclavitud del pecado mediante la vida, el sacrificio de la muerte en la cruz y la resurrección de Jesucristo de entre los muertos [redemption]

Redentor Jesucristo, cuya vida, sacrificio de su muerte en la cruz, y resurrección de entre los muertos nos libró de la esclavitud del pecado y nos trajo la redención [Redeemer]

reformarse poner fin a un error tomando un curso de acción mejor o distinto. Los profetas llamaban a la gente a reformar sus vidas volviendo a ser fieles a la alianza con Dios. [reform]

Reino de Dios el dominio de Dios sobre nosotros anunciado en el Evangelio y está presente en la Eucaristía. El principio del Reino aquí en la Tierra está presente en forma misteriosa en la Iglesia, y vendrá en su plenitud en el fin de los tiempos. [Kingdom of God]

Resurrección el volver a la vida el cuerpo de Jesucristo el tercer día después de haber muerto en la cruz. La Resurrección es la verdad culminante de nuestra fe. [Resurrection]

revelación comunicación que nos hace Dios de sí por medio de las palabras y hechos que ha usado a lo largo de la historia para mostrarnos el misterio del plan de salvación que tiene para nosotros. Esta revelación llega a su plenitud con el envío de su Hijo, Jesucristo. [Revelation]

rito una de diversas formas de celebrar la liturgia en la Iglesia. Los ritos pueden ser distintos según la cultura o el país donde se celebren. *Rito* también quiere decir el modo especial en que celebramos cada sacramento. [rite]

Rosario oración en honor a la Virgen María. En el rezo del rosario, meditamos los misterios de la vida de Jesucristo rezando el Avemaría en los cinco grupos de diez cuentas y el Padrenuestro en las cuentas que van en medio. En la Iglesia Latín, rezar el rosario se convirtió en una manera en que la gente común podía reflexionar sobre los misterios de la vida de Jesús. [Rosary]

S

Sabat séptimo día, en el que Dios, habiendo terminado su obra de creación, descansó. El tercer mandamiento nos exige que consideremos santo el sabat. Para los cristianos, el sabat se convirtió en domingo porque era el día en que resucitó Jesús y se inició la nueva creación en Jesucristo. [Sabbath]

sabiduría uno de los siete dones del Espíritu Santo. Nos ayuda a entender el propósito y el plan de Dios, y a vivir de una forma que ayude a realizar este plan. La sabiduría se inicia con la admiración y portento ante la grandeza de Dios. [wisdom]

sacerdocio todo el pueblo de Dios que ha sido hecho partícipe de la misión de Cristo a través de los sacramentos del bautismo y la confirmación. El sacerdocio ministerial, compuesto de aquellos varones que han sido ordenados obispos y sacerdotes a través del orden sagrado, es en esencia distinto del sacerdocio de todos los fieles porque su labor es la de edificar y guiar a la Iglesia en nombre de Cristo. [priesthood]

sacerdote varón que ha aceptado el llamado especial de Dios para servir a la Iglesia guiándola y edificándola mediante el ministerio de la Palabra y la celebración de los sacramentos [priest]

sacramental objeto, oración o bendición dados por la Iglesia que nos ayudan a crecer en nuestra vida espiritual [sacramental]

sacramento una de las siete formas en que la vida de Dios entra en nuestras vidas a través de la obra del Espíritu Santo. Jesús dio a nosotros tres sacramentos que nos hacen entrar en la Iglesia (bautismo, confirmación y Eucaristía); dos sacramentos que nos traen sanación (penitencia y unción de los enfermos); y dos sacramentos que ayudan a los miembros a servir a la comunidad (matrimonio y orden sagrado). [sacrament]

sacramento de la penitencia sacramento en el cual celebramos el perdón de Dios a nuestros pecados y nuestra reconciliación con Él y la Iglesia. La penitencia consiste en el arrepentimiento de los pecados cometidos, la confesión de los pecados, la absolución por el sacerdote, y el cumplimiento de la penitencia para mostrar que estamos dispuestos a enderezar nuestras vidas. [Sacrament of Penance]

sacramentos al servicio de la comunidad sacramentos que contribuyen a la salvación personal de los individuos dándoles un modo de servir a los demás. Son dos: orden sagrado y matrimonio. [Sacraments at the Service of Communion]

sacramentos de curación sacramentos mediante los cuales la Iglesia continúa el ministerio de Jesús de sanación del alma y del cuerpo. Son dos: penitencia y unción de los enfermos. [Sacraments of Healing]

sacramentos de iniciación sacramentos que son los cimientos de nuestra vida cristiana. Volvemos a nacer en el bautismo, nos fortalecemos en la confirmación, y recibimos en la Eucaristía el alimento de la vida eterna. Por medio de estos sacramentos, recibimos una creciente medida de vida divina y avanzamos hacia la perfección de la caridad. [Sacraments of Initiation]

sacrificio ritual en que el sacerdote en el Templo de Jerusalén ofrecía animales u hortalizas a Dios para dar muestra de la adoración del pueblo a Dios, para dar gracias a Dios, o para pedir su perdón. El sacrificio también mostraba la unión con Dios. Cristo, el gran Sumo Sacerdote, alcanzó nuestra redención a través del sacrificio perfecto de su muerte en la cruz. [sacrifice]

Sacrificio de la Misa sacrificio de Jesús en la cruz, el cual se recuerda y se hace presente de forma misteriosa en la Eucaristía. Es ofrecida en reparación de los pecados de los vivos y los difuntos, y para obtener de Dios beneficos espirituales o temporales. [Sacrifice of the Mass]

Sagrada Comunión pan y vino consagrados que recibimos en la Misa, los cuales son el Cuerpo y Sangre de Jesucristo. La Sagrada Comunión nos hace entrar en unión con Jesucristo y su muerte y resurrección redentoras. [Holy Communion]

Sagrada Escritura escritos sagrados de los judíos y cristianos recopilados en el Antiguo y Nuevo Testamento de la Biblia [Scriptures]

Sagrada Familia familia de Jesús en la que creció Jesús en Nazaret. Estaba formada por Jesús, su madre María y su padre adoptivo José. [Holy Family]

sagrario pieza donde se guarda el Santísimo Sacramento para que la Sagrada Comunión pueda ser llevada a los enfermos y moribundos. Se le llama también tabernáculo. Para los israelitas, el tabernáculo es el nombre de la tienda de campaña usada como santuario para guardar el Arca de la Alianza desde la época del éxodo hasta la construcción del templo de Salomón. [tabernacle]

salmo oración en forma de poema. Los salmos estaban destinados para ser cantados en cultos públicos. Cada salmo expresa un aspecto, o característica, de la profundidad de la oración humana. A lo largo de varios siglos, se han recolectado 150 salmos que forman el Libro de los Salmos en el Antiguo Testamento. Estos salmos se usaban en el culto a Dios en el Templo de Jerusalén, y han sido usados en el culto público de la Iglesia desde sus orígenes. [psalm]

salvación don, que sólo Dios puede darnos, del perdón del pecado y la reanudación de la amistad con Él [salvation]

Salvador Jesús, el Hijo de Dios, que se hizo hombre para perdonar nuestros pecados y reanudar nuestra amistad con Dios. *Jesús* quiere decir "Dios salva". [Savior]

Sanctasanctórum parte más sagrada del Templo de Jerusalén. El sumo sacerdote entraba a este recinto una vez al año para dirigirse a Dios y pedirle su perdón por los pecados del pueblo. [Holy of Holies]

santa uno de los cuatro calificados de la Iglesia. Es el tipo de vida que vivimos cuando participamos de la vida de Dios, que es todo santidad. La Iglesia es santa por su unión con Jesucristo. [holy]

santidad plenitud de la vida y el amor cristianos. Todos somos llamados a la santidad, la cual, al cooperar con la gracia de Dios, hace posible que se haga la voluntad de Dios en todas las cosas. Al hacer la voluntad de Dios, nos transformamos cada vez más en la imagen de su Hijo, Jesucristo. [holiness]

Santísimo Sacramento pan que ha sido consagrado por el sacerdote en la Misa. Se guarda en el sagrario para su adoración y para ser llevado a los enfermos. [Blessed Sacrament]

santo persona virtuosa y ejemplar que ha muerto en unión con Dios. Además, la Iglesia ha declarado que esta persona está con Dios en el cielo ahora y para siempre. [saint]

scriptórium habitación que hay en los monasterios donde se hacían libros copiados a mano. Con frecuencia, se creaban bellas obras de arte en la página para ilustrar el texto. [scriptorium]

Semana Santa celebración de los sucesos relacionados a la pasión, muerte, y resurrección de Jesús, y el don de la Eucaristía. Se inicia con la conmemoración de la entrada triunfal de Jesús a Jerusalén el Domingo de Ramos; sigue con la conmemoración del regalo que hace de sí mismo en la Eucaristía el Jueves Santo, su muerte el Viernes Santo y su resurrección durante la Vigilia Pascual el Sábado de Gloria. [Holy Week]

serafines seres celestiales que adoran a Dios ante su trono. Uno de ellos purificó los labios de Isaías con carbón ardiente para que pudiese hablar por Dios. [seraphim]

Sermón de la Montaña palabras de Jesús que figuran en los capítulos 5 a 7 del Evangelio de San Mateo, en las que Jesús revela cómo Él ha dado plenitud a la ley de Dios entregada a Moisés. El Sermón de la Montaña comienza con las ocho Bienaventuranzas e incluye la oración del Padrenuestro. [Sermon on the Mount]

sexismo prejuicios o discriminación en razón del sexo de una persona, especialmente discriminación contra la mujer. El sexismo crea conductas y actitudes que fomentan una visión de los roles sociales basada sólo en el sexo de la persona. [sexism]

soberbia imagen falsa de lo que somos que exagera lo que nos corresponde como seres creados por Dios. La soberbia nos pone en competencia con Dios y es uno de los siete pecados capitales. [pride]

solidaridad actitud de fuerza y unidad que conduce a compartir los bienes espirituales y materiales. La solidaridad une a ricos y pobres, débiles y poderosos, y crea una sociedad donde todos dan lo que pueden y reciben lo que necesitan. La idea de solidaridad se basa en el origen común de la humanidad. [solidarity]

T

temor de Dios uno de los siete dones del Espíritu Santo. Este don nos conduce a un sentimiento de admiración y portento ante la presencia de Dios debido a su grandeza. [fear of the Lord]

templanza virtud cardinal que nos ayuda a controlar nuestra atracción al placer de manera que nuestros deseos naturales se mantengan dentro de sus límites apropiados. Esta virtud moral nos ayuda a optar por usar con moderación los bienes creados. [temperance]

Templo casa donde se rinde culto a Dios, construida originalmente por Salomón. El Templo proporcionaba un lugar donde los sacerdotes podían ofrecer sacrificios, adorar y dar gracias a Dios, y pedir su perdón. Fue destruido y reconstruido. El segundo templo fue destruido por los romanos en 70 d. de C. y nunca fue reconstruido. Parte del muro exterior del monte del Templo se conserva aún hoy en Jerusalén. [Temple]

tentación atracción, que viene de fuera o de dentro de nosotros mismos, que puede llevarnos a no seguir los mandamientos de Dios. Todos somos tentados, pero el Espíritu Santo nos ayuda a resistir la tentación y a optar por hacer el bien. [temptation]

testimonio el transmitir a los demás, mediante nuestras palabras y acciones, la fe que se nos ha dado. Cada cristiano tiene el deber de dar testimonio de la buena nueva de Jesucristo que ha llegado a conocer. [witness]

Tierra Prometida tierra prometida originalmente por Dios a Abraham. Fue a esta tierra que Dios dijo a Moisés que llevara al Pueblo Elegido tras ser liberados de la esclavitud de Egipto y donde recibieron los Diez Mandamientos en el Monte Sinaí. [Promised Land]

Torá palabra hebrea que significa "instrucción" o "ley". Es También el nombre de los cinco primeros libros del Antiguo Testamento: Génesis, Éxodo, Levítico, Números, y Deuteronomio. [Torah]

transubstanciación la transformación única del pan y el vino en la Eucaristía en el Cuerpo y Sangre de Cristo resucitado, aunque las apariencias de pan y vino permanecen [transubstantiation]

Trinidad misterio de la existencia de un Dios en tres personas: Padre, Hijo, y Espíritu Santo, donde cada una es Dios, todo y entero. Cada persona es distinta sólo en su relación a las otras. [Trinity]

U

Última Cena última comida que cenaron Jesús y sus discípulos la noche antes de que muriera. En la Última Cena, Jesús tomó pan y vino, los bendijo, y dijo que eran su Cuerpo y su Sangre. La muerte y resurrección de Jesús, que celebramos en la Eucaristía, fue anticipada en esta cena. [Last Supper]

una uno de los cuatro calificados de la Iglesia. La Iglesia es una debido a su origen en un Dios único y a su fundador Jesucristo. Jesús, mediante su muerte en la cruz, unió todo a Dios en un cuerpo. Dentro de la unidad de la Iglesia, hay una gran diversidad debido a la riqueza de los dones dados a sus miembros. [one]

unción de los enfermos uno de los siete sacramentos, en el cual la persona enferma es ungida con óleo santo y recibe la fuerza, paz, y coraje para superar las dificultades que conlleva la enfermedad. A través del sacramento Jesús brinda al enfermo sanación espiritual y perdón de sus pecados y, si Dios quiere, también sanación al cuerpo. [Anointing of the Sick]

V

viático Eucaristía que recibe el moribundo. Es el alimento espiritual para el viaje final que hacemos como cristianos: el viaje a través de la muerte hacia la vida eterna. [viaticum]

Vicario de Cristo título dado al Papa, quien como sucesor de San Pedro, tiene la autoridad de actuar en representación de Cristo. Un vicario es alguien que y está o actúa por ella. [Vicar of Christ]

vida eterna vida con Dios después de la muerte y que nunca acaba. Es concedida a aquéllos que mueren estando en amistad con Dios, con su gracia viva en ellos. [eternal life]

vida religiosa estado de vida reconocido por la Iglesia. Dentro de la vida religiosa, varones y mujeres pueden responder libremente al llamado de seguir a Jesús viviendo sus votos de pobreza, castidad, y obediencia en comunidad con otros. [religious life]

Vigilia Pascual celebración de la primera y más grande de las fiestas cristianas: la Resurrección de Jesús. Tiene lugar la tarde del primer sábado que sigue a la luna llena que se observa después del primer día de primavera. Es en esta noche de vigilia antes de la mañana de Pascua que los catecúmenos son bautizados, confirmados y reciben por primera vez la Eucaristía. [Easter Vigil]

virtud actitud o forma de actuar que nos ayuda a hacer el bien [virtue]

virtudes teologales aquellas virtudes que nos fueron dadas por Dios y no alcanzadas por esfuerzo humano. Ellas son: fe, esperanza, y caridad. [Theological Virtues]

Visitación visita de María a Isabel para contarle la buena nueva de que habrá de ser la madre de Jesús. El saludo de Isabel forma parte del Avemaría. Durante esta visita, María hace su oración de alabanza a Dios: el Magníficat. [Visitation]

vocación llamado que se nos hace en la vida para que seamos las personas que Dios quiere que seamos. También es la forma en que servimos a la Iglesia y al Reino de Dios. Podemos ejercer nuestra vocación como laicos, como miembros de una comunidad religiosa, o como miembros del clero. [vocation]

voto promesa deliberada y libre hecha a Dios por aquellas personas que desean dedicar de forma especial sus vidas a Dios. Los votos dan ahora testimonio del reino que ha de venir. [vow]

Vulgata traducción de la Biblia al latín que hizo San Jerónimo del original hebreo y griego. En la época de San Jerónimo, la mayoría de los cristianos ya no hablaban hebreo o griego. La lengua común, o vulgata, era el latín. [Vulgate]

Y

Yavé nombre de Dios en hebreo dado por Dios a Moisés desde la zarza ardiente. *Yavé* quiere decir "Yo soy el que soy" o "Yo hago existir". [Yahweh]

Acknowledgments

Excerpts from the English translation of *Rite of Marriage* © 1969, International Commission on English in the Liturgy, Inc. (ICEL); excerpts from the English translation of *Rite of Baptism for Children* © 1969, ICEL; excerpts from the English translation of *The Roman Missal* © 1973, ICEL; excerpts from the English translation of *Rite of Penance* © 1974, ICEL; excerpts from the English translation of *Rite of Confirmation, 2nd Edition* © 1975, ICEL; excerpts from the English translation of *Pastoral Care of the Sick* © 1982, ICEL; excerpts from the English translation of *A Book of Prayers* © 1982, ICEL; excerpts from the English translation of *Book of Blessings* © 1988, ICEL. All rights reserved.

Excerpts from *The New American Bible with Revised New Testament and Psalms* Copyright © 1991, 1986, 1970 Confraternity of Christian Doctrine, Inc., Washington, DC. Used with permission. All rights reserved. No portion of the *New American Bible* may be reprinted without permission in writing from the copyright holder.

96 Excerpts from *Hearts on Fire: Praying with Jesuits* © 1999, The Institute of Jesuit Sources: St. Louis, MO. All rights reserved.

Illustration

Bandelin-Dacey Studios: 4, 52–53, 54–55, 76–77, 134–135, 148, 149, 165, 172–173, 234–235, 250–251, 252–255
David Diaz: 127, 201
Fran Gregory: 6, 14, 15, 30–31, 46, 109, 116–117, 133, 151, 156, 157, 167, 174, 225, 243
Monica Liu: 124–125
Peter Siu: 93
Susie Weber, Weber Design, Inc.: 276–277

Photography

Unless otherwise acknowledged, photos are the property of Loyola Press. When there is more than one picture on a page, credits are supplied in sequence, left to right, top to bottom. Page positions are abbreviated as follows: (t) top, (m) middle, (b) bottom, (l) left, (r) right, (bkgr) background, (ins) inset, (cl) clockwise from top right.

UNIT 1: 1 © Erich Lessing/Art Resource, NY. **2** (bkgr) Biblioteca Medicea Laurenziana, Florence, ms. Plut. 12.21, c. 1v; (ins) © Erich Lessing/Art Resource, NY. **3** (t,l) © Mitchell Funk/GettyImages; (t,r) © David Young-Wolff/PhotoEdit; (b,l) photodisc; (b,r) David Woodfall/Getty Images. **5** (t,r) By permission, The Julian Shrine, Norwich, England. **7** New Mexico State University Art Gallery Collection. Acc. #1969.3.6. **8** (bkgr) © Chris Cheadle/Getty Images. **9** Pascal Crapet/Getty Images. **10** (t) By permission, The Julian Shrine, Norwich, England; (m) © Jim McGuire/PictureQuest; (b,l) Myrleen F. Cate/PhotoEdit; (b,r) George A. Lane, S.J. **11** (l) © Mark Burnett/Stock Boston; (t,r) © Seth Resnick/Stock Boston; (b,r) © Kathy McLaughlin/The Image Works. **12** © Robert Lentz/Bridge Building Images, www.BridgeBuilding.com. **13** © Alinari/Art Resource, NY. **15** (all) photodisc/Getty Images except second from bottom © Michael Newman/ PhotoEdit. **16** © The Crosiers/Gene Plaisted OSC. **17** © Tony Freeman/ PhotoEdit. **18** (t) Najlah Feanny/CORBIS; (m) photodisc/Getty Images; (b,r) © Benelux Press/PictureQuest. **19** (l) © Richard T. Nowitz/CORBIS. **20** Musee du Louvre, Paris/Art Resource, NY. **21** (t) © Bill Aron/PhotoEdit; (b) Hulton Archive/Getty Images. **22** © Roger Wood/CORBIS. **23** © David Lees/ CORBIS. **24** (bkgr) Getty Images. **25** Private Collection. **26** (t,l) © Reunion des Musees Nationaux/Art Resource, NY; (b,l) Daly & Newton/ Getty Images; (r) Art Resource, NY. **27** (t,l) Myrleen F. Cate/PhotoEdit; (t,r) photodisc/Getty Images; (b,l) © Mary Kate Denny/PhotoEdit; (b,r) © Cleo Photography/PhotoEdit. **28** © Robert Lentz/Bridge Building Images, www.BridgeBuilding.com. **29** Courtesy of Enrique de la Vega. **32** (bkgr) © Dennis Flaherty/Getty Images. **33** © Tony Freeman/PhotoEdit. **34** (t,l) © David Young-Wolff/ PhotoEdit; (m,l) Myrleen F. Cate/PhotoEdit; (b,l) © Michael Newman/PhotoEdit; (b,r) © Novastock/PhotoEdit. **35** (t) © Kathy McLaughlin/The Image Works; (m,l) Richard T. Nowitz/ CORBIS; (m,r) © Cleo Photography/PhotoEdit; (b) © David Young-Wolff/ PhotoEdit. **36, 37** From the worldwide competition: "Children of the World Illustrate the Bible." By MallMedia Publishing House. www.bible2002.com. **38** (bkgr) © The Crosiers/Gene Plaisted OSC.

UNIT 2: 41 Courtesy of St. Alphonsus Liguori Rectory. **42** (t) Painting of St. Alphonsus Liguori and St. Gerard Majellan by J.W. Printon CSSR, shown by gracious permission of St. Alphonsus, Chicago, IL; (bkgr) Courtesy of the Congregation of the Most Holy Redeemer; (b) Printed piece courtesy of Liguori Publications. **43** (l) © Giraudon/Art Resource, NY; (m,r) © The Crosiers/Gene Plaisted OSC. **44** Courtesy of John D'Or Prairie Reserve. **45** © Paul A. Souders/CORBIS. **46** © Erich Lessing/Magnum Photos. **47** © Burstein Collection/CORBIS. **48** photodisc/Getty Images. **49** © Jeff Greenberg/PhotoEdit. **50** (t) © Myrleen F. Cate/PhotoEdit; (m) © David Lees/CORBIS; (b) © Mark Richards/PhotoEdit. **51** (cl) photodisc/Getty Images; © Mary Kate Denny/PhotoEdit; © Chris Salvo/ Getty Images; © Barbara Peacock/Getty Images; © David Young-Wolff/ PhotoEdit; (m) photodisc/Getty Images. **56** Gustave Doré/Dover Publications. **57** © Charles Gupton/Getty Images. **58** (t) photodisc/Getty Images; (b,r) Gustave Doré/Dover Publications. **59** (t) © David Frazier Photo Library; (b) © Mary Kate Denny/PhotoEdit. **60** (t) Nicolo Orsi Battaglini/Art Resource, NY; (b) Reunion des Muses Nationaux/Art Resource, NY. **61** Nicolo Orsi Battaglini/Art Resource, NY. **63** © The Crosiers/Gene Plaisted OSC. **64** (bkgr) © Bruce Dale/National Geographic Society/Getty Images. **66** (t) Al Podgorski photo of May 13, 2002 reprinted with special permission from the Chicago Sun-Times, Inc. © 2002; (m,r) © The Crosiers/Gene Plaisted OSC; (b) © Brent Jones. **67** (t,l) © Dana Edmunds/ Getty Images; (t,r) © Yellow Dog Productions/Getty Images; (b) © Walter Hodges/Getty Images. **68** The National Gallery, London. **69, 70, 72, 73** (all) © The Crosiers/Gene Plaisted OSC. **74** (t,r) © The Crosiers/Gene Plaisted OSC; (m,l) David Young-Wolff/PhotoEdit; (m,r) Myrleen F. Cate/PhotoEdit; (b,l) © SW Production/Index Stock Imagery/PictureQuest; (b,r) © Chris Hellier/CORBIS. **75** © The Crosiers/ Gene Plaisted OSC. **78** © "Children of the World Illustrate the Bible" from MallMedia Publishing House, www.bible2000.com. **79** © The Crosiers/ Gene Plaisted OSC. **80** © David Young-Wolff/PhotoEdit.

UNIT 3: 81 © Jesuits of the Missouri Province. **83** (t,l) © Lawrence Migdale/Getty Images; (t,r) © Sean Sprague/SpraguePhoto.com; (b) Bes Stock. **84** (l) © Myrleen F. Cate/PhotoEdit; (t,r and b,r) © The Crosiers/ Gene Plaisted OSC. **85** © Tony Freeman/PhotoEdit. **86** (t,r) © Erich Lessing/Art Resource, NY. **87** Courtesy of Sts. Volodymyr and Olha Ukrainian Catholic Church, Chicago, IL; (b) Courtesy of Dr. Elizabeth Hudgins. **88** (bkgr) © The Crosiers/Gene Plaisted OSC. **89** © Paul Chesley/Getty Images. **90** (t) © Steve Skjold/PhotoEdit; (b,l) Cameramann International/Milton and Joan Mann; (b,r) Myrleen F. Cate/PhotoEdit. **91** (l) © Michael Newman/PhotoEdit; (t,r) © Don Carroll/Concept; (b,r) © Myrleen F. Cate/PhotoEdit. **92** © Franklin McMahon/CORBIS. **93** (t) © David Kamba. **94** © Tony Freeman/PhotoEdit. **95** (t) © The Crosiers/Gene Plaisted OSC; (b) © Cameramann International/Milton and Joan Mann. **97** © Michael Newman/PhotoEdit. **98** (t) AP/Wide World Photos; (b) The Father Solanus Casey Home. **99** (t,l) © Jeff Greenberg/PhotoEdit; (t,m) © David W. Hamilton/Getty Images; (t,r) © David Young-Wolff/PhotoEdit; (b,l) © David Young-Wolff/PhotoEdit; (b,r) © Amy Etra/PhotoEdit. **100** Superstock, Inc. **101** Private Collection. **102** © Jeff Greenberg/PhotoEdit. **103** (t) photodisc/Getty Images; (b) © David Young-Wolff/Getty Images. **104** (bkgr) © Mary Jane Cardenas/Getty Images. **105** © Michael Newman/PhotoEdit. **106** (t) © David Young-Wolff/ PhotoEdit; (b,l) Myrleen F. Cate/PhotoEdit; (b,r) David Young-Wolff/ PhotoEdit. **107** Courtesy Basilica of The National Shrine of the Immaculate Conception, Washington, DC. **108** Courtesy of the International Masonry Institute. **110** www.cuba.com.mx/galeria/cobre.htm. **111** © 2003 Board of Trustees, National Gallery of Art, Washington, Samuel H. Kress Collection. **112** Courtesy Basilica of The National Shrine of the Immaculate Conception, Washington, DC. **113** © Gary Conner/PhotoEdit. **114** (l) © David Young-Wolff/PhotoEdit; (t,r) © Michael Newman/PhotoEdit; (m,r) © Bettmann/CORBIS; (b,r) © Tony Freeman/PhotoEdit. **115** (t,l) © Jeff Greenberg/PhotoEdit; (t,r) © The Crosiers/Gene Plaisted OSC; (b,r) © Michael Newman/PhotoEdit. **118, 119** (t,bkgr) © Anselm Spring/Getty Images.